JAMES AND JIM

James & Jim

A BIOGRAPHY OF JAMES KENNAWAY

TREVOR ROYLE

MAINSTREAM
PUBLISHING

First published by
MAINSTREAM PUBLISHING COMPANY (EDINBURGH) LTD.
25a South West Thistle Street Lane
Edinburgh EH2 1EW

ISBN 0 906391 46 6

The publisher acknowledges the financial assistance of the Scottish Arts Council in the publication of this volume.

Jacket design by James Hutcheson.

Typeset by Spectrum Printing Company, Edinburgh
Printed by Billing & Sons, Worcester

Contents

Preface

DURING the course of his life, James Kennaway kept a clutch of writer's notebooks in which he jotted down ideas for his books and filmscripts, and in which he kept a rudimentary diary, chronicling the main experiences and sensations of his life between 1961 and 1968, the year of his death. He was also a voluminous correspondent and most of his early letters were kept by his mother, Marjory Ewing Kennaway (later Lady Bell), his wife, Susan, and by many of his business friends and colleagues. These papers, which either belong to Susan or are in the possession of the National Library of Scotland (see notes and references), form the basis of my biographical study. I was greatly inspired by the knowledge that James had begun editing some of the papers and fully expected to see them in print, perhaps as the material for an autobiography.

In 1981 Susan Kennaway published *The Kennaway Papers,* a selection of notes, diaries and letters which describe a period of marital break-up in 1965 and which lead the reader carefully through a triangular relationship formed by herself, James, and his friend the novelist John Le Carré (called David in that book). Wherever possible in the text, I have made reference to that publication so that this study, especially chapter nine, may be read in conjunction with it.

In writing and researching the life of James Kennaway I have been most ably and enthusiastically assisted by his widow, Susan, now Susan Vereker. Not only did she make available to me all the papers belonging to James, but she took great pains to answer all my questions and to present the story of her life with him in a frank, revealing and never uncritical way. I am most grateful to her for that help and for her generosity and hospitality during the writing of the book. No less important to me has been the understanding of her husband, Stanley Vereker, who has been a tower of strength and tact throughout the project.

For information about James's childhood I would want to thank, first and foremost, Hazel Bolton, his sister, who gave generously of her time and patience. The story of his prep schooldays at Cargilfield could not have been told but for the willing assistance of Sheila Kittermaster and Mowbray Pearson. For Glenalmond, his public school, his housemaster, Charles Millar, gave me much essential advice and information about life there during World War Two when James was a pupil. The present Warden, J.N.W. Musson, circulated old boys with a request for information and the following contemporaries answered the call: Jeremy Bruce-Watt, George Buchanan-Smith, J.D. Cameron, J.S. Liddell. I am indebted to them all.

The chapter on National Service was made easier for me through the understanding of Major Allan Cameron and Major John Durbin who also supplied useful information about the background to *Tunes of Glory*. Much of the Oxford chapter was written with the assistance of James's friend, and best man at his wedding, Denys Hodson who also helped in many other untold ways.

John Guest, James's editor at Longmans, was frank about his literary relationship with an author he much admired, and Simon Michael Bessie provided a similar view from New York where he published Kennaway's novels under his Atheneum imprint. For information about Kennaway's involvement in scriptwriting, I am greatly indebted to his friends and colleagues, James Hill, Alexander Mackendrick and J. Lee Thompson; and to Robert Emmett Ginna who produced *Country Dance* as a film and who worked with him on the film-life of Robert Capa. Prudence Downing, James's secretary, kindly lent private papers and answered questions about his working methods.

Others whom I would like to thank for replying to letters and answering queries, and for discussing with me aspects of

Kennaway's life and writing are: Alan Bell, Connie Bessie, Alan Bold, Melvyn Bragg, Stewart Conn, Gay and Tony Cox, Vivien Devlin, T.A. Dunn, Owen Dudley Edwards, William Forwood, Barbara and Murray Grigor, Chris Harrison, Francis Russell Hart, H. Kennaway, Duncan McAra, Norman McCandlish, James Maitland, Allan Massie, George Melly, Sandy Neilson, Peter O'Toole, Walter Perrie, Douglas Rae, Susie Raeburn, Harry Reid, Mark Reynard, James Roose-Evans, Richard Seaver, Godfrey Smith, F.W. Stevinson, Jane and Andy Trotman, Susannah York.

The task of writing this book has been made more easy, and certainly more pleasant, by the help given to me by the staffs of the National Library of Scotland, the Library of the University of Reading and New York Public Library. Part of the book was written in the United States and I would want to record with gratitude the hospitality shown to me by The Players, New York, and Larry Cooper, Santa Monica, California.

I wish to acknowledge the permission of the directors of Longmans to quote from papers in the Longman Archive in the Library of the University of Reading.

The Scottish Arts Council kindly awarded me a travel grant which enabled me to visit the United States in the Spring of 1983 to complete my research. I am pleased to be able to acknowledge that most useful form of assistance.

My publishers, Bill Campbell and Peter Mackenzie, have shown great tolerance in allowing deadlines to come and go. I want to thank them, and also my friend, BBC Producer Patrick Rayner, who made available to me recording facilities and who commissioned me to write *Magnificat,* a radio play, based on this book.

It has become something of a convention to thank one's partner for the forebearance shown during a book's completion. In this case, custom gives way to gratitude to my wife Hannah for being such a good companion in my search for Kennaway and for keeping me straight on various medical and psychological questions within the text.

Trevor Royle
Edinburgh, July 1983

~ 1 ~

Kennaway Country

ON a clear day, the broad sweep of the fertile vale of Strathearn is seen to no little advantage from the seventeen-hundred-foot peak of Craig Lea, a stony outcrop which dominates the valley's northern edge. Seen from its summit the River Earn flashes silver as it makes its way from distant Loch Earn to join the waters of the River Tay south of Perth. The Earn, a minor enough river in a county of many waters, flows through one of Scotland's richest Lowland valleys: some two hundred miles of good farming land, made up of modest estates, ancient parklands, rolling wooded hills and green pastures. Here, too, man has made his mark with neat, grey-stoned villages, the age-old tusks of castle and tower and the sudden elegance of mansions blessed by Reason's smile. This is Kennaway country.

On a late winter's day in February 1944, while still a schoolboy, James Kennaway climbed Craig Lea in the company of his friend, Alan Peter George Perfect, "who's the best walker in the college"[1], and from the top, both boys were able to survey young James's domain, the strath that he was later to call the "flat part" of Scotland. Directly to the south, some twelve miles away, he could make out Auchterarder, the long straggling village and the capital of Strathearn, where he had been born sixteen years before. To the south-west nestled the town of Crieff where a bevy of fond aunts offered a weekend haven and the benison of good food and attentive care during the bleak years of a wartime childhood. To the south of Crieff he could just make out his mother's birthplace, the village of Muthill which stands in the lea of the great estate of Drummond Castle, home of the earls of Ancaster. And two-and-a-half miles below the summit where the Milton Burn tumbles into the River Almond, and beyond a patch of woodland, rose the cloistered buildings of his boarding school, Trinity College, Glenalmond.

Far away in the darkening east, the smoke of Perth partially obscured the compact mass of the county town, and stretching far towards the southern horizon, the lowering Ochil Hills gave a sense of definition to his view. If he had cared to turn around and to face north, all was Highland and unexplored, as the hills of Breadalbane gave way to the peaks of distant Rannoch. Only the gash of the Sma' Glen, "exceptionally small and amazingly pretty with its razorback hills at the sides",[2] gave any clue that he was standing at the classic divide that separates Scotland into Highland and Lowland, a division that is both geographical and cultural. But it was the sixty square miles that stretched to the south in Strathearn that was of immediate interest to Kennaway: it was the country of his childhood and a place in which both sides of his family had long roots, and like any other boy of his age who has known no other land, he was deeply and sentimentally attached to it.

> Whether I like England or Scotland best I don't know, but I am more loyal to my county than either country. I am proud to be a descendent of such a stalwart line of strong normal Perthshire men. The gravestone at Gask gives me a sense of security, terribly necessary in this hurly-burly age: I can think of it standing in good Perthshire earth steadfast in all the storms, scarred but still standing in the face of the four winds and I can say to myself, "There, James, there is the symbol of the men that came before you: there is your existence and pride. You too are a yeoman even if you do not till the fields." Wherever I rove to, whatever happens to me, I will still have at least one little root stretching far down into the Perthshire earth, as deep as the traditions of my forefathers. And that is a most comforting thought.[3]

Within a few years, after he had finished his National Service, Kennaway was to sever his ties with that Perthshire background. He went on to Oxford and then to a career in publishing before becoming a full-time writer in 1957. From then until his death in 1968 he was a novelist who also wrote scripts for Hollywood, a highly-paid and deservedly successful writer who was described by one perceptive critic as "a lonely and dedicated master"[4]. He was also a member, if somewhat oldish, of the sixties' generation, living in "Swinging London", into having a good time, armed with just the right amount of money to make it all extremely pleasant, and yet like the good novelist he was, he was able to foresee the end of it all in the students' revolts and social and racial unrest of 1968. As well as London he lived in California, France, Italy and Kashmir, but, apart from brief family visits, never in Scotland. And yet, like Robert Louis Stevenson before him—a novelist and man with whom Kennaway had many affinities—the feeling of exile was strong and memories of the past were to pull at his heartstrings almost as soon as he had left it all behind him. He was to call Scotland "a bad society"[5] and he also came to affect a dislike of Scottish qualities, and yet, like Robert Louis Stevenson, in his fiction at least, he was destined never fully to break the links that bound him to that country.

His first novel, *Tunes of Glory,* published in 1956, is set in the Perth that he knew while doing his six weeks' basic training during National Service in 1946. The fictional Campbell Barracks where "no civilian rightly knows what happens behind that grey wall but everybody is always curious"[6]is recognisably the Queen's Barracks in Perth, and the theatre in which the faded actress Mary Titterington is the leading lady is Perth Theatre (Kennaway asked his publishers, Putnam, to check out both references against the possibility of either having been libelled). Set in a Highland regiment, *Tunes of Glory* examines the conflict that arises when two men from different social and military backgrounds vie with one another for leadership of the regiment: Jock Sinclair, a hard-drinking Scot who has risen from the ranks, and Basil Barrow, a professional with an impeccable military background. Their mutual antagonism is resolved by Barrow's suicide in the face of Sinclair's stubborn pride and dynamic self-destructiveness which both repels and yet attracts his fellow officers. As we shall see, although his novels were not purely autobiographical they did stem from situations, people and relationships he had observed or had been involved in and on one level *Tunes of Glory* is a reflection of the *amour propre* he felt towards the regiment with which he had served, as a Cameron, in Germany, the Gordon Highlanders.

Household Ghosts, his second novel, though, is the work that is most suffused with his Perthshire background. The dotty Ferguson family with their crumbling estate and outdated *mores* is very similar to one of the Strathearn families known to the Kennaway family (again there were libel problems) and the whole atmosphere is as much county Perthshire as light refracted through malt whisky in a crystal tumbler. The big house, the home farm, the long street of the county town, the Conservatives' dance and the neighbouring golf course, all have their real-life origins within the circumference of his childhood. Even the names have hardly been altered. Throughout his life Kennaway made little attempt to find names for his characters other than those lifted simply from people he had known in his early years. Although *Household Ghosts* is set within the narrow confines of an aristocratic family, Kennaway centred its plot on the taut, violent relationship that Mary Ferguson has with the men around her: her brother Pink who lives at second remove from reality in the childhood fantasy and the frustrated passion that he shares with her; Stephen Cameron, her ineffectual husband; and David Dow, her lover, the local boy who has made good and gone to London to carve himself a successful career in neuro-physiology. The novel was re-written as a play, *Country Dance* (1967) and was later made into a film of the same title, and just as the shifting connections of the triangular relationship remained the central theme, so also was the background firmly upper-class Perthshire.

Lochearnhead at the far end of Breadalbane creeps into his last complete novel, *The Cost of Living Like This,* published in 1969 (*Silence* was put together from four fragments and published in 1972), which traces another triangular relationship involving three very different people: Julian, an economist dying of cancer, Christabel his wife, and Sally his young mistress. Acting as judge is the vivid creation of Mozart Anderson, a football referee, who watches over the women's struggle for Julian as he makes his inexorable slide towards death. But by the time that he came to write *The Cost of Living Like This* it was the strength of the characterisation and not the strength of the narrative line or the delineation of background that counted in Kennaway's fiction. Nevertheless, it is still possible, for example, to feel the same sense of winter and of the hostile nature of snow in the north that had been present in his first novel: "Snow in those parts is altogether different from the Christmas card showers in the south. It is more serious and more sinister. Snow once meant suffering and poverty, and even starvation: it brought sorrow not Christmas."[7]

In February 1944 there would have been some snow at the top of Craig Lea and it was a constant companion during the Perthshire winters of Kennaway's schooldays, but it was not the clean snow of the mountains that was on his mind when he came to write of it so sinisterly in his novels. He remembered another cold, snow-driven winter's day at a place which lay beyond the horizon of hills to his west: near Comrie, a pretty stone-clad village to the west of Crieff where Kennaway's prep school, Cargilfield, was housed for the duration of the war. On the evening of 31 January 1941 he had been told that his father had died in distant Aberdeen, leaving his son unseasonally mature at the age of twelve. The ache of that early pain was still raw two years later when James wrote to his mother on the anniversary of his father's death.

> "This is a memorable date. I will never forget two years ago at this time of year. The weather is just the same as it was then—snowing hard. In many ways I feel it is a sad time of year but something tells me I am wrong. We may have lost, for a few years, a great help, but only for a few. I will always remember, 'with all eternity before us'."[8]

The notion of having to survive with a 'father dead' was to haunt Kennaway throughout his life and at his lowest ebbs he was to place much of the blame for his predicaments in having had to grow up without the presence of his father. As it was, Kennaway was destined to die at the age of forty, his father being forty-seven when he died, and the fear of an early death cast a long shadow over his life. The nearest he came to expressing formally his own feelings about his father and their shared relationship to their Perthshire upbringing came in 1963 when he began to work on a script called *Flowers.* Based largely on the recollections of his childhood, it traces the events of 2 and 3 September 1939 as Britain prepared to go to war again with Germany. It was an important day in Kennaway's life and one that in retrospect he saw as a changing point in his attitudes towards the society in which he lived. Until that time his childhood had been happy and secure within the protective wealth afforded by his parents—as well as being a factor his father was a successful solicitor and his mother, Marjory, was a doctor. It was the kind of comfortable middle-to-upper-class society which its members had been bred to defend to the death and when war broke out the natural reaction was to invoke again St Crispin's Day. Henry V-like, Kennaway's father made application to join the Grenadier Guards, the regiment with which he had served during the First World War. The compulsory medical examination revealed that he was suffering from tuberculosis of the kidneys and he was given six months to live. As it was, the illness dragged on for a further sixteen months which he spent in Tor-na-dee isolation hospital in Aberdeenshire. The real nature of the illness was not revealed to his children until after his death.

To mirror his father's illness and his slide towards death Kennaway chose to see it in *Flowers* as a reflection of the inner rottenness and dishonesty of the society in which he occupied an honoured position. In the script (on which Kennaway lavished much care and attention, although it was destined never to go beyond the outline stage), the fictional father is a replica of his own father: a man with a love for Scotland and a man who is in league with the land. At the start of his Crispin's Day he appears solidly married, determined to preserve his own household and that of "the big house" he serves. At the end of the day he has slept with the laird's daughter, thus revealing to himself his own hypocrisy, and also something of the dichotomous attitudes of the society which he wishes to protect. More importantly, the truth is revealed not only to him but also to his son who knows that his life can never again be the same. The metaphor of a wasting illness that can lead only to death is underlined in the final frame when the father is forced to shoot an old gundog that has lumbered out in front of his departing car.

Thus within the dramatic symbolism of a man going to war, a Henry V who discovers that he is in fact Richard II, Kennaway was able to give vent, twenty years later, to feelings that were beginning to burgeon within him in 1944. During the war he became much concerned with the nature of his society and began to see it as a tired facade, an empty shell which could never again offer him the comfort he had enjoyed in his younger years. To his mother he continued to write cautiously optimistic letters about his future and a sense of certainty shines through his Glenalmond, and, later, his National Service correspondence. But there was another, more serious side to the boy whose school reports noted his "cheerful enthusiasm". Perhaps his most important correspondent at that time was an elderly cousin on his mother's side, Edith Shaw, his "dear old cousin Edith", who lived in Knebworth, Hertfordshire. To her he confided many of his innermost thoughts and shyly he sent her copies of his earliest attempts at poetry. Consequently a very different Kennaway emerges from the confident schoolboy and officer cadet of the letters to his mother. On 19 September 1949 he wrote to his Cousin Edith in a mood that reflected the kaleidoscopic change that was taking place within him:

> The morals of this generation cannot compare with that of yours: the ordinary human charity and unselfishness is lacking among war babies. Time presses ever more and more, and the prose and poetry of the world take on the speed of the airliner and jet fighter. We have all, practically all seen men suffer starvation, squalor and disillusion; we have heard children cry. Now we have seen the ideals—the wonderful ideals of the socialists badgered by their own prophets. The world has become a tangle of cunning and crisis, of men striving to create and men striving to control. The advances and the dupes have left their marks on each one of us, and it is only when we can turn to the sanity of a sanctuary like Ramoyle [Edith Shaw's house in Knebworth] which is after all only the personification of its owner's cordial hospitality that we can see how transitory our anxieties must be. Each generation has its problem children; each its heroes and its cowards; each its difficulties. This one has seen the continent at its lowest ebb, morality, art, prosperity and charity at the nadir, but perhaps it has still to see the zenith. We have a heap of broken stones around us and a desire to build an acropolis: it is a time of great concern and trouble, but it is perhaps the bitter moments that conceive the better ones. If we can one day look at the acropolis and say, "There! I helped to build that edifice with a hundred million others" then truly we will have great reason to be happy.[9]

Such a mood of disenchantment was not uncommon amongst the generation that grew to maturity in the aftermath of the

Second World War, but for Kennaway one senses that the emotion ran deeper than for most. His background was secure, his society privileged and yet he sensed that the war had destroyed their gentility seemingly for ever. The "broken stones" of the old edifice could never be rebuilt by him, and Kennaway's "acropolis" was to be very different from those constructed by his fellows. But the letter also betrays his longing for security and it is hardly stretching a point, I feel, to see in the "sanity of sanctuary" the passing regret he felt at the loosening of the ties with the land of childhood. The imagery of the broken building with its attendant motif of a society lying in ruins around it was also to be a dominant theme in his fiction and helped to fashion the articulation of many of his attitudes.

Flowers traces the collapse of a society that has suddenly become rotten in a young boy's eyes, and that sense of decay also pervades *Household Ghosts*. The Ferguson Family, the landed gentry, are "batty, psycho-whatsit, even schizo-whatever they call it, and with a marked tendency to booze"[10]. In his younger days the foolish baronet, Sir Charles, cheated at cards, and was banished from society. And the cheating continued in the treatment meted out to his children, especially the clumsily contrived marriage between Mary and the successful, though sexually impotent, Stephen which was only arranged to halt the decline of the Ferguson estates. The family is thoroughly amoral and it is the modern man, the technocrat David Dow who recognises the predicament. "A glance at their history or literature (and especially if you count Byron as a Scot, which, after dinner at least, is permissable) reveals what lies under the slow accent, the respectability and the solid flesh. Under the cake lies Bonny Dundee."[11]

Bonny Dundee—James Graham of Claverhouse—was the seventeenth century Royalist who was also a conundrum of a man, a romantic Jacobite who led a rebellion against William of Orange yet who had previously upheld the laws of the land in his savage persecution of the Covenanters. Like his namesake, James Graham, the Marquis of Montrose, he represents a polarity of Scottish attitudes that is both cultural and national. His employment as a metaphor by David Dow is revealing for Kennaway's own expression of his attitudes towards Scotland.

Dow has left Scotland and had adopted the sterile values of metropolitan success. Stephen, though wedded to the land, has been made impotent by his connection. Only Mary emerges at the novel's end as the one character able to overcome the ghosts of the past. A similar attempt is made in *The Bells of Shoreditch* by Stella Vass, the uncompromising wife of a weak-willed merchant banker, Andrew. Inspired by the ILP ideals of her Glasgow past, she puts steel into her husband who first attacks the big-money intrigues of international finance before being swallowed up in it himself. And having failed to find strength in her husband she is also doomed to disappointment in the arms of his boss, Sarson, whose "big panther appeal" only serves to dominate her in much the same way that Mary is brought down by Dow's nihilism.

Thus, in four of his seven novels—*Tunes of Glory, Household Ghosts, The Bells of Shoreditch* and *The Cost of Living Like This*—Scotland was an essential component of Kennaway's vision. It both attracted and repelled, yet it was the dynamism of that conflicting emotion that proved to be such a tense mainspring in his writing. The strength of that coil was to enable him to explore more fully the complications of the triangular sexual relationship with all its contrasting emotions of love and pain, honesty and passion, desire and anguish. And it is significant that in every novel the characters who form the apexes of the triangle are no longer at ease in a soured society, driven apart as much as they are drawn together by its inner tensions.

Though he might not have understood it at the time, as he stood at the summit of Craig Lea that winter's day in 1944 the land that lay below him was to exert a powerful tug on his emotions. On the one hand he was to entertain a fierce pride and sentimental love for it: on the other he was to become deeply repelled by the sham gentility and discreet charm of its bourgeois society. Both views of Kennaway country were to find their way into just about everything that he was to write.

~ 2 ~

A Scots Childhood

JAMES Peebles Ewing Kennaway was born on 5 June 1928 at his parents' home, Kenwood Park in Auchterarder, the ancient capital of the valley of Strathearn in central Perthshire. That he should have been born at home instead of hospital was hardly surprising. It was then considered quite normal to give birth at home, and in any case, his mother, Marjory, was herself a doctor. Besides, Kenwood Park was exceedingly well-equipped and comfortable: it had been built for the Kennaway family in 1912, a substantial stone-built house set in some four-and-a-half acres of grounds, facing south-east across rolling farmland to the distant Ochil Hills. Like many other Scottish houses of its age and character, discretion and comfort are its key features. It has a formal garden lying to the front and south of the house, flanked by hard and softwood trees, and well to the west of the house stands a magnificent copper beech tree. Situated to the rear are the obligatory outbuildings—a double garage, greenhouses, garden store and sheds for the storing of logs and apples. In the somewhat dour village of Auchterarder, with its long, straggling main street and modest dwellings, Kenwood Park was a house amongst houses, an entirely suitable home for a well-to-do legal family with interests in estate management.

But the birth of a child was not the only event that was exciting the inhabitants of Kenwood Park that summer's day.

James's aunt Elizabeth, his father's sister, was marrying a young officer of the Dragoon Guards, Hugh McLure Gardner of Caldercruix in Lanarkshire, and the entire household buzzed with preparations for the marriage. The wedding ceremony took place in Auchterarder's West United Free Church and the reception, for two hundred guests, was held at the neighbouring Gleneagles Hotel which had been opened four years previously by the London, Midland and Scottish Railway Company to provide new standards of comfort and cuisine (plus two golf courses) for its customers. Elizabeth was given away by her brother Charles and so it was that James's father had a double cause to celebrate on the birth of his second child and only son. The marriage created a good deal of local interest and the *Perthshire Advertiser's* official photograph shows a well set up family group, the men in morning suits and spats, the bride's attendants in identical *couturier* dresses and stylish white hats, and the page-boys in obligatory jackets and kilts. On a page dominated by awkwardly stilted and starched family groups at modest village marriages, the Kennaway wedding was obviously a grand affair.

And yet, for all the financial security and prestige offered by his father's position in Perthshire society, James grew up to become distinctly uncomfortable about his past. His father was one of the best known men in the district, a good (and wealthy) lawyer, witty speaker at countless social occasions, a hero of World War One and a director of several publicly cited companies. But he was also the factor. "In England they'll tell you that a 'Factor' is the same as the landagent", wrote Kennaway of his father's calling in 1965. "Not true (nothing ever is as true as it sounds, you should know that). Of course we do much the same job: rents; fences; sporting rights; keepers; roads; ditches; forests all that. We managed that for the Grahams here; my father before me, his father, and so on. As you rightly say—as if it mattered—we have, or had, been factors for 400 years, which shows what a dull lot we are."[1]

In that imaginary letter from father to son, which forms a central part of his treatment for *Flowers,* Kennaway expended no little anguish on the profession of factor, feelings of guilt that would certainly not have been shared by Charles Kennaway who took enormous pride in his work. He was the first Scottish landagent to have conveyanced £1 million-worth of land and his more successful negotiations included the sale of the Eastern Breadalbane and Castle Menzies estates in north Perthshire, Lintrose in east and Innerpeffray and Invermay in central Perthshire. His activities also included hotel transactions; he had concluded the Gleneagles' deal and he was on the board of several well-known Scottish hotels including the Dunblane Hydro and the Great Western in Oban. His factoring work had brought a great deal of personal wealth and the social obligations that went with its acquisition. The Kennaways were not only well-off, but well-connected. Nevertheless, when James grew up he would tend to look back at his childhood with some distaste for the single reason that he felt that being the factor's son was second best to the children of the laird who employed his father. To a certain extent those emotions were fostered by time, the events of his later boyhood and also by his own literary inclinations, but in one part of his heart, James grew up to be ill at ease in the society adopted by his parents.

His father, Charles Gray Kennaway was a remarkable man by any standards. He had been born in Blairgowrie in 1894, the son of a lawyer and factor who had moved to Auchterarder to set up the family business which would be run later by his son. He was educated at Perth Academy (it became a family joke that Charles had always resented his father's decision not to send him to the more patrician boarding school, Fettes College in Edinburgh) and later at the University of Edinburgh where he studied for an arts degree before being apprenticed to the law firm of W. & F. Haldane. His studies were interrupted by the outbreak of World War One and like most other young men of his generation, Charles was no slouch in volunteering—he enlisted as a private in a territorial battalion of the Black Watch, the regiment whose traditional recruiting grounds are the neighbouring counties of Perthshire and Angus, and he was destined to spend the next five years serving in the colours. He quickly gained a commission and his chance to earn a name for himself came on the morning of 27 September 1918 after he had been seconded to the 1st Battalion Grenadier Guards in the rank of captain. At the

Battle of Premy Chapel, during which he commanded the second company, he gained distinction as being one of the three officers to survive the affair. In terms of military advantage being gained it was a petty enough skirmish, but for his day's work, and his exceptional heroism under fire, the Guards' commanding officer, Lord Gort, was awarded the Victoria Cross and something of the the mystique surrounding the action clung to Charles Kennaway for the rest of his life. After the war, he served a further year in Germany on the staff of the Army of Occupation and he returned briefly to Edinburgh at the end of 1919 to complete his legal training. With his father's help he was admitted a Writer to the Signet, one of Scotland's ancient and prestigious legal bodies, but to his father's intense disappointment he refused to move back to Auchterarder to take his place in the family firm. Instead, he acquired a post in the Ministry of Justice in Cairo and remained in Egypt until 1921 when his father died and he came back to Scotland, to settle at Kenwood Park.

Three years later, on Wednesday 23 April 1924 be married Marjory Helen Ewing, a medical graduate and the youngest daughter of G.T. Ewing of Pitkellony near Muthill. Like the Kennaways, the Ewings were an old-established Perthshire family. Since Jacobite times they had farmed Concraig which abuts the lands of Drummond Castle at Muthill, and another side of her family had been ministers of the Free Church of Scotland. One of her uncles was the well-known scientist and educationalist, Sir James Alfred Ewing, whose sister Edith was to play such an important part in James's young life: she married the Revd. Charles Shaw, minister of Dunblane, but after his death she moved to Knebworth to be nearer her brother in his old age. Majory was a lively, attractive girl, a graduate of Edinburgh, who was much sought after at country dances. When she married the tall, darkly handsome Charles Kennaway in 1924 it was considered to be one of the matches of the season, bringing together such an attractive couple from such good Perthshire stock.

Their life together was one of ease and security in which money was rarely a problem. Holidays were spent abroad to satisfy Charles's liking for travel: he was fond of saying that he knew every European capital from Lisbon to Leningrad and there was hardly a patch of the western Highlands of Scotland with which he was not acquainted. Modern motor cars, domestic servants, tennis parties, garden fêtes and country dances became essential ingredients of an agreeable social life spent in one of the most pleasant areas of Lowland Scotland. But while life in Perthshire was calm and sheltered enough with its social structure still dominated by the ascendancy of the landed gentry, in most parts of Scotland it was considerably less pleasing. The General Strike of 1926 was only two years away and in the industrialised west of Scotland, only some fifty miles away from the charm of rural Perthshire, conditions for the working classes were, for the most part, appalling. Although, to a certain extent, World War One had boosted production in the heavy industries, especially in steel and ship building, and in coal-mining, a combination of a depleted labour force and antique management had seen those once proud industries sink to a level of neglect and despair undreamt by the early pioneers of the Industrial Revolution. Housing was uniformly sub-standard and unemployment tended to be higher than in other parts of the United Kingdom. Despite the successes of the Independent Labour Party members in Scotland, the so-called "Red Clydesiders" of the nineteen-twenties, Scotland was, in the view of journalist George Malcolm Thomson, "an annex, half industrial, half sporting, of English civilisation, and tomorrow she will be a proletarian state, blind, resentful and submerged, populated by a nation of machine-minders doing the bidding of foreign capitalists".[2] It would take another war to break the mould of industrial decay and also to make an incursion into the kind of society that dominated James's childhood. For while the more populated parts of the Lowland belt suffered, rural Strathearn was still blessed by enlightenment's smile, an area of estates and tenanted farms with a strictly ordered society that began with the aristocracy at its peak and descended through the landed gentry and various middle-class strata down to the poorest farmworker. And in the middle stood the factor, Kennaway's father, later to be characterised by his son as the "unyielding factor".

Charles Kennaway was considered by many people in the district to have been a hard man, a strict disciplinarian with an awkward spiky personality but many of his detractors spoke from a sense of envy of the powerful position he held in local society. Like many successful middle-class men who lived in closed and restricted communities he was much in demand and public positions of petty authority fell easily on his shoulders. He was a Notary Public and preses of the congregation of the West United Free Church, and he sat on numerous local committees. He was also well-known outside the vicinity of his home town as a man of no little importance. In 1928, the year of his son's birth, be became President of the Scottish Branch of the National Association of Auctioneers, Estate and House Agents and held the post until 1933. Four years later he became president for the whole of Britain and when he demitted office a grateful Association presented him with a handsome silver salver at a complimentary dinner at the Mayfair Hotel in London.

Yet for all his public successes and his air of worldly authority, he was also a mature intellectual with a deep and careful understanding of his country's past and traditions. For the *Aberdeen Press and Journal* in 1940 he wrote a series of articles on Scotland's military history and he planned a further work on the Scottish clan system which was destined never to be completed. His literary monument is his posthumous novel, *Gentleman Adventurer* (1951), which is set in Strathearn between the Jacobite risings of 1715 and 1745-46. What it lacks in characterisation and strength of narrative it makes up in his attention to historical detail and in his loving delineation of the sights and sounds of the neighbouring countryside that he knew so well.

> It has been my lot to see many places and diverse countries. I have looked over the Weald of Kent, looked down from the heights of Cheviot over the fair valley of Eden; I have stood above the Moselle and the Rhine, and from Brittany have marched down to see the Loire in all its glories; yet I have never seen a spectacle so fair as the valley of Strathearn from my old home at the Braes of Ochil on a still summer's night. Of a truth, from our door one can see half Scotland—from Stobinian and Ben Lomond in Dunbarton in the west to Dunsinane in Angus on the east, the whole scene framed in the background of the Grampians; Ben Ledi, the hill of God, and Ben Voirlich continuing the line from Ben Lomond in the west, northwards by the jagged heights above Loch Earn to the giants

> Ben-y-hone and Lawers; beyond the breaks of Glen Turret and the Sma' Glen, and then to the north-east in the hazy blue distance the snow-capped heights of the Cairngorms, half-hidden by the rugged Ben Vrackie and Ben-y-Gloe.
>
> Below, the glorious plain spreads out, with the Earn winding slowly, all-silvery ever, eastwards to Kinnoull and the distant Tay. Behind it the Braes of Gask verge into the heights above Monzie and Glen Almond; while to the left rises the wooded hill of Turlum, on its side the keep of Drummond Castle, a sentinel dominating the strath and providing a stately home for its custodian, the Duke of Perth.

The story follows the adventures of the Auchterarder Jacobite, Charles Hay, the "gentleman adventurer" of the title and it smoothly mixes fact and fiction in a rollicking yarn that covers the eighteenth-century years of Jacobite comings and goings in Scotland. Unlike other writers who have touched on the same theme, Charles Kennaway's novel is not suffused with regret for the romantic passing of the Jacobite cause: rather it embraces the "heavenly Hanoverianism" and the order, peace and prosperity created by the Act of Union of 1707. Charles Hay, like his father before him, is destined to become a factor to the Montrose estates, trains as a lawyer in Edinburgh and fights bravely as a soldier of fortune in France—the author's heart may well have beaten a little faster when he considered the comparisons he was creating between himself and his illustrious eighteenth-century forebear.

The novel was published posthumously and in an act of filial piety, James did much to ease the path of its publication. He valued it as a work of scholarship, too, and made much use of its background material when he considered re-setting in Scotland the novel that was eventually to become *Some Gorgeous Accident* in 1967. (All of Kennaway's novels went through several drafts, often involving not only changes of setting and characters but also of historical period and mood.) And in a way that is entirely Scottish, that has given rise to the saying "kent his faither" (that is, a son will always live in the shadow of his father) Kennaway's mother raised the shade of her husband in a press interview shortly before *Tunes of Glory* was made into a film. "My late husband was very detailed in his descriptions. I think that his son has inherited that trait from him."[4] Not that James ever felt over-dominated by his father from a literary point of view, but from *Gentleman Adventurer* it is possible to feel Charles Kennaway's love for Perthshire, a love that was equally shared by his son during the days of his boyhood. "Health and happiness", he wrote to his mother in the winter of 1945, "lies more in the solitude of a Perthshire moor. I must have walked ten miles over the hills and moors without seeing a soul yesterday. However I had a terrific chase after three deer, for miles through the snow." That sense of communion with the wild lonely places was not just born in James by accident of geography. Like his father he felt himself to be of Perthshire yeoman stock and his sister Hazel, three years his senior, remembers his liking for walks in the hills and the interest in nature that was cultivated by a family friend, Bob Sloan in Gleneagles.

Like many successful men, Charles Kennaway expected much from his children, especially from his son, and was a strict, though never unloving, father. That he may have been an austere, even distant figure in his son's eyes probably owed more to the society in which he lived than to any distaste for domestic life. Kenwood Park, with its nursery upstairs, was run on strictly formal lines and much of the children's day-to-day lives was governed by the domestic servants, the nanny and the maid. That formality in domestic matters allied to fairly rigid standards of behaviour made James feel in later life that his childhood had been unhappy and over-disciplined. He would point to the terror he experienced when he was quizzed by his father on coming home from his first days of nursery education at Miss Dow's in Auchterarder and that feeling of being put on the line grew into a minor phobia when he was older. While working in Hollywood in 1961 and suffering from an acute depression brought on by loneliness and writer's block, he confided to his diary that "I was terrified of my father. I was ambitious as a child, pressed by my parents. I now believe too hard, and yet, underneath, lies now as has always lain, real hope."[5] And to his wife Susan, whom he married in 1951 he would admit that not only had he been reduced to tears as a child through his father's insistence on his son's ability to learn arithmetic tables off by heart but also that he was made anxious and afraid by the rigidity of his father's attitudes. Hazel, he would add, earned nothing but praise at the same time.

Those expressions of loathing came when Kennaway was himself a grown man, a husband and a father himself and they say perhaps as much about his own attitudes as they do about his father's. At the time of expressing his anger his behaviour was far from being impeccable and during the period of marital break-up that did so much to disfigure his later life it was convenient to discover a scape-goat in the relationship—or perhaps lack of it—with his father. Certainly his earliest correspondence betrays no feeling of awe or terror harboured against his father, and Charles Kennaway's own letters are full of praise and restrained love for his son. "James letter caused me much joy," he wrote to Marjory on 2 May 1940 when his son was at prep school. "He is certainly a correspondent when he tries. I quite see why the school doesn't bother much about the actual handwriting—the 'stuff' is good enough to get him anywhere. I hope he can keep it up." And James, too, in a moment of reverie when he was sixteen wrote to his mother describing all the memories of his childhood that he could muster on a winter's night in 1944. "I remember as clearly as yesterday getting a pedal car on Christmas morning and papa wheeling it up and down with his hair on end". That same letter of 10 December 1944 is redolent of the ease in which his childhood was spent and gives some indication of the comfort and protection he knew to be part of his birthright:

> I remember being in a bath tub in the white bathroom and being bathed by someone I was angry with and I began to splash them. You came in and rolled the sleeves of a black cardigan (am I right?) up and blew bubbles and all my annoyance vanished. I remember careering down a landing on a pot and various other things not to be repeated on paper. I remember a telephone waking me when I was resting in your room. There was a tennis party or something going on. I remember a housemaid with a razor blade. I remember three little bears, a big hotel and a lift . . . . more hotels and a yacht . . . I remember countless dinner parties and Hazel not liking the moon . . . I remember suffocating in a tangle of blankets in the night nursery and yelling. I remember hating these animal shows in the billiard room because Hazel's horse did not win. Parties painful and pleasant—dancing classes. Pantomimes, *Treasure Island.* Hole burnt

> in the back seat of a small Ford. A car ablaze halfway to Crieff . . . Cargilfield and things are clear from then.

Nothing in Kennaway's early memories gives any indication of dismay either at being pressed unduly hard by a stern father or of being stultified by an over-rigid social life. (And neither emotion is picked up as a theme in his later writing: Scottish fiction abounds in the potent symbol of the relationship between the repressive father and the enfeebled guilt-ridden son.) Clearly the deep tensions and feelings of personal guilt experienced by Kennaway in his adult years were a product of both of his father's early death and the vacuum created by it, and also of the sense of inadequacy in repeating what he took to be a preordained pattern. But out of the ambivalent attitudes to childhood, the alloy of love and hate, did come the confused statements of an ever-changing moral stance when he himself had reached man's estate. Those emotions need not detain us here: rather it was the happy years of a pre-war childhood that remained uppermost in his mind during his adolescence, an idyllic Eden that was to be snatched from his grasp by two cataclysmic events: the outbreak of World War Two in 1939 and the death of his father in 1941.

Despite his later protests, James did enjoy an exceptionally happy childhood spent in the tightly-knit community that was Strathearn, where there were several friendships, both family and social. There were the Ewing aunts in Crieff who lived in a comfortable three-storeyed house called Craig Dhu. It stands on the road to Comrie with fine views across the upper valley of the River Earn towards the hills of the west and it was to become an important base for James during his schoolboy years at Glenalmond. At Chapelbank, some four miles north-east of Auchterarder, adjoining the Gask estate at Dalreoch Bridge, lived Sir Frederick Bell and his family. He was a friend of Charles Kennaway, a farmer who had served with distinction in the army during World War One and who had risen to public prominence as the Vice-Chairman of the Milk Marketing Board. Later, between 1944 and 1961 he was Chairman of the Herring Industry Board and although Sir Frederick's roots were in Paisley, the Bells were one of the leading families in the district. His family of two sons and three daughters, especially Jimmy and his sister Dimps, were close to Hazel and James, and Chapelbank was very much a home from home for them. Charles Kennaway was factor to the Buchanans of Gask and in the strictly ordered nature of things, they and their children were friends too, and so James's early childhood passed in a procession of dancing classes, tennis parties, gymkhanas, "a land where it's always country and always June", as he remembered it in 1961[6]. The photographs of James during that period show him to have been a serious, plumpish, fair-haired boy, dressed in his kilt, jacket and white shirt for best occasions, secure within the bourne of a wealthy and loving family. To his mother he was especially close, anxious to please her and concerned to be by her side: in his eyes she was an unfailing but not always approachable madonna, a necessary counterpoint to the dark and mighty man he saw as his father.

His first glimpse that childhood was nearing its end came in 1935 when Hazel, his older sister, was sent to boarding school, to St Bride's School in Helensburgh where her mother had also been educated. "I remember saying goodbye to Hazel in a blue cold room with lots of other girls not nearly so nice as her and a long, cold drive back telling you [his mother] to cheer up when I was nearly in tears myself. I never did want to leave her behind in that room, and often that still comes back to me." It was to be his turn next to experience the anguish of separation from his parents when in May 1937 he was sent to Cargilfield preparatory school in Edinburgh. For the cossetted James it was a terrible occasion, painful enough to be remembered almost thirty years later and to be compared to the worst anguish of mental breakdown. "In the misery of the following lonely days I knew that the experience resembled only one other when first I was left at boarding school and screamed with fear and self pity for 3 days."[7] With a fortitude that was to be typical of his years at boarding school, Kennaway kept his tears under control and within weeks he had developed the good-natured tolerance that most of his school-fellows remember. It would have been unusual, in any event, had he not been upset by the sudden change that had taken place in his young life: only the British, it seems think it normal to send their children into the care of others at the early age of eight or nine.

Cargilfield was at that time considered to be the top preparatory school in Scotland and it set standards of educational and social achievement that were the envy of its rivals. It had been founded in 1873 to provide an introductory education for entrance to the country's leading private schools and, under its distinguished headmaster, Bruce-Lockhart, brother of the diplomatist and author, Sir Robert Bruce-Lockhart, a policy had been evolved of only offering employment to Oxbridge graduates as masters, so anxious was the school to maintain its educational primacy. When James arrived at Cargilfield which was situated in Barnton, a suburb in west Edinburgh, the headmaster was H.J. Kittermaster who was destined to steer the school through the tribulations of World War Two, and a teacher and leader who was greatly respected by masters and boys alike. The atmosphere he encouraged was carefree and relaxed. Discipline may have been strict, but the boys were exhorted to develop adult attitudes at an early age and the school captains, or prefects, promoted a code of self-restraint amongst the boys.

In that easy commonwealth James flourished and became a pupil popular with both masters and schoolmates. At the end of his first term there the headmaster was able to report with some satisfaction that "he [James] has the valuable gift of always being cheerful and being able to laugh at himself as well as at others". Several of his school reports have survived and they reveal him as a cheerfully determined boy, one who set great store by other people's opinions of him. Twice in his second year he was awarded the Industry Prize, an award given to the boy who had tried hardest, and he received the same prize again in December 1940 and July 1941. He would have preferred a Form Prize for being first in class but that his work had been recognised at all was of the greatest importance to him and to his father who maintained a keen interest in his son's progress at school.

In his letters to his father, endearingly addressed to "Dear Pop", James went to considerable lengths to chart his own progress—"I am scanning in Latin just now. 'Elegiac couplet', 'hexameter', 'trochee' and words like that are difficult to learn"—and to record the triumph of being rewarded for working hard—"when I went up to the headmaster for my day's sweets, he said, 'Very good, James Peebles Ewing'." By 1940 he was in the under-12 rugby team, the school magazine reporting that he was the "soundest forward in the pack without being spectacular", and he also played in the cricket XI, successes in which his father took considerable pride. His greatest feat, though, came in his fourth year when he founded a debating society and became its first president. The news was excitedly reported home. "We had to write a small speech . . . and I came out top. I told Mr Cranmer that you have to make them sometimes and he said 'You've got the gift of the gab.'" For it was important to James that not only should he win the approval of his father but that he should emulate him as well, and in his case that meant acquiring a poise in public, an ability to speak confidently and an interest in history and political affairs. Sometimes those virtues would be taken to extremes and ridiculed—to the amusement of his friends James would often imitate his father during school walks by telling wild and improbable stories, sending up his own knowledge.

A sense of individuality was encouraged at Cargilfield and James was extremely happy there. His parents were frequent visitors and, if anything, the separation strengthened the bond between father and son: in Charles's eyes he was giving James the education that had been denied him by his own father. But there were clouds on the horizon. The years of James's early schooling were chequered by the tension created in Europe by the expansionist policies of Hitler's Germany and by the appeasement employed by the British government under Prime Minister Neville Chamberlain.

In March 1938 Hitler had incorporated Austria into the German Reich and two months later he turned his attention to the neighbouring territory of Czechoslovakia. Throughout that summer, attempts were made by Britain and France to prevent a German invasion, culminating in the Munich agreement of September when Chamberlain secured "peace with honour" in Europe. Having breathed a sigh of relief that war had been averted—at the terrible expense of the people of Czechoslovakia—few Britons thought that Hitler could be staved off for ever and 1939 saw the introduction of rearmament and a swing in British foreign policy towards the giving of unilateral guarantees of military support to those countries threatened by Nazi Germany. On 3 September 1939 Britain declared war on Germany in accordance with the treaty of defence with Poland, two days after that country had been invaded by German troops. In most people's minds, though, the country was going to war not so much in defence of another country but in meeting head on the threat to western civilisation posed by an expansionist dictatorship. It was, in other words, a righteous battle that Britain would be fighting and that attitude was impressed on the boys at Cargilfield. "The Nazis can be Goliath and us David," wrote James to his father a fortnight after war had been declared, adding, "remember David won".

The outbreak of hostilities may have lacked the drama and excitement with which World War One had been greeted in August 1914 but there was a deep sense of common purpose and preparedness. Among the measures introduced by the government to protect the civilian population a black-out was enforced, air-raid precautions became a feature of everyday life and arrangements were put in hand for the evacuation of civilians from the major industrial cities. In Auchterarder, as in many other parts of Britain, many families were astonished to discover that women and children from nearby Dundee were to be billeted on them and the experience was a source of much unhappiness and confusion. The invasion of families from slum homes lacking basic sanitation into the genteel respectability of middle-class Perthshire was a cruel revelation for both parties and a reminder of the divisions that still permeated British society. By October most of the evacuees had returned home, more willing to take their chances there than to endure the tensions of life in an alien environment. An evacuation of another kind was imposed on Cargilfield, when the school was obliged to remove itself from Edinburgh, its buildings having been requisitioned by the army. During September the entire complement moved from Barnton to Lawers, an Italianate country mansion near the Perthshire village of Comrie. The estate had been formerly in the possession of the Campbells of Lawers who later became Earls of Loudon and it was they who had changed its name from Fordie to Lawers in honour of their ancestral home on Loch Tay-side. At the time of the evacuation it was in the possession of Duncan Stewart of Millhills, the father of a Cargilfield boy.

At Lawers the atmosphere was contented and relaxed and a sense of comradeliness pervaded the wartime retreat in the upper part of Strathearn. Masters and boys joined forces in keeping at bay the bracken which engulfed the surrounding hillside and the cleared areas became improvised games fields for rugby and cricket. "In the afternoon we go to slay bracken instead of playing cricket. Mr Stewart brings everybody a bottle of raspberry, orange or lemon drink which we are very grateful for after the very hard work." James's letter of 6 June 1940 is typical of the sense of common purpose that characterised those early months of settling in to an environment that was a world apart from the disciplined orderliness of Cargilfield's Edinburgh home. But if some of the requisites of life were missing, the estate did possess many advantages. The surrounding hills became a playground for the boys and the burn which rose behind the school on the braes of Beinn Liath was there to be dammed until an angry neighbouring farmer complained that his rough grazing was being flooded. Nature study took on a new meaning with the evidence of much wildlife. The estate possessed some of the finest trees in Strathearn (now, alas, chopped down) and there was the fascination of the mausoleum (previously a chapel) in the grounds and a Roman burial ground in the neighbouring estate of Quoig. With travel in wartime presenting its own difficulties and with petrol rationing in force, life centred invariably on the school—although James obviously felt himself to be on home territory with Auchterarder only ten miles away to the east.

Shortly after war had been declared, Charles Kennaway felt that his duty lay in serving his country and for a man in his position that meant pulling strings. An accurate picture of the type of manoeuvering engaged in by the upper middle classes to get the right kind of commission in the autumn of 1939 emerges in Evelyn Waugh's novel *Put Out More Flags* and just as Alastair Trumpington studies Peter Pastmaster "with the rapt attention of a small boy, taking in every detail of his uniform, the riding boots, Sam Browne belt, the enamelled stars of rank",[8] so too was Charles Kennaway anxious to be back in uniform.

In his case he wrote to the adjutant of his old regiment, the Grenadier Guards, offering his services in an administrative capacity in his stamping ground of twenty years ago, Egypt. He was summoned to Horse Guards Parade at the end of 1939 and it was then that disaster overtook him. On reporting for the routine army medical examination it was discovered that he had tuberculosis of the kidney and that the prognosis was not good. Although the introduction of chemotherapy has reduced the mortality rate of this disease, in economically developed countries at least, it was then a killer and much feared as a highly infectious disease, the cancer of the thirties. It was, and still is, the classic example of a social disease, not only because it interferes directly with the patient's life, but more ominously because of the effect it has on the patient's own family: quite apart from the risk of infection, the consequent isolation can produce both financial and domestic stress.

For Charles Kennaway the news that he was ill came as a shattering blow. A fit man all his life, the knowledge that his body had been invaded by insidious disease and that hordes of tubercle bacilli were laying siege to his vital organs was difficult to accept. Only Marjory was made privy to the serious consequences of her husband's illness: the army medical board had informed her that the disease was in an advanced stage and that Charles only had six months left to live. That news was kept hidden from him and he set about fighting the illness with the same ordered discipline that he had brought to bear on most of his life. It was also kept a secret from the family, and to James and Hazel papa was simply ill and would have to spend some time in hospital.[9] The children only knew that, because the disease was infectious, they would not be able to see their father in the near future. But already hardened by the exigencies of a wartime childhood and used to lengthy periods of separation, this, too, they accepted.

It was decided that Charles should be treated at Tor-na-dee, Scotland's leading infectious diseases hospital situated in the village of Milltimber on Deeside, a few miles west of Aberdeen. Founded in 1917 as a sanatorium for army officers suffering from tuberculosis, Tor-na-dee was a private hospital offering seventy-four beds in two blocks, the principal one being the old

Deeside Hydropathic Hotel. Besides providing a fair degree of comfort and seclusion, and the latest in treatment, the sanatorium also had extensive private grounds with a winter garden and putting green, for, as its director noted in the first issue of the hospital's magazine, the great enemy of the patient was boredom.

> Cure is our chief, indeed our only aim, and I am glad to say that many have attained it. The treatment of tuberculosis in our present state of knowledge, however, entails a prolonged stay in the sanatorium and the restricted routine is apt to become irksome; hence the necessity for providing suitable diversion which should not only be harmless in itself, but actually part of the treatment.[10]

With so much time on his hands, Charles Kennaway turned to the library for solace. He studied the history of the Scottish armed forces and planned a series of monographs which would trace the development of the country's cavalry, infantry and navy. In outline form these appeared in the *Press and Journal* and it was during this period, too, that he completed his novel, *Gentleman Adventurer.*

The wireless became a constant companion and he spent much nervous energy following the course of a war which seemed to be very far removed from the quiet of his Deeside retreat. Although he had been a solid Unionist all of his life, Charles Kennaway began to suspect that the British policy of centralism was placing a grave strain on the loyalties of the colonies, many of which he looked on as "festering sores", in need of either investment or protection, or in extreme cases of complete independence from London rule. The war seemed to him to be the great catharsis, a cataclysmic event that would shatter the conventions of past years and usher in an age of greater equality.

> If and when we win this war, there will have to be a fresh start made. Not the start towards peace of plenty which all of the last generation made, but towards a more strenuous mode of living, on a more equal and democratic foundation, with less class distinction, and certainly less luxury.

Although Charles Kennaway's surviving correspondence is an uneasy mixture of pomposity and impatience, a long letter to Marjory written on 2 May 1940, of which that is an extract, strikes a genuine note. Suddenly the set-up, which to him had been natural and good, appeared a tired facade; society was rotten and not fertile as he had supposed previously. It was a sense of disillusionment which James attempted to capture in his film treatment *Flowers* in which the events of 2 and 3 September 1939 are seen through his father's eyes.

By the standards of Kennaway's own writing for the screen, *Flowers* is a remarkable document, and it would have made a powerful film had it matched the tenor of the mid-sixties when it was written. In the story, which takes the form of a long, rambling letter to his son, the father, a factor in Perthshire, traces his sense of alienation from the society of the landed gentry during the weekend that Britain went to war. So close was the tale to James's own childhood that at several places in the rough notes, he simply used his own and his father's names for the fictional father, Alec White, and his son, Charles. In *Flowers*, the father turns his back on his family and on his middle-class mores, grows tired of being in the service of the rich, sleeps with the laird's daughter and goes to war with a will, thus revealing to himself an inner truth that his society is crumbling and doomed, and that revelation is also made painfully clear to his son. That much is allegory and fancy, but the background details describing the village with its long street, the factor's house and the mansion with its crackpot titled family, is carved from memory, a portrait of a Chekhovian society that Alec White (and Charles Kennaway) had been reared to defend to the death. As one note makes clear, the composition of *Flowers*, with its central image of a man in conflict with the loyalties that have fuelled his life, was James's pietas to his father long dead, and to the inner torment revealed in his hospital correspondence.

> Charles's father was factor on the Ballantyne's estate. Charles's father, I am sure; but my father? He cannot be. He is my age. The riddle is traditional—that man's father is my father's son. And it perpetually reassures me. I think I write of my childhood for my father long dead in the hope of being read by my son. And when I write of Charles I so surprise myself that I wonder if it is my father's hand that guides my pen.[11]

In theme, *Flowers* is similar to *Household Ghosts* which was written four years earlier. It is set in Strathearn amongst the habitat of the landed gentry and the laird, Sir William Ballantyne, shares with Pink several characteristics, being "an ugly, attractive, lecherous, bald-headed, rotten-toothed little man". Alec White, the factor, is, like Stephen, driven to distraction by a beautiful titled girl, in this case, Odette Ballantyne, Sir William's daughter, who in going to bed with him shows him the way to freedom from bourgeois respectability. There is also a gallery of shared minor characters—Bank Lizzie, Bun and Belle—and there, too, is the cloying atmosphere of colourless small-town Scotland, the counterpoint to the easy mores of the big house. But at the centre of *Flowers* is the relationship between father and son: Charles White sees his father as "a dark man with energy so disciplined that he has almost assumed the character of the man that he is not, but feels he ought to be". Alec's attitudes to his son are stilted and awkward and yet when Odette Ballantyne eventually rejects him for his adherence to long dead values, this scene is played out in front of his son, thus uniting father and son in a chorus of despair for the servility in which both, in their different ways, have been placed.

In a letter of 20 May 1964 to his Crieff aunts, Kennaway told them about the project and asked for their memories, not of September 1939 but of August 1914, having decided to move the storyline in time to the more cataclysmic event.

> Last autumn I laid the foundations for a book about September 3rd 1939 which I remember very clearly. It suffers however from being too clearly autobiographical in certain sections. Partly for this reason and partly for more profound ones I have now decided to move the story back to 1914. That August day, "the day the war began" which will be my title.

That change was never made, although "The Day the War Began" exists in a series of notes for a novel. *Flowers,* as it remained, does contain much that is autobiographical, as did most of Kennaway's fiction, but its real importance lies in the dramatic set of circumstances in which Kennaway placed fictional father and son, almost in an attempt to come to terms with the hidden tensions of his childhood. "We do not see into the past. We imagine scenes as we think they were", is the opening note for his treatment: not for him a "lest we forget" attitude, rather it is the past as he saw it through his mind's eye.

At Tor-na-dee, Charles Kennaway, as his fictional counterpart had been in *Flowers,* was freed from many of the restrictions of the factor's role, and to Marjory he admitted that even in illness he was being allowed to be his own man, free to read, free to think and free to write. But being the man he was, he could not unchain himself completely from his legal practice, the bonds of a lifetime being too strong, and with his usual energy and lack of distraction he continued to take a major part in the running of the firm with batches of letters to his partner James Liddell written from his sickbed. His own letters to Marjory created a helter-skelter of emotions: one day he would be elated by a sudden lightening of the spirit, the next, the misery of his bed-ridden state would dampen all enthusiasm and make him tetchy and ill-tempered. For although tuberculosis is a wasting illness it is also a cunning one—it will flatter the body with fond hopes today only to deceive it tomorrow with debilitating pain.

Looking forward to a far from certain future, Marjory decided that the best course of action would be to move to Aberdeen to be nearer her husband. She had also decided to take a Diploma in Public Health so that she would be able to step back into the medical world and earn a living should the need arise. With many regrets, Kenwood Park was let and during the summer of 1940 Aberdeen became Marjory's base and a home-from-home where there were both Kennaway and Ewing relatives. Other plans were put in hand. James would be still at Cargilfield and would then continue his education at boarding school, at Glenalmond, and Hazel, having left Lansdowne Park, was sent to Crofton Grange School in Hertfordshire, where "the countryside was lovely, but oh, so flat! How I miss the blue hills of faraway Scotland!" Although he knew that they were now safe and well cared for, Charles never stopped worrying about his children. For Hazel he had developed a special affection and her removal to England was a severe blow, but his son, too, was never far from his thoughts.

> I had a splendid letter from James to which I replied earlier in the day. He wants me, 'for the whole family's sake' to get better soon. He's also thrilled about the 1st XV and the Scouts. I told him I'm very pleased with his progress.

His father's illness had brought out a serious streak in James and during 1940 he became an earnest, slightly withdrawn boy: to the outside world he maintained a gay front but the gloom cast by illness brought winter to his heart. He changed physically, too. At Easter a bout of ringworm meant that his hair had to be pulled out, and when it grew in again it was dark and curly instead of sandy and straight, a change that gave him the ruddy, dramatic looks by which most of his contemporaries remember him. The seriousness of his mood resulted too in a determination to do well at school and his last two years there were crowned with the sort of success he felt his father expected of him. He became a patrol leader in the school Scout troop and after being made a prefect he was head boy in his final year, 1941-1942, and according to those who knew him[12], he was perhaps the best head boy that Cargilfield ever had.

To set the seal on that success, James composed "Notes on Captaincy" which he committed to a black notebook and which was handed down from one head boy to the next as a model of self-discipline. No privilege without responsibility is the main theme and even though the rules may read today as relics from a bygone age, they do indicate the depth of seriousness which James was bringing to any task that required decision and leadership.

> As head boy you must realise that the school depends on you. If you are to be any use you must be very keen on this school; so may I make it clear that unless you love this school you will be no use. However if on the other hand you love punishment you will be again useless. Never "gloat" over people you have punished: that is the worst thing you can do, so if you love this school, you will not love punishment although it is necessary at times.[13]

John Buchan became his favourite author, especially the books dealing with Richard Hannay, and James may well have taken comfort from Buchan's definition of the hero as a man who maintains his position by paying his dues to society. As James progressed through his adolescence he felt increasingly that he had a duty to accept responsibility and to heap cares upon his own shoulders. He became protective towards his mother and worried that his father seemed to be getting no better. He had good reason to be concerned. During the winter,

Charles Kennaway became increasingly weak and unwell as his diseased kidneys refused to respond to either treatment or surgery. On Friday 31 January 1941 he died of renal failure. The news was passed to Lawers and James was summoned into the headmaster's room to be told simply that his father was dead and that arrangements had been made for him to travel to Aberdeen for the funeral. Like James, no one at Cargilfield had known the seriousness of his father's illness. And so James made the journey north to bury his father in Springbank Cemetery after a service at Carden Place Church. There, on a day swept by grey, snow-filled clouds, as was the custom, he took the main cord of the coffin as it was lowered gently into the frozen earth. He was now head of the family and his responsibilities were about to begin in earnest.

James had been fond of his father and had tried to emulate him in behaviour and by example. He had been a much admired model, but James had also held him in awe and was slightly afraid of him. Now that his father was dead there was no way for James ever to express the love that he had felt for him. Instead, his emotions turned to a lifelong anguish that he had been cheated of expressing fully the feelings that he harboured for the dark man who was his father. "Dammit, my father removed himself in the most damnable way. The fellow died, work unfinished—hardly begun, restless as he was."[14] Whenever tension built up in his own life, James would place much of the blame on his father's sudden absence from his formative years. This is a common enough phenomenon and that it lay submerged within him may have its origins in the fact that he betrayed little overt emotion during the funeral proceedings. Everyone who witnessed it remarked on his manly bearing and his refusal to show his feelings even when confronted with that most nerve-racking ordeal, the lowering of the coffin into the grave. Perhaps if he had given vent to his anguish, the death could have been purged and it might not then have cast such a long shadow over his life. But that would have been the easy way out and James seems to have been determined to show the world his stoicism in the face of overwhelming grief.

After his father's death, James began to develop an ever-increasingly intimate relationship with his mother. He cared about the difficulties she had to face, worried when she looked tired, and remembered to praise her when she visited him at Cargilfield—"I was glad to see you so well last night. You honestly were the picture of health and beauty." As so often happens in an exclusive mother-son relationship he became something of a surrogate husband in dealing with, and offering advice on, domestic and financial matters: no mean task for an adolescent boy. Through the difficulties of travel in wartime, Hazel had been prevented from travelling north for the funeral and she, too, saw that her brother was becoming closer to their mother than she could ever be.

The resumption of Marjory's medical career determined the family's immediate future. Having obtained her Diploma in Public Health she took a job in Hertford with the county council's medical service and made provision to move into a rented house. Her move to England meant that affairs in Auchterarder had to be settled and in the resulting domestic reorganisation she lost possession of Kenwood Park. It had been built for J.P. Kennaway, Charles's father and the Kennaways were anxious that the house should remain in the family. A problem had arisen over Charles's will which had been written and signed by him, but not witnessed, an indication perhaps of the lack of pessimism he had felt in Tor-na-dee. Until the ninteen-twenties an unwitnessed Holograph Will, as Charles Kennaway's will was known, was considered to be entirely adequate for all purposes but it had become increasingly normal for such wills to be questioned as far as heritable property was concerned. That lack of title caused several problems in the handling of Charles Kennaway's estate, as much of his capital was bound up in property, and in the subsequent negotiations it was agreed that Broom, a house at Gleneagles, should be available to Marjory while Kenwood Park, which they had rented, would be returned to the Kennaway family. It was an unsettling move and one that provided further evidence to James that his world was falling apart. But Charles Kennaway had hardly left their education and destitute: his children were able to finish their education and there was sufficient private wealth to enable their lives to progress in the same even tenor of the past.

At the end of his final year at Cargilfield James was awarded the Gifford Medal for the best all-rounder and the boy who had done most for the honour of the school. It was a richly deserved accolade for not only had James been an excellent head boy but no one who had known him could have doubted either his sense of humour or the fortitude that had brought him through the trying winter of 1941. At the end of the Spring term, 1942, he left Cargilfield for entry to Glenalmond, an earnest boy of whom much was expected, and a son who had not forgotten to send his mother words of comfort on the first anniversary of his father's death.

> I hope you are not getting by any chance depressed at this critical time of year; I'm not except when I have a lapse, but I comfort myself with these words: "To the righteous (which I know Pop was from my own experience and every man who talks of him says he was one of the best) there is no such thing as 'Death'. 'Death' means happiness and peace from pain and hardship to the righteous—there is only one sorrow, that is we can't see him at present, but we will in time"—and so to sleep.

Those sentiments were to be expressed again and again by him on his journey through boyhood as each year brought back to him the remembrance of a cold winter's day in a snow-clad Aberdeen cemetry and the saddest sound of all—the breaking of earth on the coffin of a loved one.

~ 3 ~

Glenalmond

The resumption of Marjory's medical career in Hertford meant that a secure base in Scotland at a school with a reputation second to none was a sensible solution to the inevitable problems of separation from James. There was also the important consideration that Glenalmond's isolated position offered greater safety during the years of wartime, when even Scotland was being affected by German bombing raids, particularly on the Clyde shipyards; and the school was socially acceptable, having been founded at that point in British history when Victorian expansion needed eager young men, trained in the classics to administer the nation's world empire. That entailed an Oxford or Cambridge education and so a number of new schools like Marlborough, Shrewsbury, Repton and Radley, amongst others, were established to challenge the domination of the older English public schools like Eton, Harrow and Winchester. In Scotland, education had evolved from the village schools founded in the post-Reformation years into the town and country academies which steered their pupils through a broadly-based education to a higher learning at the ancient universities of St Andrews, Glasgow, Aberdeen and Edinburgh. It was a rare event for a Scottish pupil to go direct to Oxbridge (although many went there to do postgraduate work on scholarships founded by successful scholars of the past) and so, to meet the demands voiced by many wealthy middle-class Scottish families, a small number of schools based on the English public school system were founded in Scotland during the nineteenth century (the most notable being the Edinburgh and Glasgow Academies, Fettes, Loretto and Strathallan).

Glenalmond, which must be added to their number, is situated firmly in Kennaway country in the valley of the River Almond, a pleasing, meandering stream which rises to the east in the high, heather-covered hills of Breadalbane and which ends its seventeen-mile journey at a place which means much to Scotland's history, Scone, where it spills out into the River Tay. It was there in A.D. 838 that Kenneth MacAlpine brought the Stone of Destiny from Dunstaffnage in Argyll to establish Scone as the coronation place of the Kings of the newly-united Scotland. An Augustinian monastery was added in 1147 and it was in that historic setting, significantly at the point where the Lowlands grudgingly give way to the hills and glens of the Highlands, that all of Scotland's kings were crowned until 1651 when the Scots defied the parliamentarians and crowned Charles II their last King of Scots. The Stone of Destiny, by legend and stoutly held belief, the pillow of Jacob when he had his miraculous dream of the stairway to heaven, now rests beneath the throne of a united England and Scotland in Westminster Abbey in London. Today, all that remains of that historic past is the massive pile of Scone Palace, built for the Mansfield family in 1803 and the greater part of this ancient locality is contained within the bounds of that private estate.

At first the river valley is a gentle affair as it leads up to Almondbank and winds past Huntingtower, whose castle was the scene of King James VI's humiliation and captivity after the notorious Raid of Ruthven in 1583. But from there, above Dalcrue Bridge, the flat vale gradually transforms itself into something approaching a highland glen: Glen Almond. At its lower half it assumes the name Logiealmond and it was there that the Bishops of Dunblane, Dunkeld and St Andrews would meet when Scotland was a Catholic country, and the nearby Tower of Logie was long known by the reforming farmers of the neighbourhood as "a nest of Catholics". Both sides of the river are today served by good metalled roads and it was along those, no doubt, pretty country lanes that three gentlemen made their way in a post-chaise during the summer of 1842. Although they would probably have been more than a little diverted by the scenery and the glen's ancient past, they each had one object in mind—the discovery of a site that would be suitable for the foundation of an episcopalian seminary and a boarding school offering an English form of education. Those men were William Ewart Gladstone, a successful Member of Parliament and soon to become Prime Minister of Britain, his father Sir John Gladstone, and James Hope, a parliamentary barrister with High Church, Tractarian views. The group which they represented had been formed in the previous year, 1841, traditionally the year of Glenalmond's foundation.

Their first port of call was The Cairnies which formed part of the estate of George Patton who had offered the grounds free of charge together with the right to purchase more in the future. A lavish lunch, with a crateful of the "most persuasive champagne" had been laid on for the guests but as Gladstone was later to confide to Hope's sister, his mind had been made up at the first glimpse of the estate.

> In the neighbourhood of wild and open country well adapted to the purposes of recreation, the property . . . is neither bleak nor much exposed; above it and below it are estates apparently well cultivated. The stream on which it is placed is unfit for boating, but its banks present much variety and beauty and there are walks in the woods which skirt them, to which our scholars would have access.[1]

Although arguments about the positioning of the school on the exposed rolling hill on the south bank of the river raged on until the end of the year, it was agreed that the site did meet at least one of the conditions contained in the original proposal, that the school should be "removed from the immediate vicinity of any large town". And so, four years later, on 8 September 1846, the foundation stone was laid for the "College of the Holy and Undivided Trinity", the first pupils taking up residence the following year. Kennaway's English master, G. St Quintin, was to publish a history of the school in the same year that his former pupil was to bring out his first novel, *Tunes of Glory,* and he was quick to point out that the original cumbersome title was rarely, if ever, used: "Its official title is now Trinity College, Glenalmond. To those who live, or have in the past lived there, it is "Coll". To its neighbours, it is "The College" and to the world at large, . . . 'Glenalmond'."[2]

On its prominent site at a bend in the River Almond the school offers an imposing face to the world, even if purists protest that its ecclesiastical-style buildings are more reminiscent of southern climes than of a college in a Scottish glen. It has a fine chapel and the group of stone buildings that nestle around its quadrangle give it an atmosphere that is belied by the scattered outbuildings of the boarding houses and other school properties. Over the years it has become known as a somewhat isolated school offering an ascetic and frequently spartan education, but successive Wardens (the headmasters) have transformed those necessary drawbacks into virtues and many an Old Glenalmond boy remembers most vividly and pleasurably the practice of the "docket" which allowed the boys to go off on reasonably carefully regulated Saturday-afternoon expeditions in the surrounding hills—the "docket" referred to the route or plan submitted by each boy or party of boys.

Kennaway entered Glenalmond in April 1942, the Trinity Term, and was assigned to Patchell's House, whose housemaster was C.M.H. Millar, a scholar of Queen's College, Oxford, and the son of J.H. Millar, the distinguished scholar whose *Literary History of Scotland* of 1903 was for many years the standard work of reference to Scottish Literature. In that first term he remembers Kennaway as being somewhat small for his age—he was fourteen and stood at 5′ 2½″ with a weight of 7st. 11lbs.—and he also seemed to be easily led and over-awed by his contemporaries[3]. But in spite of the difficulties he must have encountered at being thrown into a strange environment with new rules to be learned and traditions to be accepted, Millar also remembers Kennaway's cheerfulness and smiling good nature, and his first term report noted with some satisfaction that he was "cheerful and energetic" even though he was "rather tired I think at the end of the term".

Trinity Term 1942 was a trying one not only for Kennaway, but for the school as a whole. Wartime exigencies had brought with them the need to economise and the Warden, Christopher Smith, had appealed to Old Glenalmond boys to supply second-hand blazers, sweaters and rugby strips that could be used by the boys. Kennaway, in one of the first letters that he wrote to his mother reported that some of the clothes handed on to him had come from a boy called Elliot who had once "dressed up as a lady to a dance at Harriotfield. He was there for some time when a ploughman tried to make love to him—home he hopped. Across country and over the Almond and into his dorm."[4] The same boy was also supposed to have shot a fellow pupil and to have been caught in the grounds of the school with "three bottles of beer—a whole roast chicken—a beer opener and a mug. He invited the beak who caught him to eat it—and so he did." Another equally imaginative letter, of 9 May 1943, referred to a bizarre incident which, however luridly it was recounted to Kennaway's mother, did have its basis in fact.

> The only other interesting thing is that two boys have run away, but the novelty is that they don't seem to have run home, but somewhere we don't really know. Some say that they are aiming at America, working their way over. One is said to have £30 in his pocket, though one boy saw them with over £40 or something. Anyhow, one has a lot of money and the other is a tough bloke, most desperate, and is said to have a revolver with him. Both have huge sheath knives. It is also said that they're trying to get to Hollywood to become cowboy actors—positively childish, eh what?

In this case truth was stranger than fiction. The guns may have been an invention but the startling fact was that two boys did run away from school at that time and fetched up eventually as extras at the Ealing Studios. Their punishment was banishment from Glenalmond and the Warden resisted all attempts made by their parents, including a threatened legal action, to have them re-instated. It was bad enough absconding and creating additional problems for the hard-pressed staff, but it was the fact that they had become associated with something as disreputable as the film business that finally sealed their fates. At the same time, James reported that the masters were, in fact, a fine crew and that one in particular had taken an interest in his welfare—"Daudet" Hayward who was destined to become a lifelong friend and confidant during his years at Oxford and, later, in London.

The war had brought with it more pressing problems. A vigorous black-out had been enforced and on some of the rising ground around the school, posts had been erected to prevent enemy planes from landing. The already monastically-inclined school became more isolated than it had ever been in peacetime.

A Home Guard was formed by one of the masters, Major Daldy, and eventually the school corps became a Junior Training Corps to give the boys a semblance of military training. Harvest camps were held each year throughout the war at Eassie in Angus and potato howking and other agricultural work became as important a part of the school year as exploring the mysteries of algebra and mastering Latin syntax. The war was taken seriously by the masters, although as the threat of airborne invasion receded after 1941, many were more than a little amused by the advice given to the Warden by the local military authorities in the event of an outbreak of hostilities in the vicinity of the college. The boys were to be forbidden to watch the battle, and it was thought that it would be "a great help if the boys could be amused during fighting in the vicinity. The playing of a gramophone, piano or any instrument would take their minds off what was going on around them. Tea and tuck might be issued out and harmless games of chance indulged in."[5] But as St Quintin pointed out in his *History*, it was a time of togetherness which brought master and pupil close in a sense of common purpose. "Compared with what was happening elsewhere, life at Glenalmond was wonderfully sheltered and the precautions and special wartime undertakings now seem trivial enough. Yet even 'in the day when heaven was falling' the best thing to do was to carry on in as normal a way as possible."[6]

It was his mother's intention that Kennaway should enter the medical profession and so his first terms at Glenalmond were spent on the science side which he hated. Within a year he was in trouble. His winter term report thundered its disapproval of his "crude and inaccurate" thinking and of his lack of interest in the "value of precision", whereas his English master, St Quintin, noted his interest in the set texts and that he wrote "fluently and correctly". Clearly a decision would have to be made but, for the time being, unwilling to upset his mother, Kennaway soldiered on with his science subjects and discussed with Daldy the possibilities of entering either the University of Aberdeen, or Edinburgh, in October 1945. Daldy's frank admission that additional tuition would be required to get his charge through School Certificate was met with a reply that Kennaway was confident, keen and determined "for his mother's sake", and for a further eighteen months he kept up the pretence of being a dutiful son as far as his choice of career was concerned.

Several factors combined to help him alter his opinion. He developed a love of English literature and under the tutelage of St Quintin he began writing. ("He can write fluently, perhaps a little too fluently, and his matter is good.") And to his Cousin Edith he showed those early efforts. Much of the poetry of Kennaway's juvenilia is derivative enough: sentimental or heroic, echoing the tenor of the times, but one long poem, written in 1944, despite the obvious influence of Tennyson, is a good pointer to a certain duality of attitude that was growing in strength within him.

My life—with all its labours, sorrows, fear,
Darkness, its stinging wounds of flesh and soul,
Its grievous moods, beyond my mind's control,
Its warmest tear, its coldest deathly chill,
And yet with all its happiness, its dance,
Its love, its sunny days and moments still,
Together with its spirit and its chance—
For all this is my life—seemed but a dream.

A common enough sentiment in any young man's early grasping towards an understanding both of himself and of the world he inhabits, but in Kennaway's case, his view of himself is revealing and honest. On the one hand, he was a keen and enthusiastic schoolboy, liked by one and all and admired by the masters for his personal pluck. On the other he was subject to moods of grim depression when he contemplated the void caused by his father's death. He laboured at subjects he disliked intensely to please his mother when all the evidence pointed to him concentrating on English and History. To Scotland, like other schoolboys of his age, he remained intensely loyal ("I have not wasted my sweet coupons," he wrote to his mother, "and can get excellent sweets in our humble shop, without sending home for some swagger relation to buy them from an English snob in a 'ye terrific' sweet shop somewhere in London."), while his holidays were spent with his mother in England where London's West End became a tantalising lure ("Possible shows for holidays: Hamlet, Richard III, Arms and the Man, Private Lives or The Merry Widow might also be viewed from the gods."). But during those holidays he became increasingly unsociable and Hazel remembers him refusing to join in tennis parties, a strange condition for a boy who at school liked more than anything else being at the centre of attention and using his self-admitted "easy charm and winning smile" to gain a range of favours—from the gift of a dozen eggs from a girl on a neighbouring farm to being excused paying a rail fare between Gleneagles and London when he lost his ticket.

Now, while a certain dichotomy of attitude is present in every teenage boy, the feeling in Kennaway ran deeper, partly because he was more intensely aware of the two voices that guided him, and so the myth of James and Jim was born. James was quiet and studious, a little reserved perhaps, but enthusiastic and eager to please, the favourite nephew. James at one time considered that he had a calling in the church. Jim, on the other hand, had a darker side, was introverted, yet liked to be at the centre of attention and had the winning attribute of a charm that could be used, or not, to gain his own ends. Jim was also an actor who liked strutting the stage and who was possessed of all the feelings of self-doubt and uncertainty that went with the role. To J. S. Liddell, the school captain in his last year, Jim seemed to belong to a "charmed circle . . . [and those of us who stood without] looked on them no doubt with a certain awe that precluded intimate friendship"[7], a view shared by another Glenalmond boy of the same generation, Jeremy Bruce-Watt, also destined to become a novelist, who can only see in his mind's eye a boy "distinguished by a very fresh complexion—rosy cheeks—unruly curly hair and a perpetual smile".[8] Only his housemaster, "Phaz" Millar, who knew all the boys and who retains a clear memory of the period, dimly realised that his perplexing pupil led two lives. Like the other masters he admired the boy's enthusiasm and his integrity, but he wondered how much of it was an act, performed to gain admiration. In the day-to-day running of an efficient house and in the routine business of the school he began to notice Kennaway's ability to dramatise events concerning himself—everything seemed to demand being played from his point of view, and, just as importantly, Kennaway could engineer events to make himself the centre of an activity or gathering. To a certain extent, Millar's reactions were governed by the reservations that many grown men will feel when confronted by a charming and self-confident adolescent, but in the light of Kennaway's later life, his observations are not without interest.

When Kennaway tried to polarise the James-Jim split in 1965, when he saw "the familiar James . . . becoming an unfamiliar, unpredictable and unloveable Jim", he saw its origins in his boyhood and in being pushed too hard at school through his parents' wishes.[9] Much of the blame for his condition he apportioned to his father and to his early death ("You can't do a son much more harm than that"), but his mother was never involved in the process. He always took care to shield her from any unpleasantness, and Millar also remembers that mother and son adopted the same mannerisms and patterns of speech, as if enjoying a secret joke. (Sending up the system became an important part of the Kennaway ethos, and it is not difficult to see how infuriated and excluded the masters might have felt when Marjory Kennaway visited Glenalmond.) Marjory also cultivated both James and Jim. In many of her letters she would exhort him to work, to succeed, and she would worry unnecessarily, about his future. In turn, James would be the dutiful son—"I hope you are not working too hard. We don't want you fading out at this point, so don't overwork and overtire yourself, whatever you do . . . now I'll close down, but remember not to overdo things, all in moderation, and do eat", he pleaded in his first term. But she also smiled at Jim's ploys, at the daft, comic inventiveness of his letters, glad that the bond between them was so strong.

Like the other boys, Kennaway wrote a weekly letter home throughout his schooldays and from his correspondence to his mother a vivid picture emerges of the pleasures that Glenalmond afforded him. There was piping and drumming to be mastered with the Junior Training Corps ("I have learned all the beatings necessary in the drum fairly well so now I come to the difficult part, the twiddling of the sticks. I have wounded my nose with them already.); field days with the corps ("The enemy party was under Stirling, a friend of mine so I decided to put up a fight . . . they couldn't shoot me as it would give away the position, so a super free fight ensued, me against three blokes."); work camps on the neighbouring farms at harvest time ("our end, I fear to admit, was just un petit morceau de frivolous and we began chucking potatoes at each other but at that point a josser who might have been anything from Angus McAllister to Mackinnon of Mackinnon, bore down on us with a war cry: Wha's bungin' thae ta'eys aboot doon there? One wit down the line announced "that my dear boy means 'Who is throwing those potatoes about down there?' '.") Then there were the pleasures of treading the stage ("The play went off simply marvellously and I have been congratulated personally more than once on the way I lit my pipe."); the despair of being dropped from the XV ("This has been a trying week from my point of view, for a fellow who plays in the same position as me has come up and the net result is that he played instead of me."); but above all, he relished the life of the school and its isolated position in the Perthshire hills, a feeling that was brought home during expeditions to play rugby against other Scottish schools ("The visit [to Loretto in Musselburgh, near Edinburgh] made me value my own college more than ever before . . . the part I love best of college, the hills, the burns and the colour, stands infinitely above the back slums of the east end of Edinburgh.")

In his last year at school Kennaway was secretary to the Rugby Club and gained a cap even though he could not command a place in the XV throughout the season. He became a sergeant in the corps and was appointed a school prefect ("it makes a great difference to the success and happiness of everything at Coll if the Common Room are doing their job well, and giving the right sort of lead", warned the Warden's letter of appointment in September 1945), but typically, in later life, in interviews about himself, Kennaway would always say that he won the corps' Belt of Honour and that he was the school's head boy. Reality obviously was not enough for him. Less spectacularly, he became secretary to the Historical Society, addressed them on the art of poetry and learned the business of public speaking. But it was the Dramatic Society that captured his greatest interest and it was on the stage that he gained the highest plaudits.

His first part was as Ruby Birtles in Priestley's *When We are Married,* and the magic of the first night had the desired effect.

> After we'd had cocoa and biscuits Edington and I went and beat up the Patchell's room. We were eventually chucked out by the

> master in charge so came down to the houseroom where we ate some apples (received with many thanks). We then talked to the master in charge of the play and the one in charge of the scenery, and Humph. This in the gym at the end of which is the stage. At about 11 they went away leaving behind about five of us who ragged, performed initiations, did acrobatics and generally had a marvellous time until coming on for midnight when we tore ourselves away from the beloved stage and went to bed, bathing to an extent beforehand. This today is a horrid anti-climax. Reactions from the reaction. Sad and sentimental. however inevitable.[10]

His greatest success was playing the title role in J.A. Ferguson's *Campbell of Kilmohr* in which James obviously kept Jim under firm control. "Kennaway once he had warmed up gave a very promising version of the difficult part of the Campbell. He did not, however, manage to suggest the cold, devilish cunning of the man's character. One is almost glad, for the sake of his reputation, that he did not." The *Glenalmond Chronicle* was equally enthusiastic about his last acting role, that of Jimmy Ludgrove in A.A. Milne's *The Fourth Wall,* performed in December 1945. "Kennaway acted with restraint and managed to appear quite natural and at home and not the least praiseworthy part of his performance was the way in which he helped his partner (J.N. Marshall) in sustaining the more difficult character of his fiancée."[11]

Acting in the college's Dramatic Society was important to Kennaway and he secretly thought it would be a fine thing to become an actor. After the good notices for *Campbell of Kilmohr* he confided his delight in the theatre to Edith Shaw and spoke wistfully of the necessity of having to trample down "this yearning wish". When he first came to write seriously his early efforts were directed at the stage and he continued to use his later school holidays to visit the West End theatres with his mother. So stage-struck was he that it came as no surprise to Marjory to find that during a day's absence at half-term her son had managed to beard Emlyn Williams, the director and actor who was then fast approaching the height of his powers in the theatre. And all the while his literary interests were being given much encouragement by St Quintin who by December 1945 was able to give modest praise to his pupil's English style which he found to be "more restrained and seems now quite an effective instrument".

For his own sake his English master's remarks were a much needed boost to his morale at the end of that winter term. The previous July had seen James win a long-drawn-out and emotionally draining battle with his mother over the course of his future career. It had always been assumed that he would follow a medical career and, good son that he was, he had stuck to science during his three years at Glenalmond. However, shortly after his seventeenth birthday Jim had woken up to the fact that he "cannot bring [myself] to read the stuff. It both bores and irritates me. I prefer my Browning or Shakespeare." And in the same letter of 3 July he admitted that even if he managed to qualify as a doctor, he would be "no good at my job technically but I make a reasonable healer and comforter. I live in the backwoods of Dalmally, or if I am lucky, Muthill. A very happy life. Not much income—but who cares—I have my food, my books, the countryside, a shot gun and a fishing rod. I'm quite a little hero in Muthill but alas the people of Crieff have never heard of me!" In a remarkably sustained argument he put forward his case for changing from science to English and history. He pulled at her heartstrings by mentioning the implausability of his working as a Scottish country doctor in Perthshire when he knew that she had left all that behind her. He flattered her by mentioning his hopes for a career in the Diplomatic or Colonial Services. He stated convincingly that he was "intelligent and a stickler to some extent so I have managed to keep the pace so far, but as a scientific brain I'm dud". And then he placed the clinching suggestion that she should read that last sentence and ask herself what his father would have advised: "He would shake his head and say, 'Let the boy do what he's keen at and he'll do it twice as well.' Well, wouldn't he?"

With the assistance of Edith Shaw he managed to change his mother's mind. Clearly a valuable victory had been gained but Kennaway had marshalled his forces with some care. Support came from the unexpected source of Rossitter the maths master who had taken James climbing in Argyllshire during the Easter holidays and he too had added his voice in James's cause. However tenaciously she had fought a stubborn rearguard action to keep her son on course for a settled career, Marjory later claimed that she had taken much comfort in the central argument in the letter when he spoke about the indivisibility of his talents.

> But mother, (I write this now in confidence) I feel I have been granted with more than one talent; in such a life my talent of sympathy would shine but my other talents would lie buried. On my part I would get lazier and fatter every day. I might however do this at the same time as I write and really go in for writing, but I must learn more about the English language before I can write any stuff worth writing.

In that paraphrasing of the parable of the talents Kennaway gave his mother to understand that there would be "weeping and gnashing of teeth", if like the "wicked and slothful servant" he allowed his talent for English to remain hidden in the ground. Far better, he insisted, to be one of the select who shall be given more for the riches they already possess. That term, he had also been reading Milton and was much taken with the poem *"On his Blindness"* with its insistence on the "one talent it is death to hide lodged with me useless". Whatever would happen in the future he remained convinced from that moment onwards that he was possessed of talent and that it might vaguely take him into a career in the theatre or publishing.

And so it was that Kennaway's final year at Glenalmond was spent in the secure knowledge that his future was now of his own creation, that he was slowly shedding the links that bound him to the past. He read Macaulay and Scott with enthusiasm and came to admire Stevenson's rounded ability to tell a good story. In history, Bismarck became an admired model ("a splendid chap"), and even French, which had brought him no little trouble, became less of a foreign language and more of a malleable instrument, although in later life, any language, other than English, was not a strong point. As the year progressed his thoughts about his immediate future began to take shape: with the medical career put safely to one side, a Scottish university education gave way to hopes for Oxbridge and the possibility of the English Bar. It would be, as he admitted to his mother, "an appalling risk—but isn't life rather hum drum?"

He worked hard during that last year of school and withdrew into himself and into the "charmed circle" of friends which included the mercurial Robert Spence who came from Larbert in Stirlingshire and who was destined to remain one of his closest friends in the years immediately after Oxford. He had the same literary interests and was also captain of the rugby club, an honoured position in a school like Glenalmond. Another close friend was John Denby Cameron, a rector's son from Yorkshire, who accompanied James on many of his expeditions to Craig Dhu and to Chapelbank and who played the pipes there for Hazel's joint twenty-first birthday party with Kirsty Bell. At least close friendships were allowed in sixth form and prefects had their own studies, very far removed in style from the dormitories with their cubicles, or "cubes", open-topped areas separated by thin plaster partitions in which most boys slept. To look over that partition in Kennaway's day was to invite expulsion and the masters went to a good deal of trouble to avoid any possibility of homosexuality. Even at chapel, juniors sitting in the front pews were forbidden to look upwards at the older boys sitting at higher levels opposite them. Glenalmond was in some ways a republic with the traditions and rules being operated by the boys for the boys, and sixth form offered a blessed release from many of the stultifying and minor restrictions endured by the rest of the school.

The only cloud that loomed on the horizon in that first year of peace was the threat of National Service and Kennaway was much vexed by the timing of his call-up. Under normal circumstances he would have received his papers on 1 August, within days of leaving school, but the situation was complicated by the fact that he would not by then know the result of his Higher Certificate examinations. On the assumption that he had passed and gained a place at Oxford, he thought that his service might be deferred until the following year and that he might use the intervening months at Cargilfield or toughening himself up by working on a farm. As the Warden admitted to him it was all very confusing and by the time he came to leave school the possibility of deferment until 1947 was considered to be only an outside chance. All too quickly, it seemed, the school year came to an end and with it his days at Glenalmond. He left it a more mature and self-controlled boy; the discipline and sense of tradition and order had been a much-needed corrective in a world that had seemed to lose all purpose at the age of twelve, and in a shy way he was grateful for what Glenalmond had offered him. There were new fields to conquer in his eighteenth year, dances and "society" could resume now that the war was over and though he kept up a pretence of disdaining both, in his heart of hearts, Jim, like other boys of his age was becoming increasingly fascinated by the soft allure of girls.

His last report was both good and accurate, superior to the dull and timid regularity of the swot and one that echoed the bright swaying moods of a boy who knew where he stood. His housemaster may have found him to have "a rather sentimental and over-simplified outlook, due largely to lack of experience", but he also praised his "many most admirable qualities which have helped him to make a success of his school career. Those sentiments were echoed by the Warden who noted that although "he is still somewhat easily swayed by emotion and unstable in opinion . . . he has many pleasant gifts and sterling qualities. He has made a distinctive and valuable contribution to the school life and I am sorry to lose him". Both masters seemed to think that any show of emotion or sentiment in a schoolboy was a bad thing, to be avoided at all costs, and it was left to St Quintin to add the prophetic words that he found his favourite pupil's prose style "more restrained".

Seven years later, Kennaway returned his debt to Glenalmond by writing about the school in his third published story, *The Dollar Bottom.* Although many old Glenalmond boys of fierce mien thought it to be a scurrilous account of a place they held in high regard, it is a fizzy *jeu d'esprit,* a story full of good humour that steers a careful course between adult farce and schoolboy high-jinks. It was published in the January 1954 edition of *Lilliput,* and in a tongue-in-cheek sort of way it was Kennaway's own comment on his school education. Set in a Scottish boarding school—"on the borders of the Scottish Highlands"—which is obviously Glenalmond, the plot follows the development of an insurance scheme, designed by an all-knowing junior, Taylor Two, to offer, if not physical, then at least financial cover against beatings. So successful is the "Rock of Ages" scheme that it is extended to offer cover to other Scottish public schools with the result that Taylor Two and his chums are faced either with bankruptcy or a severe beating. By dint of a careful reading of Scots Law, they avoid the former by eating their "capital" in the school tuck-shop, but they have to face up to the latter: "of course, the school prefects beat him for insolence but the scars of the battle only added to the triumph of the great defeat, to the glory of Taylor's contentment".[12] Stories of that kind—of pupils outwitting the authorities by insuring against beatings—were not uncommon in boys' magazines of the period and earlier: the *Boys' Own Paper* of 5 April 1913 included a similar story, *Pip's Diary: Being a Record of Percy Ignatius Pocock's Bid for Fame,* but it is highly unlikely that Kennaway would have read it, or others of that ilk. An insurance scheme to recompense those who have been beaten is, after all, not an unnatural idea in an environment in which beatings by cane were supposed to be good for the development of character.

Kennaway's story was a great success. The actor David Niven in later years owned to a boyish delight in the *brio* of Taylor Two's pranks and thought it would make a splendid film. The publisher Robert Lusty (now Sir Robert Lusty) wrote to suggest that he meet Kennaway to discuss the possibility of "a book including a number of such incidents with a connecting link". In fact it was not until four years later, in 1958, after the success of *Tunes of Glory* that Kennaway returned to the idea of reviving Taylor Two's fortunes. The impulse to do so came from his father-in-law who was convalescing from a heart attack and to provide him with some amusement and diversion Kennaway drafted two letters that contain the essence of the sequel *Taylor's Finest Hour* (both stories were published together with an introduction by the present author in 1981). In both letters—one is a trial run—Taylor Two and company turn their attention from insurance of bottoms to assurances about the awful matter of sex. Neither story gives away many clues about the direction Kennaway's writing would take him except that they indicate that he had learned how to characterise and how to write crisp, witty dialogue. "Inclined as before to write of a boyhood in Scotland," he wrote in 1961. These stories are not part of that intention. As light-hearted romps they show a different face to Kennaway and in some small way identify him, like many other men, as the schoolboy he never quite unbecame. They also tell us not a little about his schooldays and his reactions to a school that had meant home for him for so long. Because travel had been difficult during the wartime years many boys had been unable to go home for the shorter holidays: with relatives and friends nearby Kennaway had been luckier than most, but several Glenalmond boys of those years looked on the school as being very much a home-from-home. Little wonder that the minutiae of school life remained imprinted on their minds.

Some of the details of Kennaway's two stories have been stretched to meet the requirements of plot, but physical descriptions of the Junior Room, the cubicles, the pipe band practising for Sundays and the remote school in the hills have been carved cleanly from remembrance. In *The Dollar Bottom* environmental details are surprisingly more blurred but at least one of the characters has been reproduced faithfully in fictional form. The Bishop, who brings about the beginning of the end for the Rock of Ages insurance scheme, was based on the Right Revd. Lumsden Barkway, a formidable gentleman much given to playing to the gallery during sermons in chapel and who referred to his person, as he does in the story, as "this battered hulk of mine". A glance at the school list reveals, too, that some of the boys did exist, though none were in Kennaway's house. (It was possible to go through school without knowing well boys from other houses.) There was a Taylor, known as Taylor Two and reputedly something of an eccentric by his peers, although we may be sure that his charm comes from his creator's vision of himself as a schoolboy, replete with worldliness and amiability. The Hon. D.T.G. Browne was an exact contemporary, Bailes had been school captain before Kennaway's time and Hepburn was an older boy, the object of not a little hero-worship by the lower forms. As far as corporal punishment was concerned, beating was on the way out during Kennaway's time, although Jeremy Bruce-Watt in a memoir of the same period remembers that "ritual chastisement with a cane [was] a consistent source of excitement".[13] Quite apart from the Warden's stated dislike of its use, the wartime conditions seem to have generated an equality of effort between masters and boys and negated the need for beatings. Despite Bruce-Watt's protestations, which are born of a stated dislike for boarding school education, there is no reference to beatings in Kennaway's correspondence apart from one letter which mentions the possibility of a thrashing for giving misleading information about his Saturday docket.

The headmaster is obviously a figure of invention as are the two masters, Cuddlestone and Hobson, who play similar roles in both stories. Karl Turner's cover is easily broken but it is doubtful whether he possessed a Bible box or that his mantle-shelf was wide enough to house a glass of gin and orange. *Taylor's Finest Hour,* although it betrays an accurate knowledge of the layout of Glenalmond, plays faster and looser with the realms of possibility. The Warden in Kennaway's time was unmarried, as were many of the masters, and the fictional headmaster is allowed a more casual relationship with his pupils than would ever have been possible—in any school. Similarly, Taylor Two's sidekicks, Macbeth and Graham, travel between the school and Edinburgh in their search for books with almost reckless ease, and the story as a whole is bent more towards farce than its predecessor which has a defter, more controlled touch. From his notebooks it appears that Kennaway had toyed with the idea of creating a series of stories featuring the same boys and some of their future ploys are hinted at in *Taylor's Finest Hour.* Gambling, the wine business, property development—who could say which direction would be taken by Taylor Two, the Hon. Browne, Macadam, Macbeth and Graham?

After leaving school in July 1946 there was a short and pleasant holiday with his mother at her home in Harpenden and there was also Hazel's wedding to look forward to. She had become engaged to Martin Bolton, a Staffordshire landowner, while at Girton and they had decided to marry immediately after her graduation.

The wedding was held in Knebworth. Cameron played the pipes and James wore his kilt, and gave away his sister, in much the same way that his father had done for his sister, Elizabeth, eighteen years before. "People who have the courage to fence themselves in at twenty shouldn't be discouraged," he had written to his mother on hearing the news of his sister's engagement. "We need a bigger stronger Britain even if the flesh comes from the Kennaway side." Other letters of this period refer, somewhat surprisingly, to his own desire never to marry and to father children—he felt he would not live to do so—and he viewed his sister's marriage with cautious optimism.

For her he bought a pedigree black Labrador from Lord Balerno, the father of a schoolfriend, George Buchanan-Smith, and added the proviso that it should be named "Logie" or "Coll" in honour of Glenalmond. The wedding was a great success and with the gradual break-up of her family, Marjory returned to her public health work with Herts County Council. Her next move was to St Albans where she was number two in the county medical staff, working mainly in maternity and child welfare clinics. So that he could enlist in a Highland regiment it had been arranged that his call-up papers would be sent to Broom, the house at Gleneagles; the exact date when this would happen remained a mystery. During the summer James heard that he had been awarded a place at Trinity College, Oxford which would be his in October 1948 once his military service had been completed, so, he reasoned, at least his long-term future was assured.

~ 4 ~

The Complexion of a Soldier

In the middle of August 1946 all the doubts about Kennaway's immediate future evaporated when he began the process of being called up as a National Serviceman. Like some quarter of a million other eighteen-year-olds who would enlist in the same year, Kennaway registered for his period of military service at the local Ministry of Labour and National Service and then he awaited the arrival of his call-up papers at Broom.

National Service had been introduced in Britain in March 1939 and had continued in operation throughout the Second World War to swell the ranks of Britain's armed forces. But as war gave way to an uncertain peace in 1945 two factors combined to suggest that the losses to Britain's military strength caused by demobilisation should be staunched by some form of conscription: the arrival of the Cold War in Europe which required a powerful allied presence in West Germany; and the slow retreat from Empire which had to be covered by the army as riots and terrorism broke out at one time or another in Aden, Kenya, the Gold Coast, British Honduras, Singapore, British Guiana, Hong Kong, Nassau, the Cameroons, Jamaica, Kuwait, Zanzibar, Borneo, Tanganyika, Uganda and Mauritius. British troops also oversaw the division of the old Indian Raj into India and Pakistan and they attempted to keep order in Palestine until 1948 when Jew and Arab were left to their own devices. And National Servicemen were destined to be killed in action in wars in the Suez canal zone and in the Korean War of 1951. Although there was a long history of opposition to conscription—most

British people were suspicious of the army and regarded it as a caste apart—it took three years for Parliament to address itself to the problem and wartime conscription continued until 1948 when the National Service Act provided legislation for a fixed period of eighteen months service with four years in the reserve. In 1950 another National Service Act increased the period of service to two years with three and a half years in the reserve. Thus it was that Kennaway was called up during a period of flux when many young people hoped that conscription could have no part to play in a civilised post-war Britain. As it was, the last National Serviceman was not demobbed until May 1963.

At school Kennaway had been an active and enthusiastic member of the Junior Training Corps and his father's career had given him a leaning towards the military: in the army's eyes he would have been a prime recruit. Within a week of registering he received notice to attend a medical examination in Perth, a rudimentary affair whose purpose was to determine the grade of service to which the potential recruit was best suited. These were notoriously difficult to fail despite several well-known attempts made by unwilling soldiers to by-pass this first hurdle by ploys such as eating soap, drinking too much alcohol and keeping awake for as long as possible before the routine medical. Such a course of action would have been unthinkable to Kennaway (although his friend of future years, Peter O'Toole, and other drama students in London used to run extra-curricular classes on how to fail a War Office medical), and he passed with flying colours, at the same time taking the opportunity of telling the Military Interviewing Officer that his preference was for a Highland regiment, and, in particular, for the local Perthshire regiment, the Black Watch.

He received his call-up papers in the second week of September and was ordered to report to 58 Primary Training Corps at Queen's Barracks in Perth, the Black Watch depot, where he was earmarked to stay for his six weeks' basic training. It was a further rupture in the umbilical cord and his introduction to the world of barracks life was light years removed from the calm of his mother's home or from the douce dignity of Broom or Craigh Dhu. Countless ex-National Servicemen have commented on the rude shock that awaited them during their first days of army life when it was considered *de rigeur* for the supervising corporals and sergeants to exercise all the considerable armoury of sarcasm and violent language at their command for the simple purpose of humiliating their raw charges. But if it was a harsh training ground then at least it broke down social barriers and for middle-class boys it shattered their fastidiousness and some of the intolerance that goes with it: of the platoon of one hundred and twenty, only Kennaway and one other were public schoolboys. Certainly National Service toughened Kennaway both physically and mentally and gave him a greater degree of sympathy for the lot of his fellow men than had been allowed in his immediate family circle. When he reported for duty at the Queen's Barracks on 26 September he was passing from one world into another and he immediately took notice of the high walls that had been built to keep out the curious, to separate civilian from military society—a description which he later employed in the opening paragraph of *Tunes of Glory* ten years later. Queen's Barracks have been the depot of the Black Watch since 1880 and its massive bulk dominated the open lands of the North Inch until 1960 when during a period of military re-organisation they were abandoned and later demolished.

The army intentionally made the first few days of basic training brutal and dehumanising. From tame civilians the raw eighteen-year-olds had to be forged into fighting soldiers, capable of taking orders without question, ready to accept discipline as a fact of life and capable of suppressing their own individuality. Within minutes of arriving Kennaway had been fed, equipped with the coarse, ill-fitting battle-dress and given a letter-card so that his mother might know that he had arrived safely. From a background in which polite values and self-esteem were considered to be paramount virtues he was plunged that night into a crowded barrack room whose inhabitants he found to be "filthy" and "uneducated". His first letter home to his mother was a poor attempt at disguising his lot.

> I was sad to leave you: but I daren't now think back on that happy holiday as conditions aren't in the same world. Comparisons would be futile and most depressing . . . the awful business of hiding all your kit as it is lifted so quickly, gets me down. I'm sending pretty well all my stuff to Aunt Eliz. including the beloved cardigan . . .[1]

For their first forty-eight hours of army life the members of 1 Squad A Company were introduced to the mysteries of spit-and-polish: how to burnish boots to a mirror sparkle by first burning the leather on the toe-caps, how to achieve a razor-edge crease in the battle-dress trousers by first carefully shaving the rough worsted, how to fold kit into precise army regulations with the help of cardboard squares and how to control the narrow confines of your "bed space". It was all very efficient and all very impersonal and belittling. But then a miracle happened. The company sergeant—who took a shine to Kennaway and promoted him to "a sort of local acting unpaid unthanked very lance corporal"[2]—pleased with his recruits' attempts to achieve a modicum of progress towards military standardisation, awarded his squad a forty-eight hour weekend pass. This unlooked for piece of good fortune allowed Kennaway to bike up to Glenalmond where he spent a cheerful two days watching rugby matches, attending chapel and meeting up with fellow Old Glenalmonds who also looked on their old school as being a useful retreat from the rigours of the real world. One of his former masters, W.C. Hayward, realising that Kennaway had been made miserable during his "first horrible hours in Perth", wrote to Marjory assuring her of her son's well-being.

> James always was a good mixer and he is having no trouble in getting on well with his rather queer companions . . . he has given most hilarious accounts of his first three military days and is now obviously prepared to take all these new experiences philosophically. In some ways it is unsettling for him to be so near his old happier haunts but he realises that he must keep his two lives separate. Besides, they will presumably now start military training in earnest and there he should come into his own.[3]

He was right. Kennaway did adapt quickly and although he continued to use his weekend passes to visit Glenalmond and Craig Dhu, he threw himself totally into the life of the army and cautiously began pressing his claims for a good commission. To his mother, within a day or two of depressing her, he claimed that he would "take it as his father and uncles did before me", but he realised too that his route to the officers' mess would have to be soundly charted. To the Personnel Selection Officer, Captain Donaldson, he pointed out that the Kennaways had

Black Watch connections and he made sure that his Uncle Hedley met this important officer in the George Hotel in Perth. But James needed no such social engineering to further his ambitions: his background, his experience and his enthusiasm were sufficient qualities to persuade the military authorities that he was officer material.

Within a week of arriving at Perth, Kennaway had discussed his future most earnestly with Donaldson who told him that he could either opt for an easy life as a corporal in the Intelligence Corps whose "cap badge is a pansy, resting on its laurels", or, "he could stand up to four more months foot slogging" and try for a commission.[4] He chose the latter course only to be told that his papers had already been sent up to the Black Watch as potential officer material. His name was earmarked for a War Office Selection Board the following February and whilst his fellow recruits were dispersed amongst the regiments of the Highland Brigade, once the six weeks of basic training had been completed, Kennaway was posted as an officer cadet to 2 Coy 30th Training Battalion which was stationed at Pinefield Camp near Elgin.

Once there he found that training had begun in earnest (a good deal of his time in Perth had been spent bringing in the potato crops on local farms). He was instructed in basic field tactics and he discovered the joys "of dashing about in clouds of dust sticking bayonets into straw sacks and yelling blue murder: my blood was amazingly hot and at the end I stood foaming and stamping with a lust to kill anybody and anything straightaway. A German prisoner standing by only just saved the life of a cat which crossed my path."[5] (Most National Service recruits remember that part of their training best of all—the zombie-like plunging of a bayonet into a sack held from a gibbet, learning how to kill in one of the nastiest ways possible.) But life in Elgin offered other pleasures too. He was granted weekend leaves which could be spent at neighbouring Forres where another uncle, Harry Ewing, kept the Carlton Hotel. He had travelled widely as a young man and James was greatly beguiled by his outrageous stores of wine, women and song. Despite the gloom of winter it was a happy enough time and his mood of cautious optimism refused to be dispersed when all Christmas and New Year leave was cancelled. He brought in 1947 on guard picquet at Pinefield but, typically, he was not be denied. Two days later had had used his "winning smile" to charm the duty officer into awarding a four-day leave and he wrote exultantly to his mother of the charms of Chapelbank in the snow, of the peace offered by Glenalmond and the ever-present hospitality of the aunts at Craig Dhu.

It was at that time that his mother toyed with the idea of returning to work in Scotland by taking up general practice in Perth. It was an attractive proposition for a woman who had spent so much of her war separated from her roots and orphaned from her children. Part of her wanted to come back to the tender trap of the Kennaway fold, but a sensible voice reminded her that she could never be completely independent as a widow in douce middle-class Perthshire. James was a confidant of her concerns and it was probably an indication of his own feelings towards Scotland that he urged her to remain in England, adding the clinching argument that his own future lay outside the country of his birth.

> You must think sometimes, and wonder what you are doing away, alone in Herts when the land that you know so well is still there to welcome you. You must regret sometimes not having taken the chance of a job in Perth near me—especially if I am to be in Edinburgh next. There must be a horrible temptation to come back and to live again amongst those you really know. In a smaller sort of way my visit to the college similarly fascinated me. I wished it could happen all over again: but I looked and was glad that I was going somewhere else while I had the strength: surely it is defeat to return to one's nursery when there are equally pleasant places elsewhere. I know I have the glittering prizes of ambition fulfilled before me: you have little in that way. But look at Hedley mother, and think again. The time will come when you will be ripe for retirement, but it is not autumn yet: not nearly. Every time I think of you in England, alone, I am proud: and I am convinced that you are right to remain there. When your medical autumn comes in a few years you will finish up with me, only as far away as Oxford, when you might be in Gleneagles, moping and squabbling with non-cooperative neighbours and relations. Think how much better rest is, after hard work. Enjoy life and know that I am enjoying mine: know too that I mean you one day whatever the odds and whenever that day comes, be it sooner or later, I mean you to be as proud of me as I am of you.[6]

Like several of the longer speculative letters that Kennaway wrote to his mother there was a good deal of self-fulfilling prophecy to his musings as he attempted to make sense of his life through putting pen to paper. But a subtle change was taking place in the mother-son relationship. The forbearance he had shown previously in dealing with her personal and business affairs had turned into a real sense of mature responsibility. From merely enjoying the animal high spirits of schoolday holidays with her, he now used his leaves to squire her around an increasingly busy social life. Shortly before he moved on to Eaton Hall in Cheshire to continue his military training he spent a celebratory week's leave with her in London in the middle of April seeing all the best shows, drinking champagne and dining out, smoking Sobranie cigarettes and riding in taxis without fearing the cost. But best of all, he admitted in his letter of thanks of 20 April, "I had a really comfortable and carefree week with my dear, dear mother". By his own admission the army had strengthened Kennaway physically. He had filled out to a healthier eleven stones and in his kilt and officer cadet's blouse the serious dark-haired boy would have made up a handsome couple with his still youthfully attractive mother as they indulged again their shared love of the theatre.

Throughout his National Service Kennaway's letters to his mother remained warm and loving, couched in the terms of intimacy that he had cultivated at Glenalmond. He chided her for not shaking off colds and during the course of that winter of 1947 when almost the whole of Britain was brought to a standstill in the harsh Arctic conditions, he worried about her well-being and pleaded with her not to be sparing of coal fires and warm clothes. He also took to mentioning girlfriends in his correspondence. There were dances in Elgin and during the period following his W.O.S.B. there were visits to Edinburgh for dinner-dances at the Caledonian Hotel in the company of the Vass family, whose son Donald had been at school with him. With each letter that he wrote he took care to dispel his mother's fears that he would get too involved by laughing off the attraction of the girls he met. "Never mind you needn't worry just yet as the climate here doesn't favour much of that sort of thing. Figures are clad in elephantine tweed coats and stockings of five-ply wool: all cosmetics wasted on faces the colour of the North Sea", he wrote before leaving Scotland for his officer training in Cheshire.

His mother was also able to help him out financially and to provide him with the smart civilian clothes expected of the gentleman cadet and it is an indication of the Kennaway's comparative wealth that Marjory was able to purchase a new Sunbeam Talbot motor car in 1947. Most British cars constructed that year were destined for export as the government strove to pay off the frightening war debts and to stave off the crisis in sterling which was to lead ultimately to the devaluation of the pound. The country seemed to be stumbling from one crisis to another. Coal was in desperately short supply and the bitter cold of the 1947 winter was the harder to bear because of the lack of real nourishment caused by rationing and the absence of raw foodstuffs. Bread was rationed for the first time in a year of peace, petrol was almost unobtainable and long queues became an accepted part of the British way of life. As far as the majority of the population would have been concerned, Kennaway's description of his Easter leave that year could have come from the pages of a pre-war novel. Although he would complain—albeit cheerfully—about having to wear his father's old clothes, he was one of the luckier ones.

Having been one of the four cadets, out of eighteen candidates, to have made a successful bid for a commission in February, he transferred in June to Eaton Hall, once the seat of the Duke of Westminster, but then, with Mons at Aldershot, the army school for training National Service officers. Situated near Chester, it is a gaunt, late nineteenth-century building set in magnificent parklands and for the majority of the cadets it offered an early introduction to the closed society of the regiment and the officers' mess. During World War Two Eaton Hall had been an off-shoot of the Royal Naval College, Britannia, and the army guide to the place noted somewhat wryly that the utility buildings and huts constructed as lecture rooms detracted from the "grandiose dignity of the main building". Cadets arrived in batches of sixty every fortnight, so training was continuous, emphasising drill, physical training, instruction in weapons, fieldwork and all aspects of military law and administration, with the final intention of producing a "young officer, keen to do his best during National Service, and qualified to be given a platoon which, with more practical experience, he will be able to command efficiently[7]. From the very outset, Kennaway made it his intention to match that ideal, showing the same kind of energy and enthusiasm that had marked his school career.

"This truly is a hectic sort of dump and when one isn't on parade one seems to be getting ready for the next one," his first letter to his mother complained, but within days his tail was up and he was able to report that he was achieving by far the best results of his intake. His company commander was Major Allan Cameron, an officer in the Queen's Own Cameron Highlanders and the brother of the chief of Clan Cameron of Lochiel. During the three-day battle camp at Warminster he made Kennaway "colonel in charge" of his platoon ("not altogether to my surprise," reported Kennaway) and despite his failure to beat off a second "enemy attack" on his camp, Cameron was more than satisfied with his star recruit and years later was able to remember him as being "a really nice lad, enjoyed life to the full, very popular with his fellow cadets and had the personality and leadership qualities that gained him promotion to under-officer rank".[8] That early promotion put Kennaway in the running for the coveted Belt of Honour, the award given to the top cadet at the end of each course. Kennaway felt that he stood a fifty-fifty chance of achieving it. He shone at tactics and in leadership, the practical qualities required by any good officer, but surprisingly his military theory let him down and the lead that he had built up over his rival, Robin Farringdon, was whittled away by the relatively low marks he gained in the administration course, leaving him a very close second.

His course at Eaton Hall was not all work. Hazel lived within striking distance at Croxdon Abbey, a rambling country house adjacent to the ruins of a Cistercian abbey in the Staffordshire uplands where he was a welcome visitor. His mother visited him and Chester itself was a magnet for weekend passes with its narrow streets, antique pubs and a NAAFI club offering dancing to all hours with "very modern girls". His schoolfriend Spence was stationed in Germany with the Royal Engineers and Cameron was in Palestine, and gradually as those school friendships slackened he became immensely friendly with a fellow cadet, Alasdair Hilleary. With his wealthy and aristocratic background, his Eton education and his restrained man-of-the-world attitudes, Hilleary was an immediate source of attraction and interest to Kennaway. His family owned land at Bernisdale on the Isle of Skye and he was privy to the kind of personal allowance that made flying to London for a weekend leave look a simple fact of everyday life. James was both impressed and charmed by his friend's good looks and soigné manners and the two became firm friends, enjoying one another's company to the full. Until then, James had associated gentry with the scions of Strathearn: here was a man who enjoyed his company for its own sake and not because he was the factor's son. Alasdair Hilleary became an important and formative figure during the period at Eaton Hall and it was with a sense of boyish delight that the two cadets found themselves posted to the same regiment at the end of the course.

James had pressed hard to join the Black Watch, even going to the extent of asking his mother to arrange for a regimental kilt,white dress stockings and white horse-hair sporran to be sent to him from friends in Perthshire. When Lord Wavell, the colonel-in-chief of the Black Watch, visited Eaton Hall in the middle of July, Kennaway managed to get in a few words of self-promotion, but the regiment's lists were full and he was told that he would have to look elsewhere. Help came from his company commander, Major Cameron, who suggested that Kennaway and Hilleary apply to his own regiment, and so it was that the end of the course saw the two cadets emerge as second lieutenants in the Queen's Own Cameron Highlanders. James was well pleased with himself; he had missed the Belt of Honour award by a narrow margin, but the authorities were more than satisfied with him—and he had managed to find his way into a Highland regiment.

The Queen's Own Cameron Highlanders, the 79th Regiment, had been raised in Lochaber in December 1793 by Major Charles Cameron of Erracht. Although his ancestors had fought on the Jacobite side during the uprisings of 1715 and 1745, Alan Cameron was one of a new breed of Highlander who looked to London and Hanoverian prosperity as the best goals for himself and his country. He may have retained a sentimental interest in the Stuart cause but by the end of the eighteenth century that was confined to a knee-jerk sentimentality for the "king over the water" and the white cockade of the Young Pretender, Bonnie Prince Charlie. The failure of the 1745 Jacobite rebellion had signed the death warrant for the old Highland social system: the clans were broken up and disarmed, the evictions began, many of the chiefs were lured away from the traditional homelands, the kilt was barred and the Highlander dishonoured. But out of those ashes rose the Highland regiments as we know them today. Prime Minister William Pitt, recognising the prowess of arms of the Highland soldier, encouraged the raising of clan regiments during the American War of Independence and many remained in service to become regular units of the British army. Thus, the defeated, sentimental and decentralised Scots took a fierce pride in their regiments, in their peacock uniforms and in the stirring martial music of their pipes and drums. No less worthy of admiration were their feats of arms: names like the Argylls, Gordons, Seaforths and the Black Watch became an important part of Scotland's modern tradition and a colourful substitute for a lost national identity.

Until 1897 the Camerons as the regiment was better known, had been the only single-battalion regiment in the British army and that sense of compactness made them a tightly-knit community, fiercely loyal and aware of their fighting heritage. They had fought in the Napoleonic campaigns and had taken part in many of Queen Victoria's little wars of Empire. During World War One they had won fifty-two battle honours and of the six battalions raised during World War Two, the Second Battalion gained universal approbation throughout beleaguered North Africa for being the last regiment to surrender at Tobruk. The First Battalion stayed in Malaya as part of the British Occupation Force and took part in the unpleasant jungle warfare against communist guerillas during what has come to be known as the "emergency". The method of dealing with the enemy consisted largely of using independent fighting patrols to cover large areas of the unfriendly terrain and during the campaign—the only successful defeat of a guerilla army since 1945—British techniques of jungle warfare reached a very high standard of efficiency. The prospect of serving overseas seemed not to daunt James: to his mother he wrote that it was all part of the business of growing up and more importantly perhaps, of gaining valuable experience. As it was, the Fates took a hand in his future and instead of receiving his marching orders he was ordered, along with Hilleary, to report to the Highland Infantry Training Centre at Redford Barracks in Edinburgh. The Camerons, it seemed, were replete with subalterns and the two potential officers were told that they might well be ordered to serve in other Highland regiments.

James took the change of plan philosophically and went on a fortnight's leave at St Albans. On arriving there he was somewhat chagrined to find that Hazel, who was also staying there, had been invited, with some friends, to take tea with George Bernard Shaw at his home in the neighbouring village of Ayot St Lawrence . Somewhat upset at missing out on an obvious treat (but one which Hazel had thought a bore, adding to his misery), James wrote Shaw a cunningly designed blandishment on 25 September

Sir,
I am no fond regarder
Of pompous interview,
But I come from Auchterarder
And I'd like to chat with you.
I know you're getting older
And have little time for me,
But the army's made me bolder
So I'd like to call for tea.
Otherwise I'm on a very short leave.
Yours etc. JEK.

A few days later came the reply, not the hoped-for invitation, but a kind "rebuff", pleasing enough in its own way but not the same as taking tea and strolling round the garden with the sage of Ayot St Lawrence.

Would you, by Gum! I'm sorry
But many thousands more
Are in the self-same hurry
So I must bar my door.

I have not tea enough for you

Nor teacakes in my larder,
And so send this rebuff to you,
Dear Lad from Auchterarder.
GBS

James sulked. He had started writing a play, a callow, Buchanesque intrigue called *"Political Pieces"*, that survives uncompleted in holograph, and he was anxious to meet the one man in the country who exemplified all the strengths of the English dramatic tradition. After all, he reasoned to Hazel, he was becoming increasingly addicted to the idea of a career that might embrace writing—a legal career with lots of spare time was an agreeable thought—and an interview with Shaw would have meant much to him. Even though he was in his ninety-first year, Shaw still enjoyed receiving company at his home, but only when he was in the mood. His biographer Hesketh Pearson remembered asking Shaw a year later if he could bring down an admirer in order to shake his hand, only to receive the reply: "I don't want to see anybody, and I don't want anybody to see me. You don't know what it is to be as old as I am. Do you suppose I want the great G.B.S. to be remembered as a doddering old skeleton?"[9] James was perhaps fortunate to receive such a witty retort and the Shaw letter became a valued possession; and is now in the Kennaway Papers in the National Library of Scotland.

At the beginning of October Kennaway moved north to Edinburgh and was attached, with Hilleary, to Cameron Company in the Highland Infantry Training Centre. He was also appointed Signals Officer but the greater part of his three-month posting was spent in a military limbo and with only potato-lifting squads to break the tedium, barrack life could have hung heavy on his hands. Luckily Edinburgh's social life lay at his disposal and through his cousin Mavis in Barnton and Donald Vass he had an easy *entrée* to various parties and dances. There were dinner-dances at the fashionable De Guise restaurant in the Caledonian Hotel, flirtings with equally fashionable girls, an Eve of Trafalgar Ball and in December the social highlight of his time in Edinburgh, the Highland Ball in the Assembly Rooms in George Street. There were rugby matches to be watched, including stand tickets for the Australia-Scotland game, plus in Rose Street to be visited (Paddy's Bar became a firm favourite) and subsequent hangovers to be coped with (". . . my batman brought me a cup of tea and I strengthened myself with one of Alasdair's most potent Turkish cigarettes"), all faithfully recorded in his weekly letters home to his mother. All in all he enjoyed a relaxed time in Edinburgh, made more pleasant by the relative freedom experienced by the officers of the Highland Infantry Training Centre. The cigarettes were Turkish or Sobranie, the drinks whisky and champagne, the girls pretty, the dancing fun and flirtations not meant to be taken seriously. "The champagne gave the party that touch of gaiety it might otherwise have lacked," he wrote of a party at the De Guise that had failed to live up to expectations.

To continue the illusion of living in Waugh's *Decline and Fall* or *Vile Bodies,* both favoured novels, Kennaway and Hilleary would hire a Rolls Royce limousine every Saturday in order to do their shopping in Princes Street in a degree of comfort. It pleased them to watch commissionaires scuttling across the pavement to open the door for them and to see fellow shoppers enviously pondering the identities of the two swells in the aged, upright Rolls Royce, It was an image of himself that Kennaway never quite lost and one that he admitted to enjoying out of all proportion to the cost; in Hilleary he had found a boon companion well prepared to make some of his fantasies come tantalisingly true.

Kennaway left Edinburgh on 20 December, sending his mother a telegram, "Kill all fatted calves", and after a short Christmas leave he left St Albans to take up a posting to the 1st Battalion, Gordon Highlanders, then serving with the British Army of the Rhine in north Germany. The battalion had been part of 30 Corps during the invasion of Germany in March 1945 and after a peripatetic fifteen months was stationed in Essen at the Meeanee Barracks where it had been busy regrouping itself under the command of Lt. Col. B.J.D. Gerrard, previously the commanding officer of the Gordons' 5/7 Battalion. Essen, the home of the Krupp factories, had been bombed heavily throughout the war and the Gordons' barracks were set in the midst of a "devastated land, amid sullen people surrounded by the plainest countryside Germany possessed".[10]

During those early months of peacetime the British pursued a vigorous policy of non-fraternisation and through a civilian Control Commission, backed up by the army, they attempted to impose a colonial form of government on the British Zone which included the industrial Ruhr as well as the important port of Hamburg. The majority of the 26,000-strong army of administrators were ill-equipped for the task fo bringing order to a war-torn Germany. Most had little knowledge of the country and were prejudiced against the people by wartime propaganda; others were retired colonial civil servants who wanted to rule Germany as if it was a protectorate peopled by an alien and ungovernable race. "You are about to meet a strange people in a strange enemy country," warned a British army handbook. "When you meet the Germans you will probably think they are very much like us. They look like us except that there are fewer of the wiry type and more big fleshy types. But they are not really as much like us as they look." Naturally, the outrage caused by the discovery of the concentration camps had excited public indignation in Britain and memories of the horrors of the Nazi regime were still strong, but the British policy of alienation made immediate post-war Germany an unhappy, sullen colony. Not that conditions were bad for the army of occupation. On the contrary, the armed forces and the staffs of the Control Commission enjoyed a high standard of living: their quarters were in the buildings that remained unscathed and the provision of duty-free luxuries meant that most had a higher standard of living than was on offer in austerity Britain.

Despite the annoying restrictions placed on them by the government—and by 1948 non-fraternisation was being ignored, especially by the troops—life at Meeanee Barracks was comfortable enough. Rough shooting provided ample game for the officers' mess, drink and cigarettes were very cheap, a double whisky costing 2½d, and there were dances in the various civilian and officers' clubs that had been established in the surrounding area. But the 1st Battalion was an idle battalion, most of the 27 officers and 876 other ranks were war-toughened veterans and they kicked against the enforced calm of peacetime Germany. During the course of World War Two the character of the regiment had been changed by two heavy blows: many of its regular officers had been captured in 1940 when the 1st and 5th

Battalions had been forced to surrender with the rest of the Highland Brigade at St Valery, and in the following year the 2nd Battalion was part of the garrison in Singapore when it fell to the Japanese. As a result the regiment was short of officers, especially of subalterns, and a number of officers had been posted to the Gordons from other regiments or had been raised from the ranks during the war. It was a varied mess with few of the graces that were expected of a peacetime posting and when he arrived in Essen, Kennaway did not like what he saw.

> I have never thought much of the Gordons as a regiment but now that I have served with them I am sure: there is a pettiness and filth about them which is hard to believe. The subalterns instead of being a careless community together are a throat-cutting and uncharitable circle, always grumbling. They strive for regular commissions, endeavouring to catch the colonel's eye and time after time they ruin each others chances . . . their drinking and sports—which are easier here than anywhere in civvy street—are enjoyable, but I do feel in the bottom of my heart that there's more to life than a pink gin and a fräulein pulled in the back door.

One of the problems was that the battalion possessed three lieutenant-colonels, each of whom had commanded in World War Two and each of whom strove to gain ascendancy. Friction was a fact of everyday life as uneasily shifting relationships were developed by the senior officers with their juniors in the mess. The boredom of life at Essen did not help matters and dissatisfaction reached a new peak when it was learned that the Gordons were to become a single battalion regiment in 1948, thus bringing to an end the historic amalgamation of the 75th and 92nd regiments which had formed, respectively, the Gordons' 1st and 2nd Battalions.

The deepening of the Cold War with the Soviet Union and the blockade of Berlin which was enforced in April 1948 added to the sense of uncertainty and lack of common purpose within the British regiments in Germany. To compensate, in the Gordons, mess dinners became an important ritual, a reminder almost of past glories and traditions, and officers were expected to dine most nights of the week. Drink was plentiful and added to the boredom it was heady brew, powerful enough to fuel the most trivial of controversies. In his first letters home James admitted to having had more hangovers in a week than he had before in a lifetime and the pink gins and large drams of whisky, the formal mess dinner followed by the playing of the pipes, became a regular feature of the weekly routine. James behaved himself impeccably, keeping on the right side of the senior officers and the boisterous subalterns, and he observed closely everything that he saw. "As I write there is a heated argument between officers concerning Alexander and Monty. My God these army men are the most fatuous arguers: they just shout each other down and they've shouted everybody out of the room so far."[11]

One officer in the mess stood out: Captain Jock Laurie, an ex-sergeant of the 8th Argyll and Sutherland Highlanders who had been commissioned from the ranks and transferred to the Gordons during the war. A big, red-haired man, fond of his drink and proud of the traditions of the Scottish regiments, he became a focal point for some of the discontent in the mess, a man whom Kennaway described as a "notorious and most dishonest criminal" and one who enjoyed tormenting the subalterns. James admitted to his mother that one day he would write about his experiences with the Gordons and he remained true to his word, that book being his first novel, *Tunes of Glory*, published eight years later, in 1956. Although the setting is Scotland, the regiment is undeniably the Gordons and most of the characters were based on officers he knew in Germany. Jock Sinclair, the colonel whose face was "big and smooth and red and thick" was based on Captain Laurie and his personal antagonism to the colonel who supplants him, the aristocratic Basil Barrow (a returning POW) found its starting point in Kennaway's observation of the petty squabbling for authority that was such a feature of life in the mess. Certainly, he sent the novel in manuscript to his friend and fellow Gordons officer John Durbin, then serving in Singapore, to ask him to check the authenticity of the background detail. Durbin replied that he could identify every single one of the officers in the fictional Campbell Barracks.

But in spite of his protestations about the uncouth behaviour he experienced in the Gordons—and some of his distaste may have been born of prissiness—James was by no means unhappy in Germany. Friendship with the adjutant, Major Barker—"another adjutant is coming within string-pulling distance", he reported as early as March—led to his attachment as demonstration platoon commander at the British Army of the Rhine School of Infantry at Padeborn, Westfalia, a district that he found to be "not unlike Strathearn, with its little wooded bumps and large plain set between the hills". There, life went on at a more even tenor. Padeborn meant less restrictions than Essen and it also meant girls: James was not slow in finding a German girlfriend and with her he was able to escape from the cloying confines of the officers' club and the silly giggling secretaries of the Control Commission. Although he never mentioned her by name—no doubt to save his mother's susceptibilities—and she remains a shadowy figure in his correspondence, she exerted a great influence on him and his attitudes to his surroundings. Through her he began to meet German civilians, to be invited into their homes and to see the country through their eyes. "The Germans have thought of us as proud, aloof, rather hard, but beautifully mannered to our womenfolk—and what do they find? Loose living, bad manners, indulgence in place of pride and husbands most uncouth to their own wives who are out here."[12]

He also discovered the plight of the children, lost and impoverished, living amongst the ruins of the war-torn cities. Their lot became a rallying point for his emotions and in an unpublished essay which he sent home to his mother he described his revulsion at seeing a little boy in an Essen street trip over a boot, "then picking himself up, brushed his knees and ran on: assuredly that might happen anywhere in England, and to any child. Only the boot still had a foot in it." The incident prompted him to suggest to his C.O. that the Gordons should lead the way in establishing better relations with the Germans by establishing a holiday camp for their children. Although he was congratulated on the idea and it was sent up to Brigade headquarters nothing came of it during his period of service. The image of starving unkempt children in a bleak landscape, though, was to remain imprinted on his mind.

During the first week of April his calm at Padeborn was shattered by the news that Alasdair Hilleary had been killed in Palestine. After Edinburgh he had been seconded to the Highland Light Infantry, then part of the force attempting to keep peace between Arab and Jew in Palestine. On 5 April he

1. *Kenwood Park, Auchterarder*

2. *James with his father, 1930*

3. *Hazel and James, aged four*

4. *Family holiday, 1930, James holding his mother's left hand*

5. *Charles Kennaway, World War One*

was leading a platoon into a system of tunnels and catacombs below the Holy Sepulchre in Jerusalem when a booby-trap exploded killing him instantly. James was devastated by the news. "The saddest loss I've had since I was twelve." Together they had planned a life of bachelor apartments in London, a tilt at the Inns of Court to become barristers, holidays abroad, sports cars, girlfriends . . . "why did they make him so fine if he was to die like that?" he asked himself. "But he would mock my tears. I can hear him yet. 'Come on, man. We haven't much time.' Too true. His was the course of the brilliant comet—snuffed by some underhand Jew. Never let anyone talk to me of sympathy for the Jews: I have not felt more like murder in my life."[13]

Hilleary's death reminded him too much of his father's early demise and of the easy mortality that seemed to have become such an unwelcome ingredient of his young life. His letters home began to betray his anguish at life's shortness and of having to hasten the process of living—the play on which he had been working the previous summer might never be completed, he complained to his mother, and a cold shiver of angst blighted the warm April of his 1948 Spring. On his demobilisation from the army Kennaway wrote to the garage in Edinburgh which had supplied the Rolls Royce during the carefree days of a year before and asked them for an account. It came to some £300 but a grave garage proprietor replied that it was in Lt. Hilleary's name and as he had been killed in the service of his country, the matter was considered closed. It was the only dignified episode of a thoroughly unhappy experience.

After the School of Infantry closed down James returned to the Gordons where there remained two agreeable tasks to be completed before he left in August. With John Durbin he was instructed to write an account of the three battles of Minden, a duty that allowed them to borrow a one-ton truck and to tour the surrounding countryside freed from the restrictions of barrack life. And also with Durbin and two other officers James was asked to attend a dinner given by a crack Belgian regiment, the Chausseurs Ardennais, to celebrate the selection of the Gordons as their sister regiment. The Belgians distilled their own liquor, an "atomic grain spirit served in balloon glasses" and as the regiment's historian noted: "If one has to believe the description of one of these four (and the fact that his narrative veers, almost lurches from the historic present to the past tense and back again, lends evidence to such an admission) vast quantities of alcohol were consumed."[14]

Before he left the Gordons, Kennaway was taken on one side by the colonel and asked if he would like to apply for a regular commission, but "using my barrister discretion I merely said that I wanted more room to live." In the same letter he admitted to his mother that "I very nearly told him that I would rather serve in the Argentine police than in his regiment", a remark that gives some idea of his desire for freedom. Ahead lay Oxford and the possibility of putting his name down for a legal career: as far as James was concerned he was embarking on a road that would have seemed very familiar to his father twenty-odd years earlier.

~ 5 ~

An Oxford Vintage

At the beginning of August 1948 Kennaway was a free man, and he was on his way home; "incapable of taking any decisive action apart from endeavouring to keep clear of the Newcastle gaols," he reported in his final army letter to his mother. On the eve of his demob a rumour had swept BAOR that the continuing crisis of the Soviet blockade of Berlin would halt all further leave, but Kennaway's luck held, and his last military duty was the simple task of acting as an official in the divisional rifle shoot, attached to the Royal Welch Fusiliers.

The Britain to which he was returning was still held in the thrall of economic recession: rationing may have been eased by the Chancellor of the Exchequer, Sir Stafford Cripps, but access to the kind of luxuries enjoyed by the British in Germany was still limited. Not that life was completely impoverished. The incoming Labour government of July 1945 had introduced many measures, including a National Health Service to ease the social conditions of many people and a process of nationalisation of the major industries—bitterly opposed by the Conservatives—had helped to bring down unemployment, even though pre-war production levels were a thing of the past. But in spite of those improvements, Britain was a prisoner to the effects of the war and its scars—bomb craters and the ugly ruins of blackened buildings—were a blemish in many of the major cities.

Having served in war-torn Germany, Kennaway was intensely aware of the uneven tenor of the times and of the fact that the lives of many people were being disfigured by the chaos and poverty that surrounded them. The plight of the German children had touched him and in his letters to Cousin Edith, on his return home, he spoke bitterly of the lack of charity that he felt characterised his generation; and yet for all his striking of attitudes, Kennaway could not bring himself to agree with the Labour Party's socialist solutions to the problem. Like many of his class he felt that events were moving too quickly, that social change had to be gradual and effected with less of what he saw as "revolutionary fervour". And like his immediate peers he felt that the British people had made a great mistake in rejecting Winston Churchill and the Conservative Party at the end of World War Two. "Once again it is the voice calling in the wilderness: he knows best the lie of the land and when in another fifty years a re-desolated Europe discusses international peace his words shall be remembered. They then shall curse themselves for scorning the genius of the age and the historians will record the supreme tragedy of our indifference to his words."[1]

Although Kennaway was to become an apolitical animal, before going to Oxford, and at Oxford itself, he became much involved with Conservative politics and given to day-dreaming of the delights of a safe Tory seat somewhere in England. He was a fiercely committed supporter of Churchill and on several occasions reported to his mother vivid dreams in which the wartime prime minister appeared to him and offered sepulchral advice. "I met him [Churchill] one summer's afternoon, and he was wearing a grey double-breasted suit. I asked him where his cigar was and he told me that he hated the damned things really, but had to keep up appearances. Furthermore he informed me not to get married and I would be remembered three hundred years hence!"[2] Dreams of that nature—of a dominant Churchill replete with sound advice, but lacking the priapic cigar—haunted Kennaway at various stages of his life, usually during periods of stress, and in them Churchill always appeared as a dominant father-figure offering the kind of advice that Kennaway felt that he needed on each particular occasion. (In the midst of marital breakdown in 1965 Churchill appeared to be saying to him that the protection of his talent was all-important: "Listen to nobody, defend to the end.") To a certain extent the conjuring up of

Churchill was due to the very real sense of gratitude that most people felt towards the man who had been Britain's wartime leader and a symbol of national pride during the darkest days of the war. For them, Churchill had become not just a national figurehead, but also an embodiment of British pluck and fortitude. In Kennaway's mind, though, Churchill had also become something of a personal father-figure, a substitute for the "father dead", a strong man in a world unsure of its bearings: it is perhaps hardly surprising that he should have appeared so prominently in the sub-conscious of a young man who may have yearned for the kind of security offered by the bulldog features of Britain's most famous wartime leader.

It is difficult to place an objective interpretation on other people's dreams—and Kennaway himself tended only to record the content of his dreams, rarely in early life an analysis of them—but it is clear that the Churchill dreams were important to him. Only Kennaway could say finally whether the interpretation of his dreams is correct or not, but it would seem that the Churchill figure was a substitute for the long-dead father, that the image had evolved to emphasise the importance of the father-figure and to avoid pointing directly at him should the content of the dream prove to be disconcerting. Hence the advice not to marry young intermingled with the dreams of boyhood, almost as if one part of James was urging the other to remember the boy that he used to be, and to avoid the danger of rejecting his own past. This becomes more clear when in later life James became convinced that the artist/writer within him was a "baby" and that he was "*sure, sure, sure* other writers of awkward, cut-off-your-nose-to-spite-your-face kind like myself have a baby within them to defend; and that baby is themself, but somewhere along the line the pain was unbearable and the character split, one part ruthless in defence, the other preserved in original innocence."[3] As we shall see, the protection of the "baby" was to become a vital means for Kennaway to express his attitudes towards his writing, especially at times when he felt both to be under threat from critics—either literary reviewers or friends whom he felt to have grown hostile. In other words, as he expressed it in his notebooks, gay-boy James the man had to protect introvert Jim the artist. And the clarification of that division always brought him home to the wise old man figure of Winston Churchill, an archetypal image, the source of determination, insight and understanding. Throughout Kennaway's life those dreams were to be ever-present companions and were destined to be at their most potent when he was under threat or, as we shall see, when he felt himself to be in a hopeless or desperate situation.

The Oxford that Kennaway went up to in the autumn of 1948 was still licking its wounds from its wartime depredations, a period when the undergraduate population had shrunk and when many of the colleges had housed government ministries in retreat from bomb-strewn London. It was a time of retrenchment and a time which seemed to be out of joint to people who remembered only the gayer times of Oxford between the wars. Its mood was best summoned up in the autobiography of George Scott, the distinguished journalist and broadcaster who was a contemporary of Kennaway's at Oxford (he was at New College).

> We gave special pleasure to older writers who would look back over the exciting years of their lives and draw comparisons flattering to themselves. They peered at us through their microscopes as though we were specimens of bacteria. They analysed us and categorised us and tucked us away in their filing cabinets with clever labels attached. Upon us they erected grandiose generalisations of hope or despair—and usually it was of despair. For, as they told us so many times until we were sick of the sound of their voices, or worse still, until we came to believe them, we were earnest, we were solemn, we were industrious and above all, we were apathetic. Our one purpose in life, it seemed, was to bury ourselves in our books and work as hard as possible to get a degree as quickly as possible. We were, they all agreed, dull. Not like the Thirties. Not like the Twenties. Not like the Edwardians. Not—true Oxonians.[4]

One reason why the older commentators found their inheritors earnest and industrious was that most of the undergraduates were older than previous generations had been. Some had fought in the war and most had done up to two years National Service and felt themselves to be experienced men of the world; and the austerity of the period denied the possibility of living in an Evelyn Waugh novel. (To redress the balance, it must be admitted that each generation thinks of its successors as being dull and unadventurous.)

But in spite of the cold winds that blew through post-war Oxford, it was still a place of enchantment. Like most of his contemporaries Kennaway was fascinated by Waugh, whose novel *Brideshead Revisited* evoked in Oxford a city of aquatint, in whose "spacious and quiet streets men walked and spoke as they had done in Newman's day; her autumnal mists, her grey springtime, and the rare glory of her summer days . . . when the chestnut was in flower and the bells rang out high and clear over her gables and cupolas, exhaled the soft airs of centuries of youth".[5] That image of Oxford, all dreaming spires, ancient fretted buildings and laughter off the river, remains a powerful tug on the emotions of anyone who has been at Oxford and, indeed, as an expression of the place, it is not far removed from reality. The physicality of the city does incite the imagination to conjure Oxford as an inviolate sanctury of Learning, Orthodoxy and Toryism—as James Boswell noted with such obvious approval.

For one so attuned to atmosphere, Kennaway left no such impressions of his time at university. His first letters home, a useful barometer of his feelings, are bare statements of his physical well-being and hopes for the future. Being an older undergraduate his rooms were outside Trinity College, across the road from it at 53 Broad Street. There, in a large and airy bedsitter with a view across the street to Balliol and his own college he set up house in a building that had been set aside for married couples and the more mature students. There was even "a spare bedroom on our flat where any girl friend could be put up at a pinch". At that time Trinity still retained the reputation of being a college dominated by public schoolboys and enthusiastic about undergraduates with sporting ability, and during the immediate post-war period most of them, like James, had been experienced platoon commanders leading mess- and booze-oriented lives. He gravitated towards a group of ex-public schoolboys who developed effete mannerisms of dress and language and who called themselves, "The Boys". High-spirited mischief, drink and womanising were their delights and mild disciplinary action from the "bulldogs" their objectives. James revelled in their company and his acceptance by them as a fellow spirit seems to account for the strength of his matter-of-fact attitude towards Oxford.

Against much family and schoolmasterly advice—both from Daudet Hayward and from Hazel who dismissed his choice of subject as being "a new-fangled palaver"—Kennaway decided to read Modern Greats (Politics, Philosophy and Economics, or P.P.E.) with a view to devoting his third year to studying Law. At the same time he became a student of the Middle Temple in London, a necessary step if he was to achieve his ambition of becoming a barrister. His tutor, the future Labour politician Anthony Crosland, was sceptical about his reading Law after taking an economics degree, thinking that Kennaway was being over-enterprising, but his pupil refused to be discouraged and within weeks his letters home reflected the inspiration he obviously felt at confronting the tasks that lay ahead of him. He joined the college's rugby club and found time to indulge the taste in horse-riding that he had cultivated in Germany. More significantly he became a member of the Union, the university's debating society and in many people's minds the real testing ground for a career in law or politics. The Union at Oxford is a club with its own bar and restaurant and in the debating chamber every Thursday meet the ambitious politically-orientated students to discuss the burning issues of the day, all recited to the protocol of Westminster. And just as a good maiden speech in the House of Commons can launch a go-ahead Member of Parliament's political career, so also are elegant speeches in the Union noted both within the university and outside by visiting ministers of the Crown. Critics of the institution have condemned the Union as a place for young men grown old before their time, whose debates are noted more for their shrillness than their political gravity, but despite that disapprobation, and there may be some truth in it, to deliver a graceful speech in the Union was to serve notice of one's political intentions.

James was determined to make his mark as quickly as possible. Writing to his mother as soon as 17 October he announced enthusiastically that after "some gross drinking at the Carlton Club" (the university's Tory club and affiliated to the London club of the same name), he had managed to wangle his way into a debate at Keble College and that if he spoke successfully, he "would perhaps get a paper speech in the Union for my maiden. This is very important as people stop listening after the first six paper speeches." Although the debate was postponed at the last moment he did not have long to wait and his chance came during the second week of November when he spoke in support of the main motion: "I made a maiden speech in the Union to an almost empty house at about 11.15 last Thursday. It went down quite well but there was nobody of importance there so it was a case of casting my pearls," he reported to his mother on 15 November. By the term's end his identification with the Tory faction was made complete by his appointment as secretary to the Trinity Conservative Association and his membership of the prestigious Carlton Club. In his second year his involvement increased to a new pitch when he took over the editorship of the *Oxford Tory* and canvassed for the Conservative candidate in the South Oxford constituency. His reward was election to the post of secretary to the university's Conservative Association during his second year but by then the intrigues of committee work had defeated him and politics as a burning issue began to ease itself out of his life, not to return. Shortly before the General Election of 1951 he wrote to his mother announcing his intention of exercising democracy by choosing not to vote at all, and despite her entreaties to support the Tory cause he refused to betray his principles.

Although politics may not have been the consuming passion that it was for many of his contemporaries, Kennaway's time was not wasted. As editor of the Tory newspaper he had the satisfaction of writing himself and of seeing his work in print, an important consideration for him at that period when he was still tinkering with the attempts at play-writing begun during his National Service. The position also gave him access to visiting politicians and during his period as secretary to Oxford University Conservative Association he was required to entertain leading members of the party when they visited the university. Those occasions were never less than enthralling and although by then he had abandoned all thoughts of a possible career in politics he never lost his fascination with the "big panther" appeal of that world. Here were men living by their wits, their nerve-endings constantly a-tingle, men who exercised power and controlled destinies—and men who lived in the jungle of human affairs.

Some politicians he found to be treacherous or sycophantic. After dining out with Brendan Bracken, then M.P. for East Bournemouth and Christchurch, who was known to be a political wheeler-dealer *par excellence,* he wrote delightedly to his mother that his guest was "the most reptile of all politicians. You would hate him: even I could not take his bad manners". Bracken was a curious choice of dining partner. His name had been linked to Winston Churchill since the early nineteen-twenties when he had arrived on the political scene without background or connections in the political world and had attached himself to Churchill's star. During the early days of World War Two he had been Churchill's Parliamentary Private Secretary, then he served as Minister of Information until 1945 when he was made First Lord of the Admiralty: those who hated him—and there many of their number—would insinuate that he was Churchill's illegitimate son, a rumour in which both men delighted. Bracken was a schemer, impervious to insults or social rebuffs, a man who was pleased to be thought coarse and yet who was also the cultivated director of the publishers Eyre and Spottiswoode and the founder of the magazine *History Today.* He represented the dark side of politics, the back-stabbing and the offering of gratuitous insults and even though he had no intention of falling for its lurid spell, Kennaway found it strong meat and noted its every detail. When he came to create J.T. Sarson, the "cat-man" merchant banker of *The Bells of Shoreditch,* he had Brendan Bracken partly in mind, a man like Sarson who had achieved his own potential in finance and politics at an early age by imposing himself at his own valuation.

In the Union Kennaway's ambitions were less successful. He was destined to become a pleasant, if somewhat pedantic, speaker, but he never made his mark as a political debater, preferring instead to confine himself to the casting of witty speeches larded with well-timed throwaway remarks. That failing cost him election to its committee during his second year but it did not prevent him from making a popular reputation for himself. His greatest triumph, perhaps, came in May 1949 during a debate on nationalism. Speaking in support of Scotland, Kennaway found himself falling into the trap of confusing which side of the Scottish-English border he was discussing, and when he mentioned that beggars began at Berwick, he was interrupted and asked if he meant going from south to north or vice-versa. With his eye fixed on the gallery where the female undergraduates traditionally sit, he replied, "Sir, being a gentleman, I always start from the top and work downwards!" As he told his mother, "That did the trick, and I waited for quite a while for the noise to subside." The evening's glory was made complete by "a vivacious black-haired and blue-eyed popsy" asking to meet him.

And so he met Val Mitchison (now Val Arnold-Foster, radio critic of *The Guardian*), the daughter of the distinguished Scottish novelist Naomi Mitchison. Her novel *The Bull Calves* had been recently published and it was of immediate interest to Kennaway, being set in the same part of Scotland as his father's Jacobite novel *Gentleman Adventurer* which at that time existed only in manuscript. Set in Strathearn during the same period of the Jacobite uprisings, it too is rooted in a mixture of social and domestic history and in the mythology created out of it. *The Bull Calves* had been hailed as the best Scottish historical romance since the novels of Sir Walter Scott, with its imaginary story of the love of Kirsty Haldane of Gleneagles and William MacIntosh of Berlum set against real historical events, but it was for neither literary nor romantic reasons that James enjoyed his meeting with its creator's daughter.

> All this doesn't add up to what you might think: I haven't fallen for her in my usual way or anything like that. But I am so proud that I should have been in a position—deservedly or no—for a Haldane to ask to meet me, and I thought you would like to know. It's a constantly moving world, but every now and then one catches a glimpse of things in spite of time: it is such a pity father was not here now to see how things are shaping.[6]

In the tightly-knit social world of Strathearn the Haldanes of Cloan, to which family Naomi Mitchison belonged (she had married the Labour politician Richard, later Baron, Mitchison in 1916), were very important people indeed. Their estate of Cloan is half-way up the rise of the Ochil Hills south of Auchterarder and the imposing, though strangely sombre house in the Scotch Baronial style was rebuilt during the course of the nineteenth century on the site of an older and pleasingly domestic farmhouse. It was the home of a remarkable family. Naomi Mitchison's father was J.S. Haldane, a distinguished physiologist and her uncle was R.B.S. Haldane who had been Lord Chancellor in the Liberal government from 1912 until 1915 when he had been dismissed because of his supposed pro-German sympathies. In turn, Naomi made her name both as a novelist and as a campaigner for better conditions in the Scottish Highlands and her brother, J.B.S. Haldane, was a well-known geneticist. One family of cousins lived at the neighbouring estate of Foswell and other cousins, the heirs to the Haldanes of Gleneagles, the Chinnery-Haldanes, one of the ancient families of Scotland, still lived at Gleneagles where the broken walls of their castle stood as a mute witness to their ancient heritage. The Haldanes had been lairds of Gleneagles since the twelfth century (although first official mention was not made until 1456) and one ancestor, Aylmer, had fought on the side of King Robert the Bruce during the fourteenth-century wars of independence. Although the Haldanes later became identified with the Labour movement in Scotland, as Naomi Mitchison's volumes of memoirs testify[7], theirs was still a life of landed ease which cared not for wealth or social position.

With all his memories of childhood finely attuned to the relationship of the factor to the gentry, the fact that a Haldane had asked to meet a Kennaway was an occasion of importance to James, momentous out of all proportion to its real significance. When he had been journeying north during the summer vacation of his first year at Oxford he had met J.B.S. Haldane on the train and that meeting too was excitedly reported to his mother especially as he was asking about her present whereabouts. It was a curious paradox: on the one hand Kennaway confessed to feeling suffocated by the narrowness of the Perthshire society of his childhood years and yet he continued to enjoy the *frisson* of being identified with it and of knowing those whom he took to be its social élite.

As might be expected, his earliest friends at Oxford continued to be those with whom he had shared his Glenalmond background. John Cameron was studying Forestry at Pembroke and Spence was at Worcester reading P.P.E. without much success—James was not a little pleased that his friend, and rival, from schooldays was falling behind in the race for academic excellence. Both continued to be firm friends throughout his days at university.

He also became friendly with John Mitcalfe from Northumberland, an acquaintance from Cargilfield days, whose sister Gill had been a flame during his flirtations at dances in Strathearn and Edinburgh immediately after leaving Glenalmond.

As a reward to themselves for the rigours they had faced during the previous two years Mitcalfe and Kennaway decided to spend part of the Christmas vacation travelling in Europe where their goal would be the south of France. At that time the British government restricted the overseas allowance to £50, a currency ruling that prevented all but the well-connected or exceptionally wealthy who could make other arrangements for travelling for any length of time in Europe or elsewhere. In James's case the difficulty was overcome by his mother who provided him with petrol coupons and bags of real coffee which could be sold for French currency on the black market when they reached Paris. In return James posted to his mother a diary of his trip—a delightful record of a carefree holiday enjoyed by two young men out on their own for first time in their lives. There was inexpensive wine and brandy to be drunk in great quantities at leisurely restaurants and cafés, night clubs to be visited and the *demi-monde* to be inspected, nights on the road in couchettes shared with "quasi copulating couples", and best of all, the warm sun of the south, "shirt sleeves and v. warm—ah! that's what I like about the south". There was also one "most hilarious and extravagant evening . . . which perhaps should not be set down on paper", an evening of champagne and dancing with Christian, "a Parisien girl, beautifully dressed and made up; a night club, and very, very nearly . . ." (From the army onwards, James had become less discreet in describing his relationships with girls.) On 10 December they moved on to the Italian Riviera, after spending several days in Nice, and they hurried on to Rome which captivated them "in spite of crowded transport, jibbering population and expensive food". And then it was back to London via Paris again and a chance to spend an evening at the *Folies Bergères,* so "unlike the Windmill, not in the least sordid. Wonderful sets and the dresses were a dream". Despite the shortage of money—due largely to striking a poor deal when exchanging the petrol coupons—and the real lack of comfort they had encountered on French and Italian trains, the trip had been an invaluable experience. It fired the love of travel and of life abroad that was to be a lifelong enthusiasm; and James, like many Scots brought up in northern climes, discovered that the south and the sun were both very much to his liking. And the brief journal of the tour, written on his mother's prescription pads, reflects his emotions in full: a young man's description of a young man's sentimental journey in Europe.

In Paris he had met one of Sir Frederick Bell's daughters and heard for the first time the rumour that, following the death that year of his own wife, Sir Frederick Bell was paying court to Marjory Kennaway. "Asked if I would approve were it true I answered that it was little business of mine but inferred that I did in no way approve. She smiled and said she was glad; she did not think it would do." Significantly, Kennaway left that barbed note of his feelings in his travel "diary" so that his mother would be left in no doubt that he did not approve of the match. Sir Frederick was then fifty-seven and Marjory several years his junior; they had been lifelong friends and close companions since the days of their married ease; both had grown-up children (Sir Frederick Bell had two sons and three daughters). It was natural that they should drift together in this romantic way. With James at Oxford and seemingly intent on a career at the Bar, the navigation of Marjory's life was starting to go awry and her letters to her son confirmed that she was experiencing a sense of things falling apart. The lease of her house at Holywell Hill in St Albans had come to an end and she had moved into a small flat; the public health had become a chore, she wanted to relax and work less; there were increasingly complicated trust and insurance matters to be dealt with in her husband's estate; she was not growing any younger and her children were growing away from her. Small wonder that she began to long for a period of dependence on someone else. James's solution was that she should rent a flat in London and that she should find a less demanding job so that she could spend more time with him while he was studying for the Bar examinations; he was decidedly against her getting married and throughout 1949 an uneasy tension grew up between mother and son as the question of the suitability of marriage to Sir Frederick lay unresolved between them.

During that summer he holidayed with her at Broom and then alone together at St Andrews before he moved north to Aberdeen in August to work as a very temporary cub reporter with the *Press and Journal,* a job which, as he explained to his mother he had got by the simple expedient of writing to the newspaper's owner: "Charming letter from my friend Viscount Kemsley this morning to say that a job awaits me in Aberdeen! All I have to do is state the dates . . . It is of course the same old story about travelling first class when you haven't got a ticket. If you have no experience, no knowledge, and little talent, the owner is the man to write to rather than the editor." It was a job entirely to his liking: he relished seeing his work in print, he enjoyed meeting people and as a result he made a good fist of it. When he left at the beginning of September, William Veitch, the editor, wrote to James expressing his "pleasure and even his joy to feel that you have been with us and I do hope that you yourself regard your stay here with us as not having been lost. Whatever your studies may be, a little practical experience never goes amiss." Fired by that friendly encouragement Kennaway pondered the possibilities of giving up law for journalism and wrote off to several London newspapers about job opportunities for graduates, but only one, the *Daily Telegraph,* replied and the attractions of a career in the fourth estate closed as soon as they had presented themselves to him.

While he was working in Aberdeen he met up with an old school friend, George Buchanan-Smith, who had been in the form below him at Glenalmond. He had been invalided out of the army while doing his National Service and was in Aberdeen waiting to go up to the University of Edinburgh in October. The two men spent their evenings together drinking beer in harbour pubs, walking alongside the River Dee and indulging their common interest in the theatre. During that summer the Wilson Barrett Theatre Company was playing at His Majesty's, Aberdeen's principle civic theatre, and the two discerning young men made up their minds to see all the plays in the company's repertoire, which included *Pygmalion, Love in a Mist* and *My Sister Eileen.* They were impressed, and not just by the standard of production. Two of the actresses caught their eye. George was egged on by James and they sent a message to the stage door.

Would the young ladies care to have a drink with them? They would and so an attractive young actress walked into James's life.

It was the first serious affair that was not a dancing party flirtation and James made the most of it. Each night a hired Rolls Royce would pull up at the stage door and each night the two couples would be driven down to the long stretch of Aberdeen's beach to walk in the warm late summer's nights. The Wilson Barrett's run ended in Aberdeen at the end of August when they transferred to the Edinburgh International Festival with their production of Mrs Henry Wood's classic *East Lynne.* Fired by the drama of the situation James invited his beautiful new girl friend to come with him to Strathearn where he was not a little dazzled by the sudden glamour of having an actress as his partner and first real girlfriend. When he met them again at a ball in Perth (where she had caused a sensation by turning up in a Dior new-look short dress) George Buchanan-Smith was astonished by the fierce intensity of his friend's relationship and the sense of passion with which he would discuss his affair.

News of the affair filtered back to St Albans sending alarm bells ringing and his mother's first letter to him on returning to Oxford was a dark warning about the folly of getting emotionally entangled at his young age. His reply of 10 October cautiously admitted that he would not be "foolish" but he was determined also to make the point that in the end it was his feelings that counted most. "The great point about her is that she is adult: she has no time for the gossip and trivial spites of this world, and as a companion she is as light as she is a love-maker. I like her very much." As with most youthful summer affairs, it had fizzled out by the time the year had ended, James noting somewhat soulfully on 29 November that he had been "jilted by [his] beautiful girlfriend—she has another more glamorous man. Am not heartbroken, but vanity hit good and hard."

James had good reason not to be altogether downcast at being "jilted". He too had met someone else and was falling in love with her. During his first year at Oxford he had met Godfrey Smith who became President of the Union and who was later to carve a successful career in journalism and as a novelist: he too became a lifelong friend. Through him, James was introduced to Roger and Victor Wood, identical twins who had rooms at 21 St

6. *The Best Kilt, aged twelve*

7. *County Show, James sitting second*

8. *James, right, with the Bell children*

9. *James, aged twelve, with his mother and Hazel*

10. *Glenalmond 1st XV, James standing back row, third left*

11. *The newly commissioned officer, 1947*

John Street. In the flat below lived three girls, all students at the Ruskin School of Art and as James would have it, all very easy on the eye. He fell for one of them, Mieke Wyatt and announced his intentions by gate-crashing a May morning (1949) party bearing chocolates and champagne—"breakfast consisting of cigarettes, chocolates, champagne and wild, wild women" as he later told his mother. Despite his romantic arrival, Mieke Wyatt paid little attention to his enthusiastic courting and he turned instead to her flatmate Susan Edmonds whom he took to visiting "in the evenings to consult how best he might win the much sought after and very fair lady".[8] That scheming came to naught but by early November James was constantly in Susan's company. He took her to dinner, she was his partner at the Union Ball and shortly before Christmas, after a party at a friend's flat, he realised that he was in love with this pretty, dark-haired, vivacious girl.

She was soon never out of his thoughts. He helped her to find new digs at the beginning of 1950 and to her he wrote a series of tender love letters all expressing love and devotion and also care and responsibility for her every need.

> I love you. That's the truth of it. I can't do without you. That's the long and the short of it. The evening is a longing and the morning a pining. I love you very much. I shall meet you if you tell me the exact time. I shall help you unpack, see that you are warm, make love to you, give you a drink, get you some supper, order your milk and paper, and love you for ever. Thank you for your nice voice on the telephone. Come back to me.[9]

His care and affection was not misplaced. Susan Edmonds was studying at the Ruskin—named for John Ruskin, one of the few great socialist idealists Oxford has produced—after an unhappy adolescence. Her father, Eric Edmonds who lived in Fairford, Gloucestershire and who owned a department store in Watford, had sent Susan and her sister Gyll to live with his wife's sister in Rhodesia at the outbreak of World War Two. There they had languished "unhappily and unloved" in an alien country, cut off completely from their family, the only time of good cheer being two years of boarding school in South Africa. In 1944 the sisters had come back to Britain only to find their parents divorced. Appalled by their appearance—"We appeared shortly after D-

Day (unannounced and unwelcomed on account of the censor), hotfoot off a troopship, wearing lipstick, high heels and unsuitable colonial clothes"—Eric Edmonds promptly dispatched his daughters to Cheltenham Ladies' College. It was all very bewildering and by the time Susan had arrived at Oxford she was "shy and insecure" and wary of relationships. By her own admission, Susan's father had sent her there in the hope that she would "catch a decent English husband", but James was not, perhaps, what he had in mind.

Kennaway still had eighteen months left of his university course, he was trying to tutor himself through the intricacies of the Bar exams and he was still not entirely certain of the direction of his future career. That sense of unease was a constant source of worry and although he had become "unofficially engaged" to Susan by the summer of 1950 Kennaway doubted if they would be able to marry before his Bar finals in 1952. If they were to marry earlier he foresaw a bleak, circumscribed future together, one that he knew she would hate: in a long letter to Susan of 14 July 1950 he presented the scenario that would be the first year of married life if she took a job while he completed his studies.

> Each evening you would return from work, the vegetables would need cleaning, the dinner need cooking, the socks need darning. I would help with the washing up. In this way we could together ruin your health, and our marriage in about ten months—and this is all contraceptives providing.

James's cautious attitude puzzled the Edmonds family who felt that the couple should either be engaged or not and much mirth was made at Susan's expense about the absence of a ring. ("Moreover, lest your family tease you on 'the cry goes up, how long' score, which will only make it more cruel, make them understand—or send me a note and I'll either write or come and see papa," he wrote in the same letter of 14 July.) But if the Edmonds were gently exasperated by the matter, Mrs Kennaway was less sanguine. She liked Susan but she hesitated about giving approval to an official engagement; she thought James was too young to marry and she worried, too, about letting him marry into a family in which she thought divorce was rampant, such things being unheard of in Strathearn. In later years James liked to joke that he had felt "windy" about being the first member of his family to have married an English woman and in that bluff, throwaway remark there might also have been some truth.

Fortunately for them, James's mother had finally agreed to marry Sir Frederick Bell and the wedding took place in London at St Columba's Church of Scotland on 16 September 1950. Earlier that year his mother had left St Albans and had moved into a rented flat in Knightsbridge before buying a house at 58 Hampstead Way, Golders Green, for James while he completed his legal training. The fact that his mother had married took away some of the strain from his own relationship to Susan and in small measure helped to pave the way to his own marriage, as it was then agreed that this could only take place once his legal career was settled or once he had found employment. In his anxiety to please his future father-in-law, James thought that it might be possible to abandon the Bar and to earn his living from banking or by going into business, proposals that were not calculated to gain much favour in the Kennaway camp, with all his mother's in-built suspicions about "trade".

But by 1950 James was slowly but surely growing away from her influence and the attachment to her that had blossomed after the death of his father had started to wane. They were both going to marry other people and those new alliances would obviously place a strain on the links that bound them together as James noted somberly in a letter written to Susan during the course of that summer.

> It is so strange, this business of growing up. Mother has done so much, and been the best beloved for so long. Then you come bouncing along and take such a big part of my heart I feel I'm almost being selfish not loving her the most any longer. But it's too true. I couldn't live with her for much longer now—not because of fractions, but because I can't live without you.

If there was any jealousy felt by Marjory Kennaway at the loss of her son to another woman, she did not show it even though she continued to voice her worry that James and Susan were too young to marry. Her own marriage, however, had other side-effects. It meant that her financial and legal affairs could be handled by Sir Frederick (now better known to his new family as Eric) and that the burdens of trusts, stocks and shares and insurance policies could finally be lifted from her son's shoulders. It also regularised James's private income from his father's trust which stood at £300 per year, just enough for a pleasant life at Oxford but in James's opinion, insufficient for married bliss.

For the time being they had to put up with the pangs of separation during the vacations from Oxford and, while there, with the ever-present company of their friends. James complained frequently that he and Susan never had enough time alone together when he could say to her the things he really wanted to say. Occasionally they would manage weekends away together but the cramped, hot-house style of Oxford was not designed to provide an ideal setting for intense affairs. "Love is not a traditional Oxford pleasure," wrote Jan Morris in her celebration of Oxford,[10] "if only because the traditions of Oxford are based upon bachelors' communities". She added that "it happens all the same" and during their undergraduate years James and Susan often found that their time together was a furtive affair leading to frustration and feelings of unresolved tension. It was an uneasy and unsettling time for them both.

It had been agreed that while London would be James's home in the future, Chapelbank would be for Perthshire holidays. James had always liked Sir Frederick and the Bell family had been pillars of kindness during his days at Glenalmond, but it took some time for the Bell children to come to terms with their new step-mother. Their first Christmas together proved to be a strain with all the necessary domestic and social adjustments having to be made intuitively as the holiday progressed. James did his best to jolly the holiday along but the petty bickering did take its toll. He accepted invitations to dances even though he found the girls dull and lifeless, as he reported to a grateful Susan: "none of them are educated to begin with, so all my crispest witticisms flop". He accompanied the Bells on a round of featureless festive cocktail parties: "Lady — really was the limit. She gave a party for 300 people on *1 glass* of champagne each". He went shooting and threw himself into the other necessary pursuits of a country gentleman: "I visited the country gents club yesterday for lunch which was absolute hell. Tweed clothes and tweed wits. Whisky and much manly talk. This is the club that paunched a thousand lairds". And all the while, smiling, courteous James hated it, so much so that he was determined never again to repeat the entire experience while holidaying at Chapelbank. It was his last full taste of the society that had given him so much succour and although he returned to it often enough in his writing, he told his mother that in future, visits he would beg to be excused from the social round. In spite of the obvious strain of Christmas in the north the important decision was finally reached that he would become officially engaged early in the New Year. Not only did he feel that the "unofficial engagement" was becoming increasingly farcical but he felt that it might be possible for him to complete his legal studies and find a job at the same time. Before the Christmas vacation he had received an encouraging reply from the publishers Longmans Green that there would be the possibility of an opening for him in the summer of 1951.

That he should have chosen publishing was not altogether surprising. His first attempt at play-writing during his military service had come to naught, but another play, a Noel Coward-like comedy of manners, *The Poker* had enjoyed the dubious success of enthusiastic rejection by a West End theatre management. It took as its plot the inventive idea that a group of people bound together by their social background could be projected into the past during an eclipse of the sun and that in their collective past their true emotions would emerge. Despite its lack of stagecraft and its convoluted plot, the characters were well drawn and the dialogue is crisp and to the point. On 10 January 1950, several months after it had been submitted, John Fernald, director of productions at the Arts Theatre Club had written to Kennaway turning down the play but he also sweetened the pill by stating that he was "left with the feeling that you may become a playwright of a highly original turn of mind with something to say that is worth saying. Although you have not succeeded with this play I feel that you should quickly get on with another (which I should very much like to read)." He wrote two other plays while at Oxford: *Snakes and Ladders*, a Barrie-esque political romance set in a country house south of Edinburgh on election night which is remarkable only for its fond evocation of his tutor Anthony

Crosland in the character of Tony Merton, "particularly attractive if a trifle dissipated looking. Thick, well-brushed, but purposely carelessly brushed brown hair which is cut long; a soft collar, grey suit and expressive eyes with rather heavy eye-lids. Tall and slim; suede ankle boots, and a mustard and cress tie". His other play was *Personal Friends* a romance set in Oxford: both were destined to be rejected by several managements. He had also tried his hand at writing short stories[11] and had enjoyed success with *"I want to go to Spain"*, a short humorous piece about holidaying abroad on the £50 allowance, which was published in the October 1949 issue of *Men Only*. It had elicited a good response and James had been greatly amused to receive a letter from a Spanish sherry exporter offering him the opportunity of a free holiday on his estate. Writing had become increasingly important to him not necessarily as a prop but as an engaging and vital pastime.

> I wonder sometimes [he wrote to his mother on 17 January 1950] if you realize just how much my writing means to me. I hate to be poetic about it as it does not claim to be anything more than entertaining but I feel strongly that there is hope there.

There was another reason for his renewed enthusiasm in literature: his friendship with another Trinity undergraduate, Denys Hodson, a product of Marlborough who had done his National Service in the Palestine Police. Although he was associated loosely with "The Boys", Hodson was everything that James was not: a mature intellectual who was well read in English and European literature and a socialist who despaired of his friend's petty political ambitions.

During his second year Kennaway moved into rooms in college, in Kettle Hall, an aged building in the south-east corner of the Front Quad. Some twenty-five yards away were Hodson's rooms and soon the two men became inseparable companions, sharing James's more spacious and pleasant living room on the ground floor "with Susie an increasingly common addition"[12]. The three became equally close, "a rather well known trio, sometimes thought of as a *ménage á trois* but actually not". rather as Kennaway described the triangular relationship between Tate, Donagh and Longman in *The Mindbenders*.

> In nine cases out of ten a woman in love finds a best man too.

> Practically every engagement and every love affair bears this second relationship. The couple form a solid friendship with a third party, ostensibly the man's friend, in fact the woman's second choice. Passion takes her off the ground, but doing so endangers her, runs contrary to her second instinct, security. For this reason she clings to the best man, the safe brother figure whom she books to pick up the pieces supposing something should go wrong.[13]

Denys and James were undoubtedly close at Oxford, enjoying the kind of intense friendship that youth and a university education permits, a proximity of energy and spirit that vanishes as the years go by. And Susan was fond of Denys, too, looking on him perhaps as a "second choice". In fact he was their best man when they married and remained a lifelong friend who was fiercely loyal to James even when he was at his most difficult. At Oxford he was an important influence. He encouraged James to read more widely, to investigate especially Balzac and Francois Mauriac the French novelist and playwright who won the Nobel Prize in 1952, and to indulge in a greater self-analysis of his own work. Kennaway responded to most of the advice given to him even though he continued to be suspicious of Hodson's highly specialised classical education. But it was not all serious late-night discussion.

> I remember our second summer as being a kind of "Salad Days". The weather was outstanding and we idled by the Cherwell in the Parks a good deal and found a marvellous spot in a clear stream somewhere up by Godstone with a deep pool under a little waterfall and a clear gravel bottom. We called it the Garden of Eden.[14]

They also told each other their innermost secrets, commiserated with one another over poor results or the rebuffs of girl friends, and were boon companions. In their final year they moved into superior digs at 27 Wellington Square (now demolished), run by two New Zealand ladies, the Misses Wedge, and which had a first-floor sitting room and two bedrooms. Denys Hodson remembers that Kennaway was a conventional undergraduate who dressed in tweed jackets and flannels. He still preferred his Macpherson dress kilt to his dinner jacket for dances, and he had still some of his father's dark suits which smelled fairly horribly of mothballs. During his time at Oxford he put on weight and as he grew older the fairness of his boyhood changed to a dark ruddiness and a high complexion. Most of his contemporaries remember him as being strikingly good looking.

On 5 October 1950, to his astonishment, he was invited by the Principal, Dr Janet Vaughan, to a dance which Somerville was giving in honour of Princess Margaret, as "she is anxious to dance with members of the University rather than her own particular friends and I feel it would be pleasanter if her partners were also known to members of Somerville who won't necessarily be anxious to give up their partners to the Princess for the whole evening". The invitation had been engineered by Val Mitchison and as James was the only man to receive the invitation he was mightily pleased by the honour, although his tutor remarked drily that it gave some indication of how he spent his time. (The evening did not have a happy ending. James was snubbed by the Royal party, and he returned to Susan with tears of frustration dimming what should have been a glittering occasion.) In fact, during his final year Kennaway cut down on his socialising as most of his time was being spent with Susan and Denys and also because he was belatedly making up lost time in his degree course. P.P.E. had not suited him and only the Politics course held any interest because it veered towards his favourite subject, History. He attended the lectures given by Asa Briggs and A.J.P. Taylor but as Denys Hodson remembered "it was typical of him to be more interested in Lord Randolph Churchill than in any successful statesman". And that interest was partly due, no doubt, to the very special interest that James had in his son, Winston. His special subject was Epistemology but he got little change from it and by the time of his final examinations he was floundering. To his dismay and hurt pride he was awarded a third instead of the hoped-for second.

As it was, the results mattered not. In July 1951 after weeks of patient negotiation he was offered the post of personal assistant to John Longman, to run the medical and scientific lists of the publishing house of Longmans Green. After a trial period of six weeks he would be given a salary of £500 and a permanent post. Needless to say, John Longman had little difficulty in accommodating his new assistant and so, with a good income from his salary, a substantial private income and a house in London, the way was open for James to marry Susan. They had become engaged on St. Valentine's Day, 1951, an "irrevocable step" but one which James explained to his mother had to be taken to end the months of uncertainty.

By then he knew exactly in which direction his future lay.

> I must determine just how I want to live my life, and the things I value now, and believe in, it must be admitted, are not the same as I thought they would be at this stage. It is not my object now to be a prima donna of any world, stage, politics or Bar. I think in that personal struggle you lose more than you ever gain. It is on the other hand my very great ambition to be considered one day a fine man; a man with sympathy and courage. I must be good at something, and I think—always taking writing as second course—publishing may well be the answer, even if it means starting at 0.[15]

James was not dissembling for his mother's benefit. He had gone up to Oxford with the intention of carving out a career at the Bar, he had flirted briefly with politics and he had entertained thoughts of becoming a Coward-like writer of the theatre, complete with cigarette holder and silk dressing gown. Marriage he had held in disdain and the thought of children had been automatically dismissed in favour of the life of a man about town with an agreeable amount of money in his pocket. But much had happened within those three years. His mother had remarried, thus removing a moral sheet-anchor from his life; and more importantly, he had met and fallen in love with Susan, who, he admitted to his mother, had taught him to think less about the Jim in James Kennaway and more about other people. Now James looked forward to the domesticity of marriage, to the prospect, later, of becoming a father and to spending the next years of his life in the genteel ambience of publishing. With Denys Hodson as best man, James and Susan were married on 6 October 1951 in Oxford, at the venerable Church of St Mary Magdalen.

~ 6 ~

Publisher's Clerk

IN the *Sunday Times* of 16 June 1957, James's friend Godfrey Smith, then working as the newspaper's News Editor, printed the photographs of twenty-seven of his Oxford contemporaries who had made good during the previous five years. He called them "a tumultuous post-war generation" who had spent their undergraduate days, "all living, working, drinking and quarrelling in the same square mile", and pondered the fact that although it might be considered a hothouse generation, all had made their mark by the age of thirty. Smith chose his vintage well and as events have proved, all have stayed the course and many are now well-known, household names. Kenneth Tynan (Magdalen 1945-48) was already Drama Critic of the *Observer* newspaper. Robin Day (St Edmund Hall 1948-51) had begun his career in broadcasting. Kingsley Amis (St Johns 1945-47) had published his novel *Lucky Jim.* Anthony Wedgewood Benn (New College 1946-48) had found a seat as a Labour Member of Parliament. Roger Bannister (Exeter 1947-50) had run a mile in under four minutes. Francis Huxley (Balliol 1945-50) had returned from adventures in Brazil to write his anthropological study *Affable Savages*. The remaining score had also achieved considerable personal fame and are still leaders in their chosen fields: in the bottom right-hand corner is the photograph of "James Kennaway, author of *Tunes of Glory*. New novel due soon. Age 29".

His appearance in the half-page feature was entirely justified; he was a successful and popular author and he was entertaining thoughts of launching himself into an independent career, by earning his living entirely from his pen. It had all become very different from the hopes that had accompanied his graduation and his wedding half-a-dozen years earlier. Not that he had been an unsuccessful publisher: James had launched himself with enthusiasm into life at Longmans and had become a respected member of the editorial staff. His immediate boss was John Longman, a lineal descendant of the Thomas Longman who had launched the firm "at the sign of the Ship and the Black Swan" in 1724, and it was his and his personal assistant's task to tour the British universities looking for authors who might contribute academic textbooks to Longman's medical and scientific lists. This work involved much travel. In September 1952 Kennaway attended the annual meeting of the British Association which was held that year in Belfast where "the whole time it is receptions, lectures, coffee, a drink, then write up what's done and what's spent. We've been to the Harbour Master, to the Mayor, to the Prime Minister, to the inaugural meeting".[1] While he may have found the proceedings dull and many of the scientists enclosed within the galaxies of their own research, Kennaway enjoyed the experience, using his youthful energy and charm to make a number of vital contacts. At the conference's end he felt that he had made enough of a mark for the Longman's job to be his for as long as he wanted it.

He had also been immensely charmed by John Longman's brother, Mark who was twelve years his senior but whose charm and vitality made him the friend of all who knew him, whatever their age. Educated at Eton and Cambridge he had been blessed with many advantages. Apart from his name and entree to a famous family firm, he was handsome and intelligent and his high-spirited good nature had made him one of the most attractive personalities in London's literary world. Just as he had found Alasdair Hilleary's good looks and patrician nature appealing, so too was James drawn into Mark Longman's orbit and the two men were destined to become very close friends indeed.

After their wedding and honeymoon (which began at Claridges "with sunken baths, bidets, sprays, a monstrous great bed and breakfast brought on a huge trolley and served on perfect china") James and Susan settled at 58 Hampstead Way. Although it was theirs rent-free, neither particularly liked either the house or the area.

> Nowhere are feelings less strongly felt or a man's opinion less vigorously defended; nowhere, therefore is life at a lower ebb than in the better suburbs of London—and the suburb in which Andrew and Stella lived could hardly have been more typical. It was called Temple Fortune, a nebulous area which is neither Golders Green nor yet Hampstead Garden Suburb, but boasts the worst characteristics of both. But the Vasses' neighbours (and also the rating authorities) insisted firmly that their house was in the Garden Suburb—sometimes even in Hampstead—which was a good two miles away.[2]

Just as Andrew and Stella Vass in *The Bells of Shoreditch* felt their lives, in different ways, to be circumscribed by their suburban existence, so, too, did James feel ill at ease in the part of London he was well content to call Golders Green without any of the Hampstead permutations. The road in which the Kennaways lived linked Finchley Road, the main artery of the suburb of Golders Green in north-west London to the north end of Hampstead and it bounded the quaint village-like streets of Hampstead Garden Suburb which had sprung into life at the dawn of the century with houses designed by Edwin Lutyens and Sir Raymond Unwin. It owed its existence to the indomitable persistence of one woman, Mrs Henrietta Barnett and the story of her battle to provide a better environment in London for working people is one of the better in the annals of those individuals who take on bureaucracy and win. It is also a peculiarly British tale with a sad sting in the end.

In 1889 Henrietta and her husband Samuel Barnett, a campaigning Church of England curate, who worked for better living conditions in London's East End, took to spending weekends at St Jude's Cottage on the north side of Hampstead Heath beside the famous Spaniards Inn. The white clapper-boarded house enjoyed open views across a broad expanse of farmland and it became a much-valued sanctuary for the Barnetts after their daily struggle with the filth and poverty of the slums of Whitechapel. But no sooner had they acquired St Jude's than words like "development" and "progress" began to be aired freely in the neighbourhood. So popular had the area become that builders were planning to move into the area with ideas for throwing up the kind of speculative housing that was being seen in other parts of London to meet the demands of the capital's growing, and increasingly wealthy population. Worse still, the underground railway planned to drive a line to the new suburban population. Appalled by the prospect of a railway station serving a new generation of commutors from the closely-packed suburban villas that would undoubtedly mushroom in the view from their cottage, the Barnetts set to work with a will. A Hampstead Heath Extension Council was formed, money was raised and the open land bought from its owners, the Eton College Trustees. The campaign had been fought on a shoestring budget and against the wishes of some of the members of the Hampstead Borough Council who felt that the area was well enough endowed with open spaces and that only the wealthy would benefit from the Barnett's victory. For them, Henrietta had an answer. On the remaining open ground should be built a "garden suburb, in which every house, however humble, will be surrounded by a garden large enough to be productive as well as pleasureable".[3]

It took time and energy to carry out the remaining land purchases and to raise the capital needed for the building of the houses which were built in such a way that the windows would always look out onto greenery, Mrs Barnett believing that the sight of burgeoning nature would dissuade the residents from going to the pub or to the bookmaker. By the nineteen-twenties, the idea of a garden suburb providing a home for the downtrodden masses had been diluted by middle-class encroachment; by 1951 it was the smart suburb it is today, an area in which houses change hands at prices that put smiles on the faces of estate agents. But in spite of the proliferation of expensive cars in its once quiet streets, the picturesque houses and green gardens remain an oasis in the surrounding anonymity of north London suburbia. Although Hampstead Way was not part of the garden suburb and number 58 was well removed from it at the southern end, it is easy to understand both Marjory Kennaway's reasons for buying the house and James's disquiet about living in an area which in the post-war years was becoming increasingly built-up and without any discernible character. His dissatisfaction found a ghostly echo in Stella Vass's sarcastic outburst in *The Bells of*

Shoreditch: "Oh, dear me, no, we couldn't desert the suburb and Henrietta Barnett's last remains. You've no idea how I'm going to enjoy it now."[4] Within two years of settling in, James was on the look-out for a house with character and had set his sights on the neighbouring suburbs of Hampstead and Highgate.

The return of the Conservative government under Winston Churchill in the month of Kennaway's marriage coincided with a general return to the beginnings of a new prosperity in Britain, brought about mainly by a reduction in world tension and a rapid fall in the cost of raw materials. Throughout 1950 the war in Korea and the international uneasiness it created in the relationship between the United States of America and the Soviet Union had led to fears that a Third World War was on the horizon, and ominously that the United States might employ nuclear bombs to settle the issue. Raw materials for the war effort had been stockpiled in the States, and in Britain industrial resources had to be diverted to produce new weaponry for the British presence in the United Nations force. With the lowering of import prices British industry revived and an air of optimism returned to the country. The import bill came down, prices fell, consumer goods began to return to the shops and the Festival of Britain, which had been held principally in London during the summer of 1951 to commemorate the Great Exhibition of 1851, had shown the hard-pressed British public the "future" that would soon be available to them in the shape of "contemporary" household goods and furnishings. And the heralding in of the "New Elizabethan" age on the coronation of Queen Elizabeth signified a feeling that all was well with the world, that Britain still had a glorious future and that the affluent society was just around the corner.

For a reasonably well-off couple like the Kennaways (his salary of £500 was 10% above the national average and he had his private income) the new mood of national rejuvenation was especially conducive to their future plans and in many ways they personified a typical couple of the period, with a house in the suburbs, a job in the city and a multitude of friends in the same happy position: Godfrey Smith described them later as "a charismatic couple: Scott and Zelda with manners"[5], a depiction that perhaps owed more to romanticism on his part than reality on the Kennaway's. Susan herself described her and James as being "a very ordinary couple"[6]. Denys Hodson was a frequent visitor at 58 Hampstead Way, keeping up the same intense triangle that had existed at Oxford until he, too, married in 1954. It was typical of James that he should rescue his friend from a fit of depression at two o'clock in the morning when his bachelor party went sour, but inevitably the links thereafter became less close. Robert Spence lodged with the Kennaways on several occasions usually when he was recuperating from broken love affairs and the only answer was talk and a large gin or two. There were point-to-point meetings in the country at weekends, parties in London, the Chelsea Arts Ball and when Emma, their first child was born in 1953, there was an *au pair* to help look after her. James became a member of the Savage Club and used it for entertaining his authors: London had become his playground and he enjoyed every minute of it. "Life is good to me just now," he wrote to his mother on his twenty-fifth birthday.

He was well content to venture north to Chapelbank but he avoided the dates in late summer which coincided with "the Balls, and general county season. We come to Scotland to see you," he wrote to his mother on 20 January 1954, "and so that I may take exercise on the barren mountains." There was no doubt at all in his mind that he was now a citizen of London, that although he might retain a romantic affection for Scotland, that to have remained there would have been some kind of dreadful failure, a "no" to life.

Partly, his position is explained by his education. The Scottish private schools, like Glenalmond, tend to encourage their brightest and best to look to Oxbridge and then to careers in England or abroad. Once he had reached Oxford, Kennaway knew that his career would inevitably lead him to London. That expatriation was also assisted by seeing Scotland from the objective of an ambitious young man. To his mother he vented some of his feelings about his fellow countrymen's shortcomings in much the same tones of despair that he would use when talking to his friends about his ambivalent feelings towards the place.

> Scots people are far too much concerned with what other people think, your actions and reactions over-influenced by the opinions of

> your fellow countrymen. The explanation lies jointly in the smallness of the population and the lack of entertainment. The enigma is why the last reason does not change the first reason. Presumably this depends on the higher standard of education of Scots people and the weather, the great passion damper.[7]

Scots who leave their country at an early age tend to be their fellow countrymen's fiercest critics and Kennaway was no exception. Just as other writers before had chosen to live and work outside Scotland either from personal volition or from force of circumstances—apart from Stevenson; Edwin Muir and Muriel Spark spring to mind—so too did James swear that his only possible future lay outside the country. Only Glasgow remained in his affections and played a substantial part in his fiction. "For me," he stated in an interview of 9 December 1967 with William Foster of *The Scotsman*, "a lot of the Edinburgh attitudes, harking back to a golden age, are pathetic. I think I'm a Glaswegian at heart." And in his notes to a possible adventure novel set in Scotland, to be called *Old Alliance*, and started in 1961, he placed his finger on the rivalry that exists between Scotland's two leading cities, a dichotomous competitiveness that leads to one, Edinburgh, being described as enlightened and refined, and the other, Glasgow, blighted perhaps, but energetic and fully alive. "Popularly, mistakenly, the two cities of our flawed personalities, our gimlet souls, are christened (there's blasphemy) Edinburgh and Glasgow. The first the enlightened one, purports to be the true capital while the second, the darker one, surely the larger and infinitely the more important, is conveniently relegated. Down dog down."[8] Not that he felt particularly English, or indeed, committed to living in London, for all the obvious delights it offered him; rather he felt that it would be a fine thing to live in warmer climes and he often longed, like a bird, to wing his way south.

He also clung, stubbornly, to his belief that life was short and that there was simply not enough time in which to complete all the many things that he felt had to be done. Several of his letters of this period began to be peppered with Leon Montenaeken's maxim on the brevity of life.

> La vie est brève:
> Un peu d'éspoir,
> Un peu de rêve
> Et puis—bon soir!

The death of a childhood friend in a road accident in February 1954 prompted gloomy thoughts on man's mortality and constantly at the back of his mind at low moments was the never to be forgotten memory of the "father dead". They reconfirmed within him the need to hurry himself along and to maintain a constant pressure on his life, to make sure that life was experienced to the limit.

His work began to take him more and more away from home, to Scotland, to the university towns of England and Wales and with each trip the pain of separation from his family became more acute. In May 1955, shortly after the birth of his second daughter Jane, he spent a fortnight on Longmans' business in Holland and thoroughly hated the experience. For the first time he began to think that perhaps his future lay not in peripatetic author-hunting but in a desk job that would allow him to keep his own hours: as Susan noted, his letters were charged with an "intense loneliness whenever he was away from home and his overwhelming need to be with me and the children".[9]

> I think I'm going to have to take a holiday when I come back as I'm getting nearer the edge than I've been for a long time. Every minute I'm not giving my heart to you or writing which is not directly but is very much indirectly connected with you I'm throwing life away. I simply haven't the capacity to enjoy it any more without you. Do touch the infants for me, so kindly, and tell them that they are the children of a father who has given his life to their mother and who loves them all the more for that.[10]

When he was at home he enjoyed playing a relaxed, jovial *pater familias*, perhaps compensating himself for the lack of a father during his own boyhood. In April 1954 he bought a handsome house at 8 Holly Terrace in Highgate, enjoying views over Kenwood Park and Parliament Hill and south towards Westminster. Lying to the east of Hampstead Heath, Highgate is best known for its association with the fifteenth century Lord Mayor of London, Richard Whittington, and also for its nineteenth-century literary connections when it became for writing what Chelsea had become for painting. But it was for none of those reasons that the Kennaways moved house. 8 Holly Terrace was tall and imposing with a metal verandah outside the first-floor drawing room, it commanded a fine prospect and it was a house of character, very different from the uniformity of the houses in Hampstead Way. Now in his middle twenties, Kennaway began to take stock and the end of his first quarter century is no bad time for a young man to reconsider his position, and the way forward. His young family meant that he was beginning to cut down on many of his social obligations and also that he saw less of his immediate family. Inevitably, trips to Chapelbank had become less easy to organise, and Hazel, with whom he had never been close, became something of a distant relation in Staffordshire (as he had done to his mother, he refused to be drawn into her county set on visits to Croxdon Abbey). In London he had a handful of close friends and enjoyed their society, he lacked no material comforts and yet he felt ill at ease and unsure of his bearings. As his letter from Holland to Susan explains, he disliked being absent from home on business, both because he missed his young family, and also because he wanted—and needed—more time to write. During all the moments of spare time he could harvest from Longmans, Kennaway had found idle half-hours, here and there, which could be devoted to writing. He began keeping a notebook, a habit that would last a lifetime and in it he would jot down plots for plays, stray pieces of dialogue and notes on characters—he still thought that the stage would ultimately provide his true literary metier. His first tangible success was the publication of a short, humorous story, *"It pays to advertise"*, in the June 1953 issue of *Courier* whose editor was Alan Brien, the distinguished columnist. In this piece of Edwardian whimsy about a father's advice to his son on worldly affairs—an ageing tart catches the old man's eye simply by absenting herself from her usual seat in the Lido Bar— there are some deft strokes and the story is typical of the felicity and precociousness of Kennaway's early prose style.

> The day I remember best he gave me a glass of Madeira. I suppose that was the fore-runner of the bottle of gin in the right hand drawer which is such a habit now with account executives. Then perhaps Madeira was one of his accounts: it was a great mistake to underestimate the old man. He looked like a retired major with a bone for a brain, and he was most at home on his hunter, but he was the grand cham of the advertising business, 20 years ago.[11]

For his story he received eight guineas and the encouragement to try again. Three months later he tempted *Argosy* with a portrait of an endearing Italian dominating an expensive restaurant to the shame of his daughter in a story called *"An Italian has Lunch"* which editor Diana Burfield liked for its "vivid portrayal of character", but which she rejected because it seemed to have too slight a story. *Punch* and *Men Only* also turned down sketches on contemporary manners but on 20 October that same year Michael Middleton accepted *"The Dollar Bottom"* for the January 1954 issue of *Lilliput* and for the first time Kennaway felt that his writing was being taken seriously and could perhaps be commercial, too. "I have had a good many laughs out of it and I am sure our readers will also," wrote Middleton in his letter of acceptance, adding the hope that Kennaway might like to consider other stories in the same vein and featuring the same schoolboy characters. Although he was tempted to return to Taylor Two and his friends—David Niven gave him lunch at his club, Bucks, on 15 June to discuss the possibility of making it into a film—he was too restless to stay in the confined world of the Glenalmond he had re-created, and from his pen came a string of short stories, all experimenting with style and content, none of which were published[12]

He had, though, proved to himself that he could write fiction—that he could create characters and fashion dialogue, that he could tell a story. The fee, too, was not without importance. Susan remembered that as well as a layette for baby Emma, James also "bought a ridiculous amount of very expensive scent which he brought to the hospital and which rather embarrassed me in front of the other patients because of the wild extravagance they clearly suspected".[13]

He had also begun work on a novel which he called, tentatively "The Gun Carriage" and which was to be based almost entirely on his National Service experience with the Gordon Highlanders. Later it became "The Complexion of the Colonel" before being published in 1956 as *Tunes of Glory*. It reached its first draft in August 1955 and was published the following May by Putnam. The story is deceptively simple and yet, in it, it is possible to see many of the preoccupations that were to dance through his later fiction. Striding like a colossus through the novel which is set in the Officer's Mess of a Highland regiment is the un-nerving figure of Colonel Jock Sinclair, a war-hero, hard drinker, tough fighter and macho-Scot who has come to command his regiment by way of the pipe band and Barlinnie Jail. In wartime he is a bulldog, the idol of his men; in peacetime he is a boor, the despair of the regiment's smarter officers. By the time the novel opens, his time has come: his world is about to be taken over by an officer who is everything that Jock is not—Basil Barrow, an anglicised Scot, Eton and Oxford, Staff College and Military Intelligence, a prisoner-of-war while Jock was fighting. Jock looks on his rival with all the scorn of a disappointed lover: Barrow is simply "a wee man" with "tabs in place of tits" (p.27).

Jock is the regiment in all its antiquated glory, its Highland pomp and its battle honours, a personification of its fighting spirit and its glory: Barrow can understand that, and as the regiment's historian he admires Jock for those warlike virtues, but for all that, he is mortally afraid of him.

> He seemed incapable of speaking the truth to Jock. He was almost like a son with a father too fierce: in order not to offend he told a half-truth, until the time came when he found it more natural to lie. It was perfectly obvious to him why he did this. Everything about Jock frightened him. His authority, his unpredictability, his bluntness. It was more than that. The very depth of his voice and the thickness of his arm made Barrow afraid. (p.121)

No mess could hold the two men. The wilder officers maintained a fierce loyalty to Jock while the smarter majors and the surrounding county set made much of Barrow. Following preliminary skirmishes Barrow tests his authority by introducing a dancing class for the officers, Sinclair resists the command and both men meet their nemesis at a regimental cocktail party when "the county decided to come to the colonel" (p.58). Flaunting Barrow's new regulations against dancing eightsome reels with raised arms, Sinclair leads his set in a wild dance that echoes the strength of his passions.

> For the first circle he behaved himself: he set to his partner and to the third lady, and he completed the figure of eight with reserved precision coming near to perfection. Then when they circled again he sprang off the ground, flung his hands high in the air and let out a scream to crack rock. The others followed his lead. The noise rose, the floor started to shake again, and the glass in the door rattled louder than before. (pp. 64-65)

Barrow stops the dancing, makes a fool of himself in front of the guests and his fellow officers, but it is left to Jock to play out the fatal scene. After visiting his actress girl friend, Mary Titterington, he goes into a nearby pub where he strikes a corporal piper who is in the company of his daughter Morag—not because she is in the company of a non-commissioned officer, but because she lied to him about her whereabouts that evening. That action—an officer may not hit one of his men—brings him into direct disciplinary conflict with Barrow who cannot bring himself to order the necessary court martial and who subsequently commits suicide, unable to bear the burden of his own inadequacy. The final section of the novel, "The Funeral Orders", sees Jock so filled with remorse that he orders a full-dress ceremonial funeral for the regiment's colonel, thus giving life to his dream of the regiment's perfection. "Just the drums, the whole long column, the whole Battalion of us at the slow march and just the four kettledrums rapping, beating, with a die— with a *die, dittit die, dittit die.*' (p.199)

It is a remarkably assured first novel. From the opening paragraph inviting the reader to come inside the enclosed high walls of Campbell Barracks to the last scene in the regiment's piping room where Jock hears his own tunes of glory, the atmosphere is not only accurate, but it is also enticing. The reader is being extended an invitation to become a visitor to the mess of a Highland infantry regiment and to take part in its peculiar *lares et penates.* The opening chapter, setting the scene on a mess night with the regimental silver on the table, the officers dressed in their "Number Ones" and the pipes playing, is so well described and lovingly brought to life that it would be an unimaginative reader who did not entertain a curiosity about the fates of the various officers who are being introduced. The background is a Scottish county town—in this case, Perth—with its regiment tucked safely behind the walls of the gaunt Georgian barracks, and the narrow streets full of the ghosts of Jacobites. But for all that soft underbelly of romanticism and Kennaway's cautious hints at the grandeur of Scottish militarism and the part it has played in the country's history, the level is severely monochromal. The time is winter, the weather dark and grey, lit up only by the snow which "brought sorrow, not Christmas". (p.91) That much Kennaway remembered from his childhood and the Gothic description of Perth is as finely drawn as anything out of Sir Walter Scott.

The officers of the regiment who inhabit Campbell Barracks were also drawn from memory, and, according to John Durbin, each had his opposite number in the 1st Battalion, Gordon Highlanders, with whom Kennaway had served in Germany in 1948. Jock Sinclair, as we have seen, was based on Captain John Laurie who had fought in the war with the substantive rank of lieutenant-colonel, and Kennaway admitted in later interviews[14] that the impulse to write about his fate came from the disgust he had felt at the way in which the War Office treated in peacetime promoted ranks who had served their regiments and their country in time of war. There was, though, another model for the character of Jock Sinclair. In 1870, a young crofter's son from the Black Isle had joined the Gordon Highlanders as a private; during the Second Afghan War he made his name as a brave and upright soldier capable of leading his men in action, he was promoted sergeant and caught the eye of the commanding officer of the Kabul Field Force, General Roberts (later Field Marshal Lord Roberts of Kandahar). In 1881 he was raised from the ranks and promoted a second lieutenant in the Gordons, a move that changed the course of his life and one that was unusual in the Victorian army, so severe were the differences between the world of the officer and the other ranks. During the Transvaal War of 1881 he gained further honours, fighting to the last round at the disgrace of Majuba Hill when a British force surrendered to a tiny group of Boers. Later, he was transferred to the army of the Sudan under Kitchener and his career reached its pinnacle in September 1898 when he played a leading part in the British victory at the Battle of Omdurman. His name was Hector Archibald Macdonald who was destined to become a general, an *aide-de-camp* to his monarch and one of Scotland's best-known and most popular soldiers, known throughout the Empire as "Fighting Mac".

His career came to an abrupt full stop in March 1903 when he committed suicide in a Paris hotel rather than face the charges of homosexual misbehaviour that had been brought against him whilst he commanded the British garrison in Ceylon. Had it not been for the size and strength of his personality he would have appeared merely as a footnote to history's pages, but mystery surrounded the facts of his death and for many years a legend grew up around "Fighting Mac"; that he had been sacrificed by an establishment jealous of his fame and that his death had either been faked or he had been murdered. The truth was more prosaic: Macdonald was a competent fighting soldier who could not adapt to peacetime duties and whose sublimated homosexuality led to his undoing.[15] In Scotland he had been revered as a national hero, and the Gordons, quick to forgive, kept his memory as an integral part of the regimental pantheon. To officers and men alike he was the embodiment of soldierly pluck and recruits to the regiment were reminded that just as "Fighting Mac" had risen from the ranks, so too was that possibility open to them. So strong was the feeling for him that the regiment always took his portrait with them on their overseas postings and Kennaway was introduced to the story as soon as he was posted to the Gordons in the early part of 1948. With all its drama, its pride and its tragedy the story made an immediate impression on him and although Macdonald was a very different kind of social beast than the Jock Sinclair created by Kennaway, the position in which he found himself—a ranker divorced from his past and not yet adopted by his present—was very similar to the one in which Jock was placed in Campbell Barracks in the bleak midwinter of post-war Scotland.

All the other officers owe their existences to real life people, or in the case of Basil Barrow, who remains a shadowy, half-drawn figure, represent a type of officer; in his case, as a returning P.O.W. he is an amalgam of the pre-war Gordons' officers who had spent their war in Japanese captivity. But when one considers the range of characters it is possible to realise the intensity and the sharpness of Kennaway's observation and his ability to draw rounded characters: Jimmy Cairns, the adjutant, with aunts in Crieff and an education at the local academy (shades of David Dow in *Household Ghosts*), Sandy Macmillan, the sleek major, "who was perpetually sunburnt" (p.12), Major Charlie Scott, another war veteran and Jock's treacherous friend, and Dusty Millar "the fat Quartermaster [who] had long service and a couple of tricks with a matchbox for a shield" (p.41). Even the subalterns, the minor characters, have independent lives:

Simpson who "had been a prefect at school" (p.15) is a loose self-portrait and MacKinnon, "the junior subaltern who had a face like a faun and the manner of a gentleman" is a reflection of Kennaway's dead friend Alasdair Hilleary. The bullying regular subalterns "a throat cutting and uncharitable circle", as he had described their Gordon's equivalents to his mother were also carved from memory, men like Alec Rattray, a "real pillar-box Scotsman", and Douglas Jackson "who had a head like a German". (p.40) It was hardly surprising that when the novel came to be made into a film in 1960 the actors were able to give so much substance to the characters.

It can, of course, be dangerous to read too many real-life situations into a novel and to inject fictional characters with personae drawn from the author's memory. Kennaway was always quick to point out that although "the physical image must be founded on a real person"[16] his novels were drawn from within, that he relied on observation but that nothing he wrote was completely autobiographical. Nevertheless, in *Tunes of Glory,* his prentice piece, his gallery of characters, for a man with so little real experience of the world, had to come from those he had known or what he had experienced, hence the novel's primary virtue of being a good story well told.

After some minor tussles with his editor Roger Lubbock (he objected to the "physical impossibility" of Charlie Scott's claim to have made love under water (p.26), James retorted, "No!") the novel was published in May 1956. With the rawness of its plot and its excellently drawn characters it attracted immediate enthusiasm from the reviewers. Peter Quennell in the *Daily Mail* of 10 May forecast that Kennaway would "take his place amongst the finest storytellers of the day", the *Times Literary Supplement* noted the novel's "moving compassion", John Betjeman called it an "excellent first novel" in the *Daily Telegraph* and Sir Compton Mackenzie nominated it as his Book of the Year for the *Glasgow Herald.* The *Daily Mail* presented Kennaway with its prestigious Book of the Month award, and even grudging notices—*The Scotsman* of 10 May thought it improbable that Jock could sustain any affection from his brother officers—could not but admit that Kennaway had made a very promising start. Even before publication the signs had been good. Pamela Hansford-Johnson, on seeing a proof copy in March, thought it "remarkable. Surely not a first novel? Far too sure and sophisticated in touch. If by any chance it should be, the author is quite something. If it isn't, he still is. I found it most original and moving and at the same time very subtle." Despite his openly avowed "dislike of the Scotch", Evelyn Waugh also took Kennaway's work to heart, stating firmly that the author demonstrated "a powerful natural talent which may well develop into something important".

With so much public success Kennaway's head could have been turned. Each new letter that arrived on his desk at work was sent cautiously upstairs to Mark Longman for comment. Corgi bought the paperback rights, Harpers published it in the United States where it received an equally enthusiastic reception and the BBC made it into a radio drama which was prissily not broadcast in Scotland because the BBC hierarchy there thought that it would have an adverse affect on recruiting north of the border. Kennaway took his revenge on his fellow countrymen's lack of imagination in an interview in the *Daily Express* in which he described the Scots as being "their own worst enemies due to an inbred inferiority complex. That is why their manner is often so bullying. They are on the defensive all the time. It is that attitude which puts off English people. And when they have had a drop too much, they put off a lot more."[17] And in an interview with the BBC in Scotland a year later he expanded on his theme by explaining why he preferred England to living in Scotland.

> What makes me immediately angry when I get there [Scotland] is this terrific conformism that goes on. And also, what's sadder and rather deeper is the feeling that, well, this is how we do it here, this is how we've always done it here. We like it that way, and I suppose if you're going to stay in Scotland and never move out of this teeny little circle and never want criticism from elsewhere, then fair enough. But this is the same as the cabbage in my garden and it's doing very well, thank you.

In the same interview he went on to describe himself as a novelist from Scotland, not a Scottish novelist, not for him the heather on the hills or the fishing boat coming into harbour but rather—his example—the clash between external social conformism and the innermost emotions of the girl at the tennis club. The test of Scottish-ness, both as the critics applied it to him and as he related it to his own work will be discussed in a later chapter, but it is telling that with his first book, Kennaway was aware of the problem that runs through Scottish literary society: the feeling that any book that is not identifiably Scottish is therefore not Scottish at all. (In the final part of the interview he compared himself to James Boswell, in that Dr Johnson's famous biographer had to earn his literary reputation in London. The other side of Boswell's life, his desperate sexuality, is also not without its interests in Kennaway's case.)

In fact there is much in *Tunes of Glory* that is thoroughly Scottish, quite apart from its setting and the gloom of its winter atmosphere. Jock Sinclair is typical of the heavy-handed, macho, insensitive father-figures who stalk through some of Scotland's greatest fiction: Lord Hermiston in Stevenson's *Weir of Hermiston,* John Gourlay in George Douglas Brown's *House with the Green Shutters,* Gillespie Strang in John Macdougall Hay's *Gillespie,* John Guthrie in Lewis Grassic Gibbon's *Sunset Song* are all recognisable literary forebears. They are proud and superstitious men, flawed by the self-destructive impulse that leads them into conflict with those who are nearest to them. (It must be admitted here that Kennaway in all his novels presented the main male characters as powerful men and accorded them due, almost filial respect: Sarson the banker in *Bells of Shoreditch* and Julian the economist, who might also be a knight, in *The Cost of Living Like This,* for example.) Jock is a man capable of provoking both love and fear in those who swim into his orbit. According to his mistress, the actress Mary Titterington, he is "twice the man of any o' them", "a bloody king" (p.151), a hard man who is afraid of nothing, except for the ghosts of the past (another favourite Kennaway theme, as we shall see). When he walks through the streets of the garrison town he is unnerved by the shades "who wander through narrow wynds and every human is a stranger surrounded, followed, and still alone" (p.34) and his nightmare in Mary's flat is that of "the whole Battalion . . . lined up on a grey afternoon, lined up ready to move off, and at the back . . . the gun carriage, with a platoon round it commanded by a tinker" (p.196), an archetypal image from Scots folklore which, as Duncan McAra has pointed out "is as grotesque an image as a pig playing the bagpipes"[18]. There is even a hint of that other Gothic Scottish preoccupation, the divided personality in Jock, with Barrow being his mirror image at key moments: both men feel the same "blind rage that is born of fear" (p.95), Barrow when he reprimands Jock at the cocktail party, and Jock when he strikes Corporal Fraser in the pub. Small wonder that the literary critics hoped that Kennaway would turn his talents to other novels in the same vein.

But there was another influence on *Tunes of Glory* besides those supplied by his own country's literature. Kennaway had been greatly taken with the sequence of novels of Cambridge life, "Strangers and Brothers" written by C.P Snow, and of those novels, *The Masters,* published in 1951 can be counted as a contributory influence in the creation of *Tunes of Glory.* Snow's novel opens in mid-winter and conjures up immediately the raw cold outside and the "blaze of firelight" and comfort within the medieval rooms of the Cambridge college. Here too is a closed society—the fellows of the college with all their shared rituals of fine wines and mannered conversation in the combination room—and here too is a competition for power between two men, Paul Jago, the mercurial Senior Tutor and heir-apparent, and the challenger, Thomas Crawford, a man of science. And surrounding them, like the officers in the mess, are the other fellows, each of whom is a roundly drawn character: Brown, who like Jimmy Cairns, cares for the good of his society, Eliot, like Simpson, the good prefect, Nightingale, like Rattray, the impervious, life-denying lout. There are other comparisons. Just as Jock contributes to his own self-destruction, though his wilful behaviour, so too does Jago wreck his chances through his unpredictable behaviour, and both men face ruin through the defection of a friend—Charlie Scott in *Tunes of Glory* and Chrystal in *The Masters.*

Significantly though, it is both novelists' fascination with the trappings of power that brings both books into the same orbit, that and the vaulting ambition of both protagonists. Snow's novel was concerned with a wider debate and the sequence of which it forms a part is a chronicle of a changing age and of one man's—Lewis Eliot's—part in it. (By the time Kennaway came to write *The Cost of Living Like This,* the economist Julian and the creation of the Cabinet Office are very un-Snow-like creations, so far forward had Kennaway's techniques evolved.) In comparison with *The Masters, Tunes of Glory* is a raw, though vividly written first novel, fired by Kennaway's ability to create a rounded central character and a tangible background. Kennaway was still learning his craft and he was reading widely. Snow was a model in this novel, so too was Waugh, and he was reading the work of other novelists who would also influence him—Mauriac, Dostoyevsky, Hemingway and Ford Madox Ford. Slowly, his life was revolving around writing and writing only, and the development of a mature literary sensibility. *Tunes of Glory,* he noted in his diary five years later, proved to him that he could write. What had to come next was the evolution of a style of writing that would be capable of embracing the themes that he knew existed in his first novel—the pain of self-discovery and breakdown and the extremes of love and hate in man's mental make-up.

The publication of *Tunes of Glory* also brought with it a greater involvement in the literary world and Kennaway became that much sought-after beast: the bright young author. He became a member of the team of the Critics' Programme on BBC Radio and on 10 April 1957 he was invited to accept a fellowship of the Royal Society of Literature. He wrote for *The Bookseller,* the book trade's weekly magazine and he took up occasional reviewing in the national press, usually on Scottish subjects which he subjected to much good-natured scorn. His publishers wanted another novel in the same vein as *Tunes of Glory* but it simply was not possible. His next attempt, *Coming of Age,* collapsed at the half-way stage and was condemned to the bottom drawer. Instead, he turned to film and to writing for the cinema in an attempt to find a new means of interpreting his experience and his dreams to a much wider audience.

~ 7 ~

Movie Man

FIVE months after *Tunes of Glory* had been published, Kennaway had fixed on his next literary project: a novel to be set in Strathearn which would attempt to touch the mores of a landed family whose ancestry contained many skeletons. To begin with he thought that it might be called *Twist and Bust* and an unposted letter to his mother suggests that it would be set in Gask House near Auchterarder, although it would have nothing to do with the Buchanans, the family who lived there. Having conjured up the idea, he then had to shelve it and it lay dormant until 1958 when it re-surfaced through several drafts to become his second novel, *Household Ghosts.*

In that same letter, written on the night of 22 September 1956, Kennaway, for the first time, attempted to come to terms with his writing and his own attitudes towards his creativity. The letter, like many others he wrote in periods of deep introspection, was never posted because, he admitted to his mother, "it might worry you", but it was kept and was found later in his papers after his death. Not only is it a remarkable document in its own right, but it is also a key means of understanding Kennaway's condition during the ten years that were still to come. Firstly, writing had become for him, the most important and closely guarded element in his life.

> It is becoming more and more ludicrous to pretend that the point of my life is anything other than writing. All the day and half the night I think of nothing else. For days on end I am totally immersed in the work. Where it will lead, except to megalomania, it's hard to see, but

> the facts have to be accepted. The curse of it is that it gets out of hand. The only way to get away from the difficulties one's encountering in the work is to live hard, nearly to blaze, to drive places quickly, see things, do something else intensely.[1]

It was not writing for its own sake. Through it he wanted to discover the truth about himself and about other people, to approach the general human condition. Behind that energy was a feeling that his life had been too comfortable and that he lacked the basic experience with which he could mine that seam of unalloyed truth. To make that discovery, though, might be a painful process, causing anguish to himself, and perhaps, also, to others.

> One's living more intensely than most people but the equation doesn't equal happiness: then life doesn't equal happiness; pain and danger is part of it, always have been, and ever shall be.

As explanation for that notion that fiction could be a mask for truth, Kennaway turned it on himself again and pointed to the well-spring of his father's death and to the traumatic effect it had created on his young life: "the idea that I shall see my children grown up is immediately, automatically dismissed". Although he was clearly excited by the dramatic concept of prophesying an early death for himself—the artist being cut off in his prime is a morbidly attractive myth—Kennaway did feel, and continued to feel that he had to pack as much experience into as short a time as possible, almost as if he was making up for lost ground. When one's range of experience has of necessity been narrow, as Kennaway's had been, the thought of death was bitter gall. He had seen his father die, his work uncompleted and he did not want to suffer the same fate.

> Just now I want to blaze, in every direction, right or wrong, just so I shan't sink with too much left undone, too much never tried, too many sensations missed.

In the letter he also resurrected, for the first time since Glenalmond, the idea of the two men within him, the man, who worked for his living, and the artist who wanted to create, to write, to blaze.

> I've remained a child, more of a child than before, even in some directions; and in others I've outstripped my contemporaries. I suppose I'm what is called an outsider now. No team spirit, no

> society in the accepted sense. A lot of amusing acquaintances, a handful of friends who are becoming less not more close, neither English nor Scottish, nor richer nor poorer, uneasy.
>
> But God, how much better it is than being with the 90%; than being a potato. One should count one's blessings, even if it implies one's conceit.

It was a fairly accurate portrayal of his circumstances. He was twenty-eight. *Tunes of Glory* had brought him a good deal of public success and it had persuaded him, too, that he could write, that there was hope for him there. His way forward, though, was circumscribed by domestic circumstances. He had a young family—his sons, Guy and David, would be born in 1957 and 1959 respectively—and he had a decent and well-paid job in publishing. At Longmans he still had to make the round of British universities seeking out scientific authors, the only compensation being that he now began to take notes about the people he met and about the scientific problems which they faced in their daily work. Everything he did now was grist to his literary mill.

Clearly though, a decision would have to be taken about his future and his route was chosen for him not by the world of books but by the quicksilver world of the movie business. During the summer of 1956, trading on the success of *Tunes of Glory,* he had been commissioned to write an original script for producer Michael Relph of at Ealing Studios. This gave him not just finance in another league from the rewards gained in royalties from his first published book, but it also introduced him to the art of writing screenplays. Here, having a good idea was not enough: he had to structure it into a proper narrative, develop characterisation and create dialogue, all within the bounds of short scenes. Form and design suddenly became as important as the content. As a result, the first draft of the script which Kennaway wanted to call *Firefly* reads more like notes for a novel than a screenplay, and indeed, when the film was launched as *Violent Playground* in the Spring of 1958, critics voiced their disapproval of the "over-literary script".

The film was set in a modern housing estate in Liverpool and in plot it shared several similarities with *Blackboard Jungle,* an American film starring Glenn Ford and Sidney Poitier, which had caused a sensation when it had been released on both sides of the Atlantic in 1955. Both dealt with juvenile delinquency, *Blackboard Jungle* being set in a high school and *Violent Playground* in the modern sprawl of high-rise urban development, and both were designed to make audiences feel uneasy about the modern young. But for all its similarities to its American cousin, *Violent Playground* was a determinedly British film under the direction of Basil Dearden who had made that classic police drama, *The Blue Lamp,* with Relph in 1950. It had a strong documentary emphasis and Dearden was careful to bring out the solid virtues of the family relationships enjoyed by the central character Johnny Murphy, the "juvenile delinquent". The story centres on young Murphy's delinquencies—he enjoys setting fire to property—and his estrangement both from his family and from the society in which he lives: there are good stock portraits of his sister, his priest, his teacher and the policeman with a heart of gold under his cast-iron exterior. Most of the film is very predictable—and dull—until it builds up to a shocking climax in which Murphy sets fire to a hotel and then barricades himself in a school classroom with twenty tiny-tots and a sten gun, threatening to shoot them one by one should the avenging police attempt to arrest him. In a scene of great power and tension, as Murphy calls out his demands, it becomes obvious that he is a crazed and terrified boy who may well commit murder in his desperation to escape. At that point the writing is tense and clipped, free from the platitudes of the earlier, domestic scenes and the sense of impending horror is stark and tangible.

To find the correct balance and to evoke the atmosphere of antagonism that many young people were feeling towards the police at that time, Kennaway spent some time in Liverpool, but as the script was being finalised during the autumn, reality came to the rescue of art. On 10 October in Terrazanno, Italy, two mad brothers, armed with guns and dynamite, burst into the local school and held to ransom ninety-two children and three teachers, threatening to kill them unless various unspecified demands were met. The news electrified the entire world and it occupied the headlines during the siege and its aftermath: one of the teachers eventually attacked the gunmen and the police swept in to save the children from their ordeal. Kennaway kept every cutting describing the event and around it he was able to fashion a flashpoint of tension in what was a run-of-the-mill film.

Violent Playground was filmed in 1957 with David McCallum as Johnny Murphy and Stanley Baker as the C.I.D. man who is unwillingly transferred to the post of Juvenile Liaison Officer in Liverpool, thus bringing him into direct contact with the problem of juvenile delinquency. The other stock parts were played by Ann Heywood as his sister, Peter Cushing as the priest and Clifford Evans as the schoolmaster. It received a Royal Film première at the Odeon Cinema at Marble Arch on 3 March 1958 and by the standards prevailing at the time, it was not an unsuccessful film.

The Relph-Dearden partnership had been nurtured in the immediate post-war years at Ealing Studios under Michael Balcon. There, with other talents like Alexander Mackendrick, Monja Danischewsky and Pat Tennyson, Balcon had produced, in association with the Rank Organisation, a series of popular films depicting British life in all its variety, or as Balcon put it, "British films must present to the world a picture of Britain as leader in Social Reform, in the defeat of social injustices and a champion of civil liberties"[2]. With films like *Passport to Pimlico, Whisky Galore* and *Kind Hearts and Coronets,* they brought a sense of professionalism to the British cinema with highly literate scripts and elegant visual precision. With its celebration of community life on the one hand and its attempt (largely unsuccessful) to confront big issues on the other, *Violent Playground* was very much in the Ealing tradition even though, by the time it had been made the famous studios had been sold to the B.B.C. (1955) and the company was destined to pass out of existence by the end of 1959.

But by then British society had taken another turn. The last remnants of wartime rationing had disappeared in June 1954, there were television sets and other consumer goods in the shops as affluence became more widespread, especially with the introduction of the successful American import, hire-purchase. Rock and roll was being heard in the land and political and social agitation led to protest and demonstration. Thousands of young people flocked into Trafalgar Square to voice their disapproval of the folly of Suez in 1956; the Campaign for Nuclear Disarmament came into vociferous being with the march to Aldermarston its annual pilgrimage. In the theatre "kitchen sink" drama was all the rage and at the Royal Court Theatre in London John Osborne gave birth to the angry young man. Authors like John Braine, Stan Barstow and Allan Sillitoe wrote novels that sprang from working-class experience and during the late nineteen-fifties it became *de rigeur* for writers and artists to proclaim their provincial origins, although, it may be added, that most ended up the decade in the south-east writing metropolitan or cosmopolitan fiction. Residence in London was still desirable in spite of the brief provincial revolt. Although that social mini-revolution did not affect Kennaway directly, his baptism in the world of the sharp ten-per-cent men and the barrow boys of Wardour Street gave him an introduction to the *degagé* world of the communications business. And he was fortunate that his entry was made in the company of Relph and Dearden, two Ealing men who placed great store in writers' cinema—both men became seminal influences on Kennaway's attitude to script-writing.

The relative degree of success enjoyed by *Violent Playground* and Kennaway's general liking for his brave new world—wheeling and dealing for scripts was to become an enjoyable part of his work—encouraged him in the belief that he could make reality of the hopes that he had expressed to his mother in the unposted letter. By the beginning of 1957 he was completely immersed in his writing and by the following year he had begun work on the early drafts of *Household Ghosts.* The crunch came in April 1957 when he was offered the post of manager in the Longmans offices in Hong Kong with the implication that it was a necessary stepping stone towards a seat on the board. Had he taken it he would have become one of the youngest and most successful publishers in London, but his reaction was to cut and run as he explained in his letter of resignation of 16 April:

> Hong Kong is a tempting offer. Before I am tempted further let me say no: no, immediately: no, before I've talked with Mark: no, thanks.
>
> Hong Kong has precipitated a deeper crisis. Clearly I've got to be author or publisher. Every reason in the world points to the second career, but for the one compelling reason. I don't want to do anything except write.
>
> Sadly, therefore, I make my exit.

> I think you've treated me extraordinarily generously and I've enjoyed myself very much. But if I don't push out the boat now (whether I'm a flop or a success in the end) I feel that I'll look back and say: "Oh, you coward!"

Clearly it had been a difficult decision to take. Longmans was a good firm and Mark Longman had become, increasingly, a close friend and a committed colleague. He was about to enter the jungle of the film world and there was no other book immediately in sight, but as he explained to his mother on the day that he wrote his letter of resignation, there were some safety precautions.

> My intention is to work completely freelance for a minimum period of one year. If by the end of that year I've been forced to live on capital rather than income then I shall return to publishing. Mark has already asked me that in the event of my not making good as a writer I should go back and see him before going elsewhere. Evidently there would always be a place at Longmans and as a matter of fact I don't think it would be very difficult to find a job elsewhere.

In fact, Longmans went one better and kept him on on a very part-time basis for a further nine months until he felt that his boat had been well and truly launched. The move, though, frightened his mother no end and she wrote in great alarm to James that the ladies of Auchterarder would think "freelance" too vulgar a calling, a complaint which James laughed off: "Freelance does sound disgusting and a little like a tart, but just say writer or novelist. People will fall for that much more quickly." In preparation for the great adventure, he reported that new clothes had been bought, the wine cellar stocked and insurance policies bought: James was anxious that neither he nor his family should be caught short-handed.

He wrote in his study at the top of the house in Holly Terrace, but soon he preferred taking his work downstairs into the kitchen where he could be surrounded by children and comforting noise—like John Buchan, who encouraged people to be with him in his study while he worked, James, too, liked company while he wrote. In the evening he would sit with Susan and read the work to her and she became his first line of encouragement and inspiration—*Household Ghosts* was dedicated to her. Having never mastered the art of the typewriter he wrote all his work in an elegant and careful longhand and each script or novel went through several drafts: often from the back of old Longmans' proof copies through different shades of writing paper, the whole becoming a kaleidoscope of yellows, blues, reds and pinks. He wrote quickly and expressively, cutting back in draft after draft to reach the state of economy of word and imagery that he felt characterised all the best fiction. To achieve that degree of self-absorption in his writing, Kennaway believed it to be necessary (for himself, at least) to build himself up into a state of tension and implosion with the result that the writing would usually emerge as an inchoate mass, full of insight and invention, but entirely lacking structure. Then, all passion spent, he would often react like a thoroughbred and tear up the manuscript if it did not meet with his approval or with the approval of any colleague who was party to his work. The survival of at least four drafts of each of his principle novels and scripts is mute witness to the bulk of creativity necessary to fuel the subsequent quality of writing.

Reading also became a vital component of his working methods and he read widely, catching up on the lean years of his education. Francois Mauriac, the distinguished French novelist, was an avowed model and his novel of 1923 *La Baiser au Lépreux* influenced considerably the creation of *Household Ghosts.* Mauriac's novel is notable for two virtues, both of which impressed Kennaway: the subtle evocation of life in the claustrophobic village in the *Landes,* and the study of sexual assassination in the unsatisfactory relationship between Jean Péloueyre, the physically repulsive son of a widowed landowner and Noémi D'Artiailh, a docile virgin, who is tricked into marriage. When Jean dies of tuberculosis Noemi is trapped within her marriage contract and is forced into the resigned servitude of nursing her ailing father-in-law as he begins the long journey towards decay and eventual death. As well as telling a good story, Mauriac also created a world which he invited his readers to enter, a technique that Kennaway had also employed in *Tunes of Glory* and one which informs the ambience of *Household Ghosts.* and just as we feel mutual sympathy for victim and assassin in the relationship between Noemi and Jean, so also did Kennaway adopt the motif of a highly charged, though unsatisfactory sexual liaison between Mary and Stephen, her impotent husband in *Household Ghosts.* Both are created to excite the readers' sympathy. Kennaway was also impressed by his "master's" (as he referred to Mauriac in his notebooks) highly charged studies of love as an impure and hopeless emotion, and he admired Mauriac's ability to express his fiction in theatrical terms, allowing the narrative to progress through the development of character and through the composition of crisp, believable dialogue. The other novel which gave him much pleasure was *La Noeud de Vipères* (1932) with its dark central motif of a family torn apart by its sinful impulses and its struggle towards a desperate kind of Grace.

What Kennaway had not bargained for when he left Longmans was that Kennaway the novelist was now going to have to play second fiddle to Kennaway the movie man, and during the next ten years, until his death, an uneasy tension grew up between the twin states of his art. Not that the movie was bad to him. His involvement in film brought with it many lasting friendships with the producers, directors and writers who had been associated with Ealing and who were now working on their own account after the closure of the studios. Basil Dearden and Michael Relph who had founded Allied Film Makers in 1959 offered him encouragement and employment and for them he wrote *The Mindbenders* which was released in 1963 after a long gestation. For Ronald Neame, a director of some solid major commercial successes, he wrote the screenplay of *Tunes of Glory.* J. Lee Thompson, a director and writer who had run the gamut of British film-making from comedy to psychological tension became a valued colleague and boon drinking companion; but by far the most important personality and authoritative voice encountered by Kennaway belonged to the magisterial figure of Alexander "Sandy" Mackendrick.

Born in 1912 in Boston to a Scottish family who had emigrated to the United States, Mackendrick had been educated at Glasgow School of Art and had entered the film industry as a documentarist in 1937. He was considered to have been the most inventive of the Ealing team and his work on films like *Whisky Galore!* (1949), *The Man in the White Suit* (1951) and *The Maggie* (1954) had earned him the reputation of being a director who could combine comedy with satire and a radical concern for social structures. His wry and subversive view of the industry was a much-needed antidote to the hard-edged cynicism of the money-minded denizens of the world of the producers and financiers, and his encouragement and criticism of Kennaway's filmwork made him both mentor and father-figure to a young man taking his first tentative footsteps in the industry. Later, James would show him just about everything that he wrote and any note of disapproval could lead to the destruction of the script, so necessary to him was Mackendrick's guidance. More importantly, perhaps, Sandy Mackendrick became a good friend in a world in which friendships only lasted as long as the last successful film.

The friendship of those older men was also important from a domestic point of view. A chorus of disapproval continued to be heard in Auchterarder and it took the combined forces of Dearden and Relph, if not to silence them then at least to still their shrillness. They both journeyed north with James in November 1957 to explain to his mother that her son's involvement in scriptwriting need be neither haphazard nor vulgar. Their letters of thanks for the Bell's courteous hospitality emphasised their hunch that James had made the correct decision to leave Longmans and to join with them in a common purpose: the making of good British films. Relph's letter of 3 November was especially persuasive and did much to allay Lady Bell's fears—although to the end of her son's life she continued to wish that he would settle down to a proper job.

> I believe, in common with a great many people much more qualified than I, that James has a very considerable and important literary talent. It has been with this very much in mind that I have given any encouragement to his writing films. I believe that the film business can give him financial security whilst at the same time enabling him to exercise his writing talent in a way that seems to interest him very much.
>
> My only concern is one that I have constantly expressed to James. This arises from the fact, that, unless I am greatly mistaken, he will shortly be one of the most sought after writers of films in this country. He will be offered large sums of money for his work and it will need great self-discipline if he is to devote as much time as he should do to his other literary work.
>
> From what I know of James I believe he is quite capable of this

> self-discipline and will keep his film wok in true proportion to his career as writer.

For Michael Relph he began work late in 1957 on a screen adaptation of *Tunes of Glory* with the producer's firm intention that the character of Colonel Jock Sinclair should be played by Jack Hawkins with Alec Guinness in the supporting role of Basil Barrow. However, Guinness, fresh from his success in *Bridge on the River Kwai* declined the part as he felt that the Barrow role was too close in character to Colonel Nicholson, the obstinate British officer who against all the odds built a bridge for the Japanese enemy and in so doing showed a good deal of British stiff upper lip. Kennaway experienced several difficulties in making the adaptation. Whereas the novel worked as a unity through its finely drawn and highly charged atmosphere of a Highland infantry mess, in film terms that ambience came across as a glorification of the military ethos, a dangerous shift of emphasis in a Britain that was still smarting from the humiliation of the Suez military expedition of 1956. Although there were gung-ho producers at Ealing who applauded the idea of making a traditional British military caste film, for many years a studio stock-in-trade, the script adviser, Ken Tynan, was forceful enough to demand that changes had to be made in Kennaway's first draft script, in a memo to Sir Michael Balcon on 13 January 1958.

> There is a lot of army-worship in it—this, incidentally, was the reaction of Sandy Mackendrick to whom I showed the script. I am beginning to wonder if it is either possible or desirable nowadays to make a film about the army which does not at any point condemn (or even *discuss*) the purpose for which armies exist . . . I seriously believe that unless Jock goes completely insane at the end we shall appear to be endorsing not only him but all he stands for—including officer-worship, the need for a tough, bloodthirsty army, and the need for National Service. In short, without meaning to, we shall have made a Fascist picture.

Mackendrick's warning added to Tynan's reasoning forced James to think again and throughout January 1958 he worked hard on the script, levelling out the rough edges and instituting two important changes that would make the central characters more believable: that Jock would indeed be seen to have had a mental breakdown and that Barrow, before his suicide, would question the basic tenets of his calling. Also, the minor characters were given sharper attitudes and Mary Titterington, the actress, was brought into stronger perspective as a character who could understand and influence Jock. However, these changes were temporarily to little avail when Ealing went cold on the project after Jack Hawkins declared himself unavailable and the script was put into cold storage.

The failure for the moment to get *Tunes of Glory* off the ground did nothing to dampen the company's interest in Kennaway. He was under contract to the Rank Organisation who regarded their Ealing associates with grave suspicion and who expected their contract artists and writers to provide good wholesome family entertainment. From their plush offices in South Street in London's Mayfair, Rank executives would sniff prissily when Ealing projects were discussed, half expecting them to be, if not downright anarchistic, then at least to be its dreaded half-brother—intellectual. *Tunes of Glory,* with its powerful military flavour and its central theme of a clash between *officers* was music to their ears.

The next film on which Kennaway worked blew a different and unnerving kind of note, one that might be popular, but one which might also be disconcertingly subversive. Jazz. In the late part of 1957, Michael Trueman, a director, had teamed up with the Mick Mulligan Band to draft out a film proposal that would paint a picture of youth in the late nineteen-fifties in their true colours: a large group of young people without the vote who were expected to do National Service and yet who were aware that military training might well be superfluous in the advent of the nuclear age. These youngsters, Trueman argued in a memo to Sir Michael Balcon, were tired of being exploited by film-makers as being coffee-bar adolescent rebels without a cause, or as the mindless teenie-boppers characterised in such Elvis-look-alike films as *The Tommy Steele Story* or Frankie Vaughan's *These Dangerous Years,* both of which had been released in 1957. Jazz was altogether different as Trueman attempted to explain in a memo that manages to gloss the truth while at the same time never ridding itself of a soft-centred air of patronisation.

> It [jazz] was once regarded as the symbol of the roaring twenties and dancing daughters; a disreputable irresponsible sound. Now it

> has not only become classical music in its own right but is drawing immense audiences of young people all over this country and most others; bands of young jazz musicians are growing like multi-capped mushrooms,, playing to either dancing or just listening audiences. Jazz used to be synonymous with drink—now the brewers could die where they stand as far as the majority audience is concerned. Their tipple is coffee, Coca-cola or squash. The slightly older professional jazz players do drink but they are approximately in their thirties. The present relationship between Jazz, the men who play it, and the audiences is exciting because it reflects and symbolises so much the feeling and spirit of today's young people.[3]

The world that Trueman was attempting to portray has been pleasurably evoked in George Melly's autobiography *Owning Up* (1965) which lays bare a world of pubs, clubs and coffee bars; of drinking and whoring, and of the intimate world of a group of extroverts bound together by their household gods of jokes, funny voices and a distinctive, private vocabulary. In another context, Melly, a Blues "shouter" with the Mick Mulligan Band, has described the post-war, revivalist jazz generation as being remarkably similar to the clientèle described by Trueman, even though the director's sense of virtue may have been over-rampant when he composed the memo—"both its executants and their public were mostly into their twenties before the movement was even under way . . . this was further underlined by the fact that although enthusiasm for the music cut right across the social spectrum, it contained a surprisingly large minority of middle- and upper-class adherents and even a few elderly and distinguished advocates who had found a taste for the music before the war".[4] In other words, the film would be very different from those depicting the teds who wrecked coffee bars and who ripped up cinema seats in the wake of their adulation for the new gods of Rock and Roll, Elvis Presley, Bill Haley and Buddy Holly.

Nevertheless, although Balcon was enthusiastic about the proposal, he forsaw problems of authenticity and atmosphere and rightly demanded a story-line before giving his go-ahead. Trueman had spent some time with the band and they had presented him with a spectacle of the jazz-man as drunken raver and as Melly admitted, they had "camped it up like mad". To get behind their defences and to evolve a story which would be worth telling in cinematic terms, Kennaway was deployed in the spring of 1958 to accompany the Mick Mulligan Band on its tour of the northern circuit. Here was a world that was still alien to him, one of late nights, gargantuan drinking bouts and cramped, uncomfortable travelling in a Volkswagen mini-bus with a group of strangers who, to begin with, did not take to the conservative, well-mannered and well-groomed James.

> To start with he hated us very much. In The Bodega, at the end of his first night on the road, he stood, his eyes full of angry tears, and beat his clenched fists against the wall.
>
> You're all shits!" he shouted. "I hate you. I hate you."[5]

Breaking into any closely-knit group of people is always disquieting, and the Mick Mulligan Band, as Melly's book makes clear was united both in its passion for anarchistic behaviour and in its unsociable attitude to strangers. They tried freezing James out of their discussions, employed a vast repertoire of voices and in-jokes, increased their bad behaviour to heroic proportions—both to alienate him and to impress him. Kennaway, in turn, quickly discovered that if he could not beat them, then he would join them and as Melly admitted, "he turned into a real raver". That fascination for naughtiness, for drinking to excess, crashing parties and playing fast and loose with life took a grip on him: he may have enjoyed high-jinks in the army and taken part in undergraduate horseplay at Oxford but through the band he was coming into contact with the everyday lives of other people, even if that experience was heightened by the roving-minstrel-like nature of the band's calling. It was all very revealing and a taste for *nostalgie de la boue* was to become an increasingly vital ingredient in his life—and Mick Mulligan and George Melly both became part of his pantheon of acquaintances in the world of entertainment.

By June, Kennaway had drafted out the story-line and had written the first script of a film that, in deference to the band's inventive vocabulary was called "The Dicks in the Wagon". It was a simple and unpretentious story: Johnny, an Oxford undergraduate in the middle of exams, is persuaded to "sit in" with a jazz band, spends a weekend with them, has a crisis of conscience about his future, almost falls for jazz, but with minutes to spare on the Monday morning is delivered at the gates of his college by the band who then drive off into the golden dawn . . . The script is redolent of life on the road and replete with the kind of jokey language that Kennaway had experienced during his time with the band and the film, had it been made, would have been notable for its sharp observation and documentary-like ability to create vivid scenes of people at work and play, a concept very much in line with the Ealing tradition. Later that summer its title changed to "One Night Stand" and a final script, *The Saints,* was put up for production on 16 September 1958. It was never made. A week later, Balcon's company was sold and another jazz, film, *It's Trad, Dad!,* was made instead.

Despite the failure of his two pet projects to get off the ground, Kennaway had learned much about the challenging and highly technical world of writing screenplays and his writing was gradually being reduced to that necessary concentration required to hold both a producer's and an audience's attention. Film had also brought with it the reward of financial security but however pleased he was with the promise of his own performance and however much Jim had enjoyed the slapdash Spring, James worried about the neglect of the novel. In order to get down to some solid writing and to re-charge his batteries, he persuaded Robert Spence to accompany him to Lerwick in Shetland, the principal town in Britain's most northerly group of islands and an ideal place for uninterrupted writing. During October he put up in a "semi-commercial hotel overlooking a grey sea" on Lerwick's waterfront—the hotel was literally on the very edge of the harbour—and there he began work again on the novel that he had called *Twist and Bust,* but which he had told his mother at the beginning of the year "may be called The House that Adam Built, maybe Household Ghosts, maybe Scottish Baroque. It's extremely artificial . . . I'm afraid it's too difficult to sell well."

His intention was to write about a closely-knit family whose past ghosts return to haunt them and to dominate their actions at a time of great stress. To begin with, he had thought of setting the action in a house like Gask, but in Lerwick he rewrote the novel completely to set it in a generations-old printing firm in Edinburgh, called J. & R. Hope, which name was to be the title of the book. He reported back to Susan that he was "still going strong, though God knows how much of it is readable", a sensible enough assessment as the work, as it exists in manuscript, is a mass of contradictions, false starts and overblown prose. Whenever Kennaway got into difficulties with his work, he would attempt to write his way out of trouble and the evolution of *Household Ghosts* is a fair example of his methods—later still, it assumed another mantle, being called *A Letter from Torquil.* Part of the problem lay in the fact that, unlike his experience with *Tunes of Glory,* he was writing from imagination and not from experience. This entailed placing an entirely artificial story in a background that he knew well—which is why he abandoned false Edinburgh for familiar Strathearn in the final text. Out of the mass of writing that was put on paper in Lerwick came the realisation that the novel would have to be called *Household Ghosts* to express its main theme, that it would have to be set in a country mansion and that it would have to include the character of "Pink", Kennaway's most memorable creation, who began life as the wayward, black-sheep partner of the firm of J. & R. Hope.

Greatly invigorated by the change of scene, James returned home to London and his family in time for Christmas. With a successful year behind him, a novel on the stocks and further film work in the offing, he began to question the sense of staying on in London. His writing could be done virtually anywhere, he had enough material for his novel, his finances were secure and living abroad was still relatively inexpensive, especially if the family chose carefully and travelled out of season. After taking a long hard look at the domestic budget, James and Susan decided that if, they let Holly Terrace, most of the following year could be spent abroad and after sifting through the likeliest places, they picked on Alassio, on the Riviera di Ponente in Liguria, to the west of Genoa in northern Italy. It was a good choice. The Italian Rivieria was then still relatively unspoiled, not the popular holiday resort that it became in the late nineteen-sixties, and the coastline was still dotted with villas occupied by people who wanted to avoid the winter fogs and frosts of northern Europe. Besides, there was a tradition of British artists and writers living abroad and James was greatly taken by Dr Johnson's dictum that a man "who has not been to Italy is always conscious of an inferiority" and he knew, too, that across the bay, in Tuscany, had lived a man who was becoming increasingly a romantic literary hero—Lord Byron.

The Kennaways took up residence in Alassio, at Villa Garassino, in the early summer of 1959 and that was to be their home for the better part of that year. The children accompanied them and a governess was employed to give them daily lessons so that Emma's and Jane's educations would not suffer: as Susan remembers, it was a time of great togetherness and domestic calm, James revelling in his role as head of an extended family. Each day he would leave the villa and write furiously in a local café or taverna, the hubbub of noise never disturbing him as he never learned Italian and the friendly ambience reminding him of working at home in the kitchen in Highgate. There were several expatriate British families in the neighbourhood for company but James was becoming less demonstrative in his social life, more wrapped up in his writing and, on the surface at least, less sociable.

One reason for this change in his point of view was that his writing was becoming all-consuming and more difficult to achieve. A first draft of *Household Ghosts* was completed, he continued his work on a film project for Dearden called *The Visiting Scientist* (later to emerge in 1963 as *The Mindbenders)*, and he began work on drafts for two novels that he wanted to write in the following year, *Settling Down* and *Old Alliance*, both of which he hoped would be potboilers that might take off. In the April before leaving London, he had spent some time with Sandy Mackendrick, talking to him about the structure he hoped to apply to *Household Ghosts*, and both men travelled up to Chapelbank to savour fully the atmosphere of rural Perthshire. During the course of the journey back to London, Mackendrick interested his protegé in a project that was to be, on and off, a lifelong issue for Kennaway and one that still haunts Mackendrick[6]: a film about Mary, Queen of Scots. Like most Scots, both men were deeply moved by the story of Scotland's tragic queen, but both shared the same idea that it should be told stripped of all romanticism and presented in terms of *realpolitik*. It was Mackendrick's idea that the film could be made within the conventions of a Chicago gangster movie without playing it in the period of the nineteen-twenties, and that Mary could be seen in terms of the dichotomies that run through Scottish life. She was a tall, beautiful, cultured woman who stepped from the *politesse* of France in 1561 into the rough-house of Scotland whose capital city, Edinburgh, was little better than a shanty-town ruled by robber barons. ("A Mexican border town with bandits", as Kennaway described it.) There she married the effete Darnley, was raped by the rough Bothwell and found herself plunged into chaos by the diversity of her emotions towards them, while at the same time having to deal with a nobility that took out contracts on their enemies and who brutally murdered her secretary David Rizzio. Mary herself would be played with a mature sensibility allied to a velvet sensuality, able to make the dark figure of John Knox fall for her, and in the foreground would be the Machiavellian Sir William Maitland of Lethington, Secretary of State, and the one man who pulled all the strings at Mary's court. He would have been the central figure in the film, a foil to Mary's bright energy.

James fell in with Mackendrick's proposals with enthusiasm and for two years a hot-house correspondence sprang up between them in an effort to iron out the intricacies of a tortuous historical plot and to make the characters and their relationships understandable to an audience in film terms. It was left to Kennaway to provide much of the dialogue as Mackendrick plotted the overall structure and their resulting correspondence[7] is a remarkable example of stream-of-consciousness creativity as ideas, many half-formed and contradictory, poured on to the paper—most of the letters are at least twelve pages long. Mackendrick had been nursing the project for eight years and although it never came to fruition, James's involvement—which reached its climax in 1961 in a make or break effort to win funding—gave him fresh insight into the ways in which characters related one to another and something of the self-destructive nature of Mary Queen of Scots found its way into his creation of Mary in *Household Ghosts* and Stella in *The Bells of Shoreditch.* Mackendrick had just experienced a spell in Hollywood, directing *The Sweet Smell of Success* for the Hecht-Hill-Lancaster partnership but although that film had won plaudits for its sour satire of corruption in the newspaper business, he was considered to be something of a brittle maverick in America, a director who could be hard on his writers. James thought otherwise, not just out of loyalty, but because he looked on Mackendrick as being the one genius he knew in the movie world: from him he learned some of the savage self-criticism that he knew he had to apply to his own art.

One problem of living in Alassio was that James felt distanced from what was happening to his various projects in London. At the beginning of August he flew back to meet Dearden over the possibility of scripting a film for Sydney Box which would be set in Tangiers and which would be a thriller with an international cast. Again, the deal fell through and Kennaway was beginning to wonder if indeed his star was waning; had it not been for the loyalty of Dearden "who fought for hours on my behalf, without hope of personal interest in the deal", he told Michael Relph that he would have seriously considered begging Mark Longman to take him back into publishing. It took him a further year to understand that in the never-never world of film-making it could often take years to make a movie, that vast sums of money could be poured into projects that never took off and that talent could be bought and sold like a new line in a supermarket: once he got the hang of it, Kennaway looked on his negotiations with producers as a necessary part of his day-to-day work. In October his agent, Graham Watson of Curtis Brown, was able to report that *Tunes of Glory* had re-surfaced and when the Kennaways returned to London plans were well advanced to produce the film with Alec Guinness to play Jock and, as James told his mother on 18 November," this means a film on the scale of Bridge over [sic] the River Kwai, Guinness and international cast for American and world distribution, director Ronald Neame who I have to meet today."

The plan was to shoot the film mainly on location at Stirling Castle, the regimental headquarters of the Argyll and Sutherland Highlanders who would also be employed as extras, but there were problems. The War Office felt that *Tunes of Glory* presented the army in a bad light with its story of mayhem in an officers' mess and a suicide, and at a time when the whole National Service question was under discussion, they felt that any collusion between themselves and the film's producers would be bad for recruiting. In the end they chose that typically British escape route—the compromise. Soldiers could be used but they would be Irish Guardsmen and not Highlanders, a tartan could be worn provided it was not regimental, some scenes could be shot at Scottish locations but not at Stirling Castle which would have to be rebuilt as a studio set. In an entirely unashamed *volte face,* when the film was premièred in Perth, the Black Watch used the occasion for a recruiting drive and to Kennaway's anger the performance was attended by the General Officer, Commanding Scotland, as well as by several officers in uniform.

The film's leading players were Alec Guinness in the role of Jock Sinclair, John Mills as Basil Barrow, Gordon Jackson as Jimmy Cairns, Dennis Price as Charlie Scott and Kay Walsh as Mary Titterington and so strong were their interpretations, in that they breathed real life into the characters, that it is now well-nigh impossible to have seen the film and then re-read the novel without their performances springing into the mind's eye. The film also introduced Susannah York in the minor role of Morag, Jock's daughter. She was distantly related to James through his kinship to the Bells and she played leading roles in two other films that he scripted: *Country Dance* and *Battle of Britain. Tunes of Glory* was given a Gala Performance at the Leicester Square Odeon on 1 December 1960 and opened in Britain and America to a fanfare of praise from critics and audiences alike. The *New York Times,* a newspaper not normally noted for its gentle treatment of British films, saluted it handsomely, especially the "magnificently observed" acting, and the reviewer, Rosley Crowther, also picked up the notion that the "professional soldiers are not just fellows to please themselves but the guardians of a stern tradition and a selfless responsibility". In Britain it was considered a triumph, "a thundering good film" was the verdict of London's *Evening News*—other papers were equally enthusiastic—and in the United States, Kennaway's script was one of five nominations for the Best Screenplay awarded by the Academy of Motion Pictures, Arts and Sciences. The coveted Oscar finally went to Richard Brooks for his script for *Elmer Gantry* but the nomination increased Kennaway's own personal stock and just as the novel had made his name, so, to his exasperation (he had found both easy to write), did the film cement it.

At the years end came the first call to work in Hollywood but his he refused, preferring to concentrate instead on the first drafts of a play he had been persuaded to adapt from *Household*

Ghosts, called *Country Dance*, which he had sold to the Tennant organisation and which he hoped would be directed by Sandy Mackendrick. Events suddenly seemed to be overtaking him and he was caught in the dilemma of having to concentrate on his writing while at the same time keeping his name to the forefront of his producers' attentions. Not that he had nothing to keep him occupied. Other projects which he worked on in 1960 included a film outline called *Country Cousins* which, like *Household Ghosts*, occupied rural gentry territory in Perthshire; *Palladini*, a property/crime fiction based on *Settling Down*;a remake of *Captain Blood* which eventually so angered him that he walked out on it in disgust at the producer's attitudes; a piece of whimsy—an outline for a remake of a musical of Rene Clair's classic film of 1936, *The Ghost Goes West*, which would have included a part specially written for that fine Scottish character actor, Duncan Macrae.

By far the most long-reaching decision taken in 1960 was his return to Longmans, not as an employee, but as an author: "I'm coming to Longmans and I'm coming for life," he wrote to Mark Longman on 14 June. Roger Lubbock at Putnam had shown little enthusiasm for publishing *Household Ghosts* and James had instructed Graham Watson to make the change for editorial and financial reasons. Harpers also turned down the book for publication in America and it was sold instead to Atheneum, a company which had been established in the previous year by three New York editors, one of whom, Simon Michael Bessie, had been at Harpers when *Tunes of Glory* was published, and who knew and liked James and his work. For his part, Kennaway now felt that he was back in the fold amongst friends who would offer help and understanding.

> Let us play this one along with enthusiasm, knowing that James is much disposed to being published by you and by us. I should say here, and should have said earlier, that this is something which I welcomed with very considerable enthusiasm. I have always wanted to be his publisher and I take very seriously and also with delight the prospect of this coming about.[8]

Mark Longman's letter to Simon Michael Bessie, written that summer, is a fair statement of the faith that both publishers had in their author. Both were prepared to take a chance on his difficult second novel, and Longmans' faith was expressed in an advance on royalties of £450—a generous amount when it is compared to the £150 they paid for fellow author David Storey's novel *Flight into Camden* that same year. In his first letter to Mark Longman, James had written that money was not important to him but that he had to keep up his market value which was a fair enough remark: what mattered most to him was that at Longmans he would be edited by John Guest, one of London's most creative publishers and an editor who had revitalised Longmans literary list.

> As far as the editing of the books is concerned I want John here because I always have needed and always will need considerable editing. The thought of his support in this way is, sans blague, a relief to me already, and is one of the chief reasons for my real sense of happiness at coming to Longmans. So he must edit personally. Nor must he ever be afraid to suggest all sorts of changes etc. I believe my reputation in the film world, which even if you don't know it, is bloody good, comes mainly from the fact that I'm prepared to say that a good deal I write is crap, and start again. Quite often, by the way, I should be told to stop rewriting, because things are getting more crappy, not less.[9]

The relationship between both men was a happy one, James rarely failing to take Guest's advice, especially when he was in danger of being too oblique in his approach—like all good editors, Guest tended to take the reader's side when he reached an impasse with his authors. To Bessie, Kennaway had admitted that *Household Ghosts* had been a most difficult novel to write and that some three million words had been expended in its creation and although he could have written another straightforward book like *Tunes of Glory* he wanted to dig a little deeper, to create characters without any material existence, to live inside his novel while finding a voice that would be his own. He was not content to repeat the success of his first novel, feeling that *Tunes of Glory,* because it had been easy to write, had been something of a cheat. The result was the impressive *Household Ghosts,* a novel that most critics think his best piece of work[10], yet when it was published in June 1961 it attracted curiously ambivalent reviews from the British critics.

By the time of its publication it had moved in time and space from the Lerwick-born ramblings and was fixed firmly in a country house in Strathearn, although the setting is neighbouring Strathmore, perhaps in an attempt to dissuade his mother's friends from thinking that they had appeared in it. There, the Fergusons, a landed family with several unwholesome domestic skeletons including suicide, cheating at cards and homosexuality, live in isolation from the community which tradition forces them to inhabit. Sir Harry Ferguson is a cold and remote widower, his son Charles Henry Arbuthnot ("he had been Chuff-chuff before he was old enough for gin") is an ageing Billy Bunter who has opted out of responsibility, and his daughter Mary has been forced into marriage with impotent Stephen, a farmer who has revitalised the estate, the only thing that he is good at. A lover, David Dow, a local boy made good as a neurophysiologist in London, bids for her after a country dance and their affair and its ramifications is the novel's basic plot. Mary runs off to London with Dow, but finding her emotions unrequited by him, in much the same way that her sexuality is thwarted by Stephen, she abandons him, becomes pregnant by a stranger at a party and eventually returns to Scotland to compromise and a sterile marriage. The only relationship which approaches any degree of satisfaction for her is the childhood bond to Pink, a love that is expressed in terms of memories both of the shared lack of love from a distant father and a dipsomaniac mother, and the ritual of games and funny voices left over from the nursery. At the novel's end, diminished by Mary's action and feeling the absence of her love, Pink slumps into madness.

Within that framework Kennaway accomplished a great deal that was new in his writing. The atmosphere, from the opening scenes of the Conservative dance in Dow's Academy, to the claustrophobia of the Ferguson's house is evoked subtly and enticingly by not concentrating on physical description but by following the characters' reactions to it. The Fergusons are rounded three-dimensional creations who are fully established within the space of the first dozen pages through the strength of the dialogue. Adjectives are kept to a minimum and it is the characters' relationships to each other that build up their presence, not the author's insistence on describing their physical or mental make-up. With David, Kennaway employed a different technique, that of the first person narrative through his unposted letters to Mary.

> I remember your bracelet fell down your wrist as you watched the dancers creeping round, most of them, rolling Hunt Ball-Night Club style. You weren't drinking whisky any more. That added another German touch. Lager, now. You leant your head back until your hair pushed against the climbing bars, and there were dark shadows under your eyes, giving you, rather alarmingly, and suddenly, a great deal more sex. (p. 47)

Although this method, that of intercutting scenes from past and present and altering the mode of narration, presents problems for the reader in discerning the narrative flow, *Household Ghosts* is not the difficult novel that many reviewers imagined it to be. It does, though, mark a turning point in Kennaway's writing and presents the themes that he was to pursue in his later fiction.

Firstly, he saw Mary as a life-enhancing force surrounded by sterile men who imagine themselves to be in love with her, a characteristic he also found in his other later fictional female characters. Secondly, the dynamism of the triangular relationship and its shifting permutations came to be the one force in his writing that really touched him, and thirdly, he articulated a belief that failure was an important virtue, that disaster could hasten either success or despair: in this case it was the latter, with Sir Harry ruining his life by cheating at cards in much the same way that Lt. Col. Sir William Gordon Cumming had in the Tranby Croft affair during the reign of Queen Victoria, a story which fascinated James and one that was to recur again in his writing. Briefly, what happened is this: Cumming was caught cheating at Tranby Croft, the home of his host, Arthur Wilson. Because he did so in front of the Prince of Wales, in order to avoid a scandal he signed a declaration that he would never again play cards, and there the matter might have rested. But scandal reared its ugly head later when the details of the affair were released to the press and Cumming sued Wilson and his fellow players, citing the Prince of Wales as a witness. The resulting scandal was colossal with the press getting a great deal of fun out of the discomfort of the main protagonists—a cartoon of the Prince playing cards with the motto "Ich deal" was one of the wittier effusions—and the trading of innuendoes and market in backbiting was as great as it was in that scandal of Kennaway's own lifetime, the Profumo affair which involved prostitution and treason amongst Britain's upper classes. The Tranby Croft affair was to re-surface in later drafts and was to have provided the central theme for the plot of an unfinished novel of 1968, *Round and Round the Wedding Ring,* but it was less the historical interest in the matter that excited him than the blurred motives and the resulting anguish that was heaped on the culprit's family—although Cumming won his case there were few who did not believe that he had in fact cheated at cards. As a boy James had been told the story by his father.

Finally, *Household Ghosts* introduces us to the idea of the "obligatory scene", another Kennaway preoccupation and one that he had borrowed from William Archer,[11] a Scottish-born drama critic who had made his name and reputation by introducing British audiences to the work of Ibsen in *fin de siècle* London.

> In ninety-nine cases out of a hundred the obligatory scene is never played. The people concerned so dislike the idea of a heavy emotional struggle that they walk off in different directions, one perhaps, rather faster than the other. They leave their problem, whatever it may be, in mid-air. In a year or two, or even a month or two, because it has been succeeded by so many others, equally acute, the situation disintegrates. The traces of it, by a tacit agreement between the parties, both of whom are now convinced that they are older and wiser, are felt, but socially ignored. (p. 124)

As it is articulated by David Dow, a sexual relationship cannot develop between two people until the lovers confront one another with a blazing intensity. If they evade that point of commitment, they will never be responsible one to the other and it is David himself who fails to play that scene, preferring instead to be like "the tinkers who move on; who invite experience but flee from consequence' (p, 175). When David's relationship with Mary ends, it is he who is to blame for his sterile lack of commitment, for his failure to say "I love you" at the right time. That sense of evasion, that unwillingness to face up to emotional responsibility colours the last four novels and the idea of the "obligatory scene" is an important prop to an understanding of the shifting nature of sexual relationships in Kennaway's fiction.

Not that *Household Ghosts* is an entirely sombre novel. Pink's role-playing includes some splendid moments of high farce and the dialogue is witty and assured, especially in the weaving of the childhood word-games played by Pink and Mary, but what makes the novel such a distinguished piece of writing is Pink's observation of the "process of predestinate tragedy" which imbues the Ferguson family, and the understanding of the destructive power of Calvinism in the face of love as it is evoked in the relationship between Mary and David, she casting herself in the role of Scotland's tragic queen, he in the shade of John Knox.

It was also a novel that gave Kennaway many problems in its creation. In its early stages, when it was bigger in ambition and more dynastic in concept, he worried about people from his childhood days recognising themselves in the characters he had drawn. The society of upper-class Scotland tends to prefer discretion and privacy, and it is very much "a way of life furbished but ultimately flawed by anglicisation" as Magnus Magnusson noted in his preface to the reprint of *Household Ghosts* in 1981. Hating publicity or scandal-mongering, they live with their own particular mores apart from the community and it was precisely that atmosphere that Kennaway wanted to capture, the idea that the Fergusons had failed to adapt to the changing needs of a modern world, hence the myths woven by Pink and Mary to explain away their family's ghosts. For those reasons the typescript was screened carefully by the Longmans lawyers and only family pressure prevented at least one Strathearn family from taking legal action because they felt that the Fergusons had been drawn in their likeness. (Only one episode has its origins in fact: Sandy Mackendrick gave him the story for the absurd Uncle Arbuthnot's suicide in Dundee.) To his diary Kennaway noted that although the characters in *Household Ghosts* may have begun their existence in real life, by the time they hit the page, they had been transmogrified into creatures of his own creation: "To this added simply me: i.e: my extension from given fact—never investigation of somebody else's life and build up from there. Observation usually short-lived. *Usually*. Notable exceptions? No, I think I'm alright."[12] In other words, although like *Tunes of Glory* he knew intimately the background he had created, the characters in *Household Ghosts* were very far removed from any real-life model, for example, Stephen is based very loosely on Denys Hodson.

One reason why James had experienced such personal anguish in the creation of *Household Ghosts,* and in the same diary entry noted his "vague disturbing feelings about people recognising themselves" was that he was not really writing entirely from experience and worried, therefore, about the fictional consequences. Like other writers who had been granted success at an early age and whose life had been one of almost unbroken ease, he was concerned that his lack of failure or disaster might blight his ability to experience life to the full. He did not know what lay below the characters he had created, and so he had to sweat blood to conjure it up, to write and then rewrite until he, too, felt that degree of despair that he admitted could send him to bed weak with headaches and exhaustion. This torment, the growing belief that, as a too successful man, he had been denied access to disaster, led him to believe that he had to court it, that he had to push himself towards the brink of the abyss. It was at this point in his life that the writings of Ortega Y Gasset began to come into sharper focus. Just as the Spanish philosopher had influenced the novelist Malcolm Lowry with his belief that the novelist is involved in the process of writing his own life, so did James come to imagine that, lacking the extremes of emotional experience, he had to create them in order to be able to continue writing. Later he would claim to be confused by the difference between fiction and reality, and at low points would believe them to be one and the same thing.

In an attempt to concentrate his thoughts and to keep a record of his sensations and ideas, James began a writer's journal on 7 February 1961. The journal, kept at odd moments in spiral bound notebooks, is not a conscious record of his life and writings in the Thoreau sense of it being a mirror-image, rather it is a device for dealing with bits of information that are not immediately useful. In parts, the notebooks are little more than a means of jotting down stray pieces of dialogue and isolated ideas all conveyed with much nervous energy. It was only in 1965, during the period of his marital break-up, that the journal became a record of every thought and every action, almost as a medium for writing his life instead of living it. Through his first journal it is also possible to trace the creative torment that built up in him during the early part of 1961. Hollywood had raised again its troubling head with an offer to script a film for a princely $50,000 that would put him beyond the realms of uncertainty about the future. Ronald Neame had suggested him as the writer for MGM's adaptation of Max Catto's novel *Mister Moses* which was to be produced by Frank Ross: it was a tempting offer that frightened James. Firstly, he did not believe that it was possible for him to adapt another writer's novel, and secondly, he did not want to abandon his literary projects, especially the Mary Queen of Scots proposal which was beginning to raise a head of steam. In the end Mackendrick persuaded him to go, to gain some experience in Hollywood while he pushed out the Queen's boat in London. Kennaway decided to say, yes, on the strict understanding that his family would be able to join him in California.

At the beginning of June he flew to Los Angeles. It was his first time in the United States and although he had friends there in the shape of Ronald Neame and Lee Thompson, his first few days were spent in a fit of uncontrollable depression. "I was very tired," he wrote to Susan on 9 June, "and very sorry for myself here and booked a plane home, but several people, including Lee Thompson, persuaded me I was a cunt as this looks an easy job". It was small wonder that he felt down in the dumps. New York, with its familiar landmarks and the hustle and bustle of Manhattan is well enough known to movie-goers of any nationality even before they have set foot in the place, but Los Angeles is something else, a dehumanising mass of freeways and endless boulevards punctuated by parking lots and shopping centres. This city only possesses the myth of the good life, the seductive promise of lounging on sunlit beaches with the paradise of eternal sunshine and a ranch-type house in Beverly Hills. The reality can be overwhelming, an end-of-the-world vision, to those who have been nurtured on the home-grown American legend of Hollywood, the dream factory. Faced by the oppressive heat of early summer, the long distances and by the sheer lack of character in the urban sprawl, all exaggerated by an unnerving bout of home-sickness, Kennaway's first impulse was to run away.

> . . . this central part is hell beyond all description with bitches in big box cars—(not one of which, may I add, have I even spoken to. I've never felt so sexless anywhere). The feeding is gross to a degree.

> There is less straight vulgarity than I'd anticipated, more kind of limbo-like Hampstead Garden suburb life, and everywhere is miles and miles to the next place. A taxi from Lee's hotel to, say, Ronnie's studio covers probably seven miles, all built up, along one or two streets. This scale is what strikes me.[13]

The Frank Ross production company had put him up at the Beverly Crest Hotel on the Wilshire Boulevard, one of Los Angeles' main thoroughfares and once he had grown used to the notion that friends who lived in faraway San Fernando Valley or Santa Monica could actually visit him, that Los Angelenos thought nothing of driving several miles just to have a drink, Kennaway began to enjoy himself.

Lee Thompson became a special friend, introducing him to the bars and nightlife that flourish on Sunset Boulevard and once his homesickness had worn off, James threw himself into Los Angeles life with a desperate air of recklessness. He was new in town, he was successful and good looking, and with British manners still very much in vogue, he made good use of his attributes. Within a fortnight he had cornered enough of the local action to make Ivan Moffatt, self-styled leader of the British community in Hollywood, remark that he had accomplished in three days what most Brits took a year to uncover.[14] For the most part, his "bad" behaviour amounted to nothing more than drinking too much, going to "topless" night-clubs and gate-crashing parties, the kind of naughtiness that is tolerated when the perpetrator is a success. But involvement in the movie business in California also meant easy access to sex, and James took full advantage of the facility.

All of a sudden, courteous James found that unruly Jim could be given full rein at night. There had been the odd casual affair in the year before and he had lusted after one or two women in London but nothing serious had ever happened: here in relaxed, sun-soaked California, sex was a different matter altogether. Not that he wanted to be unfaithful to Susan—his letters home still echoed to the numbness he felt at being absent from her and the children—it was just that casual sex with different women, many of them extremely beautiful, appealed both to his vanity and to the boy within him who had never quite grown up. It was all something of a joke and he was quite secure in the knowledge that in the West Coast dream factory no one would kiss and tell. Relax kid, they told, have a drink, get yourself laid. Later, James would explain away Jim's extra-marital excursions to Susan by telling her that it was "an essential part of the creative part of his writing, a necessity"[15] By sleeping around, Kennaway felt that he was merely carrying out what had to be done to release his creativity: to have denied that would have implied the destruction of his talent. To have pretended that Jim did not exist would have been pointless and unproductive, and this led him to the argument that he had to seek out darker alleyways than the easy path of his life had hitherto led him. Put another way, he launched his belief that the artist within him was the child, that the child had to be protected and spoiled. It is significant that Lee Thompson, his partner in many of the episodes, looked on their behaviour as being no more than childish[16]: picking up call girls in nightclubs, smuggling girls out of hotels, flirting outrageously, all done with a good measure of boyish exuberance, as if whoring was the greatest joke in the world.

Artists, of course, have no licence to behave less well than other people, although many will at one stage or another in their lives. For James, guiltless sex was an ideal; he had no intention of leaving Susan, although to test her reactions he would eventually tell her something about his little affairs. By then, as Susan admitted in *The Kennaway Papers*, there would have been little point in breaking up the marriage on account of a petty affair that had ended months ago, one that had not materially damaged their relationship. He would also argue that casual affairs did not necessarily mean that he was being totally unfaithful to his wife and family and if pushed on that point he would return to the argument that sex was a necessary dynamism for the true artist, a double morality that became increasingly acceptable as the dawn of the sixties introduced a new sexual awareness in western society.

If California encouraged James to enjoy himself without guilt, working in Hollywood brought him into contact with writing for the studio system, the hardest part of his West Coast apprenticeship. For the first time since he had left Longmans, he was required to work in an office on the lot, and to accomplish this tiresome task he brought insolence-with-a-smile. On his first day at the studio he parked his car in a space belonging to one of the company's presidents, and on being told to remove it by the commissionaire, he merely answered that he was Lord Kennaway. The following day, his new name appeared on his office door.

Having been offered a sizeable amount of money to work on the script of *Mister Moses*, a dire contemporary parable based on Biblical source material, Kennaway felt it was his beholden duty to do his best. But the fact that it was somebody else's novel and not an original script prevented him from giving 100% effort, no matter how many hours he spent wrestling with the intricacies of the plot and the characterisation. By the summer's end he had tired of the film and had removed his name from the credits. (when it was released in 1965 it was a flop, in spite of a moving performance from Robert Mitchum as the saviour of an African tribe.) The tension within him, between an almost puritanical necessity to give his money's worth, and his desire to concentrate entirely on his own work, made him brooding and introspective in those quiet moments when late-night fun did not claim his attention. As a consequence, his diary for that summer is particularly arresting: uppermost in his mind were thoughts of childhood, of the mutability of life and an attempt to delineate his writing in terms of religious experience.

> It's summer: hedges full: buz buzzing, white clouds drifting in blue sky. With a satchel on our back on a dusty road. The van that passes, hoots, and the man waves but does not stop. We know each other, are pleased to salute each other but go about our way. It's foolish to deny that we all have this picture of heaven. Just as girls when babies are born so often will ask where did it come from, the patient who is aware of death coming, and whose pain is not too severe will fall in love with death and always there are the green fields, beyond them is a stream: we know that. Cattle too. These are our needs. give us this day . . . [17]

Several of the extracts from this period were published in *The Kennaway Papers* (pp. 75-86) and they present a very different picture of James from the Jim that only Hollywood knew. Here was a man struggling to touch the well-spring of his art, wrestling with the forces of love and hate, hope and indifference, forces that were laid deeper in the mind than he had ever been prepared to admit. He had taken with him to California the manuscripts of *Settling Down* (now called *Mainstream* and based, loosely on the Goldsmith elopement) and *Old Alliance,* both as antidote to the inevitable grind of script-writing and as the raw materials for his next novels. On his return to Britain later that year *Mainstream* was submitted in its raw state to Longmans who rejected it on the advice of their reader, Doreen Manton who felt it made "too many unrewarded demands on the reader".[18] It was abandoned, a fate that also befell the other still-born novel.

At the end of June Susan had arrived in Los Angeles with the family, James noting that "with Susan, end of 'solitary', sanity has of course returned. Ramblings in previous pages recognised for what they are—turmoil; leading in the end, one hopes somewhere, but so unsettled that they're not workable yet".[19] No matter how connected they might have been, the diaries had in fact been a source of comfort to him during that period of "turmoil", a means of siphoning off much nervous and creative energy. To accommodate his newly-arrived family, James had taken a house at Tancras Beach, a few miles north of Malibu, at 32504 Pacific Coast Highway, the long rambling road that skirts California's southern coastline. It was a long wooden building on the dunes with a Jacob's Ladder leading down to the beach below, possessing too few rooms for a long stay but ideal as a summer residence, and like most American houses, well-equipped with the kind of gadgetry that was still a luxury in Britain. With the wooded hills in the east reminding them of Alassio and the roar of the Pacific waves below, the Kennaways were well content with their isolated summer house. Lee Thompson had taken a beach house nearby so there was no lack of intellectual stimulus or excuses for fun in the evening, but after the frenzy—largely self-inflicted—of June, that summer was one of fun for all the family, with beach parties, swimming and games on the beach at the end of the working day.

The crunch came at the end of August when he decided to write himself out of *Mister Moses*—instead of turning in a treatment that evoked the religious drama of the novel, he turned it into a comedy, a concept that did not appeal to the producers. The loss to his exchequer he claimed to be at least £700 a week, but he was unrepentant, claiming that Kennaway the movie man was determined not to sell short Kennaway the novelist. An added impulse to leave Hollywood was that the tyrannical Alfred Hitchcock had offered him the script for his adaptation of Daphne du Maurier's story *The Birds* which was to become one of Hitchcock's greatest successes. While it would have been a tremendous feather in James's cap, he realised that to accept the commission would mean an end to his ambitions as a novelist, and also to impose exile on himself and his family in California. After discussing the offer with Susan he turned it down and began making preparations to leave. Most of his British friends thought him mad, but he received support from an unexpected source, David Selznick, one of Hollywood's greatest producers, who told him: "This is a lotus land, You'll stay here and you'll never write another word."[20]

~ 8 ~
All You Need is Love

The Kennaways were not England-bound in September. After travelling across America by train they took a ship to Barcelona from New York and then travelled on to Mallorca to spend the rest of the year there, on a Mediterranean island which, in its country districts at least, was not the lurid tourist trap that it is today. (A late nineteenth-century Spanish guidebook describes Mallorca's chief characteristic as being "its collection of strange and eccentric foreigners" and the island has always been a welcome haven for British writers.) During their American interlude James had kept in more-or-less constant correspondence with Longmans about his future literary plans and John Guest had been kept up-to-date with the progress of the novels that had accompanied James to the States.Originally, Mark had hoped to be in Mallorca at the same time as the Kennaways, but they had long since departed for London when James and his family arrived at their house, late at night, and following a hair-raising drive in an antique taxi. But there were other friends there in Sandy Mackendrick and, improbably, in Jim Godbolt, one-time agent to the Mick Mulligan Band. The Kennaway's house was at Cala D'Or where despite "the fleas, the smells and the thunder" James was quite prepared to put up with some discomfort to save money and to try and salvage *Old Alliance.* "We're still swimming," he told Mark in the same letter of 2 November[1] "and we're just about the only people here". For Christmas they made their annual ski-ing pilgrimage to Courchevel in Savoie, France: the pattern their lives was taking was now fully confirmed.

On returning to Longmans, as an author, James's friendship with Mark had taken on a more intimate standing and during 1962 the two men were to be very close. For his part, James was rather dazzled by the concept of inherited wealth and by the continuity of power and social standing suggested by the old-established family firm like Longmans. He also allowed himself to be fascinated by the aristocracy, and Mark's wife, Lady Elizabeth, a daughter of the 10th Earl of Cavan, interested him in much the same way as the gentry of Strathearn had beguiled him in earlier years. But in this respect he was not a mere *parvenu*, anxious to seek out their society; rather he admired the notion of an aristocracy, of breeding and inherited manners, allied to social authority, and the Longmans represented that ideal to him. Perhaps there was still something of the factor's son in him, the boy who felt himself to be on the outside of a charmed circle that also drove him towards cultivating his friendship with Mark Longman. When the two familes were together, as they had been previously in Alassio, James and Mark would sit up late together, talking endlessly into the early dawn, often to the despair of their wives who felt excluded from the masculine, clubman's patina of their discussions. They enjoyed one another's company greatly and if James admired his publisher on account of his undoubted glamour and social standing, the feeling was reciprocated.

Their friendship had other, more practical attributes for James, and during the course of the year, Mark Longman was to put at his author's disposal some of his firm's not inconsiderable assets. James had been offered a filmscript for a film which would be set in India and he would have to spend time there doing the basic research, but, unnerved by his Hollywood experience, he did not as yet want to be tied down to any one project. Nevertheless, he did want to visit India on his own terms because he felt that it would yield a new set of experiences, enough perhaps for a film of his own creation, or a new novel. Mark offered to help by setting up the trip through the firm's Delhi office where his representative, a Mr Kohli, would iron out any local difficulties that James might encounter in the country.

It was decided that he should travel out in May and that Susan and the family should follow later for an extended holiday in

Kashmir, but the absence of any sizable film projects, together with more extended travel and the lack of any real financial success with *Household Ghosts,* meant that in 1962, money suddenly became a problem. James had admitted to Mark that he needed at least £5,000 a year to meet the household expenditure which "on tour" had to include money for a nanny and a governess, and that he could not do with less. To save his author any financial embarrassment, Mark opened for James a general account of £3,000 with the firm on which he would be permitted to draw and which would be repaid in stages as film deals were finalised. It was a remarkably generous offer, cementing the relationship between author and publisher and yet at the same time allowing James to feel that, however difficult might be the births of his novels, Longmans trusted him.

In return he entered into an agreement with Longmans that they should have the novel based on his next film, *The Mindbenders,* which was due to be released early in 1963—the book of the film was to have been written by someone else and only issued in paperback, but James felt that it would make a useful hardcover edition if he wrote it himself. The script had begun life in 1958 at Ealing under the working titles of "The Visiting Scientist" or "If this be Treason" but it had been shelved because its subject, that of brainwashing, had been thought too far advanced for its time. Its fortunes revived in 1961 when Basil Dearden persuaded Dirk Bogarde to play the role of Longman, the Oxford scientist who takes part in experiments involving sensory deprivation. The novel received goodish reviews, but the film was savaged by the critics, not because the script creaked, but because no one would believe that brainwashing experiments involving sensory deprivation could be made in a civilised country. The critics' ignorance angered Kennaway. He had invested a good deal of time and effort researching the scientific background and he had first come across mention of the experiments while visiting Oxford in the early fifties when he was a Longmans' editor. That he was correct in his assessment of the military and strategic part played by those British experiments—in *The Mindbenders* the scientists place their volunteer in a diver's suit suspended in a tank of water, cut off from the world—was borne out in 1979 when the Freedom of Information

12. *Engagement photograph, 1951*

13. *James's and Susan's wedding, 6 October 1951*

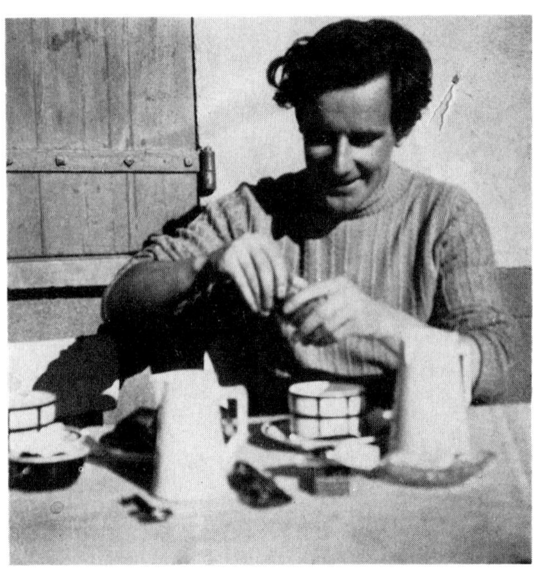

14. *Holiday breakfast, France, 1953*

15. *James, Susan, Emma and Jane in the garden of Holly Terrace, 1956*

16. *8 Holly Terrace, Highgate*

17. *Pensive in the garden, Holly Terrace, 1957*

18. *James, 1960*

Act in the United States revealed that Britain had been co-operating with the C.I.A. in experiments similar to those employed by Kennaway's fictional scientists.

> The meeting (dated 1 June 1951 between representatives of the British, Canadian and American governments) discussed "research into the psychological factors causing the human mind to accept certain political beliefs aimed at determining means for combating communism and selling democracy" and "research into the means whereby an individual may be brought temporarily or perhaps permanently under the control of another".[2]

The British film critics who so disliked *The Mindbenders* for what they took to be overstated sensationalism could not have known about British participation in those brainwashing experiments. What was understood was confined to the treatment of American prisoners in Korea: the world had not yet fully woken up to the psychiatric treatment repressive governments meted out to political dissidents or to the military application of "mind-bending" in interrogating prisoners. (In 1978 Britain was criticised in the European Court of Human Rights for allowing its army to use such methods in Northern Ireland.) In contrast, American reviewers of the novel picked up on those aspects and on the fact that the story had been suggested to Kennaway by experiments in British and American universities. Kennaway is not usually thought of as a writer with political or sociological concerns, yet the main events and preoccupations of his day are never far from the surface of his novels. *The Mindbenders* is by far the most explicit but, as we shall see, in his remaining novels he cast his eye over the period, the sixties, and commented on the political scandals that saw in the decade, the phenomenon of "swinging London", and the student unrest and race riots of 1968 that helped to bring it to an end.

On 20 May 1962 he flew to Bombay and then straight on to New Delhi where he was met by Mr Kohli and whisked off to his hotel, the Imperial. His first impressions were good, and that same night, fighting off fatigue, he wrote to Susan, comparing the country to Mexico—"men by the roadside huddled talking in the shadow of the trees. A great many ruins about the place as if there'd recently been a war"—and the official attitudes to Italy—"there seems to be a lot of people getting in on wearing uniforms, talking to each other behind desks". He went on to warn that proper tropical clothes should be bought for the children and that they should come prepared to find an alien country, quite different from anything they had experienced before in their travels. And yet there was no sense of despondency in his letter, in spite of the warnings. There was none of the terror that had met him in Los Angeles. Instead, the sights, sounds and smells of the warm Indian night breathed a new familiarity: "It's a place to slim, to fast, to grow richer, we hope, in the mind." He felt at home there and began to wish that he had not arranged to spend more time in the city, but his first priority was to finalise the plans for his family's visit: it had been decided, after much prior consultation with Mr Kholi, that they would spend the summer on a houseboat on the lakes near Srinagar in Kashmir. Two days later he flew there to scout out the territory.

If Dehli had offered the promise of contentment in a new country, then Srinagar confirmed it. "This is it, this is it, this is it," he exulted in his first letter about a country that was part India, part China, with hints of Scotland in the blue faraway mountains, the familiar streams and lakes and the quiet reserve of its people. The houseboats, too, were a surprise and a novelty, far removed from the homely hulks dotted along the banks of the Thames. These were large palatial affairs with accommodation for servants, "deluxe special houseboats, fitted with all the modern facilities—all sorts of excellent delicious food and service provided on board", the advertisements had promised and the Kennaway's vessel, "the good ship California", was indeed an ideal holiday home, even though it lay moored on the Dal Lake in a setting that was reminiscent of Henley. Once they had moved in, the boat was taken downstream to the quieter waters of the Nagine Lake. There they followed a well-accustomed path. During the early part of the day the older children would do their lessons in the walnut-panelled houseboat and in the later afternoon there would be expeditions by boat and pony to explore the surrounding countryside, and all the while, sometimes up to ten hours a day, James was writing, completing the final draft of *The Bells of Shoreditch,* his novel about marital infidelity and scandal in the city.

As had become customary for him by then, it was causing him no end of trouble, partly because he did not know the background he was exploring and also because the male figures surrounding Stella Vass did not possess the life he had managed to breath into her. Stella's avowed ILP Glasgow background, incidentally, was inspired by stories Sandy Mackendrick had told James during their Mallorca interlude. To Mark, James wrote in some despair that the novel might well be a still-born monster.

> . . . the city mentality had proved much more difficult than one would have guessed, explanation tending to destroy "art" in all the drafts until now—you can guess the sort of thing, little essays about the rate of interest "slipped in", one thought, but in fact sticking out like sore thumbs. However, all along I've felt that it's possible to get some sort of unity into this novel (which was in Tunes of Glory but lost in Household Ghosts) and at last, touch wood, that seems to be coming. At present I'm trying to make a clumsy, in parts journalistic piece into a poet's novel, with that certain accuracy and economy that never comes except by drafting and drafting again.[3]

But if the thought of the unfinished novel filled him with despair, the same letter shines with his love of Kashmir, expressed in terms so glowing that Mark was persuaded that it would be a fine thing if he was able to join his chum there, come the autumn.

> Houseboat life is all organised [wrote James], no worries; but I'll be your agent, because there are some bad ones (and besides, I need the 10%). Food isn't all that special, let's face it, and beds are hard, but on the other hand there are some very special things. Service, view, atmosphere—all wonderful. Tomorrow, to give you an idea, is Sunday. I rise at 5.30 to go fishing with servant and gillie in tow. Last outing, also on a Sunday, I caught 9 lbs worth of brown trout in a stream so like Aberdeenshire it became ridiculous. . . yet two miles away there are rice paddies. One day I did some hill walking, up to 10,000 feet, having to keep an eye open for wolves, bear and leopard. And did I keep my eyes open. Did I . . .

The owner of the company which operated the houseboats, Haji Karima Ramzan Goroo became a friendly neighbour for James while he waited for his family to arrive, and his brother was one of the fishing accomplices mentioned in the letter. This was a real lotus-land, not the dream palace conjured up by California but the balmy solitude of an out-of-the-way part of the world that could easily ensnare the unwary. James admitted that he had to struggle fairly hard with himself to get down each day to the business of writing, realising that but for his puritanical work ethic, fishing, walking and lazing could easily fill the waking hours of the day. However, the family's arrival brought with it a different set of problems. In spite of all attempts to maintain high standards of hygiene, the children inevitably fell victim to stomach upsets which became increasingly debilitating as the summer progressed. David, now three-years-old, was particularly unwell and had to be taken into the local mission hospital, which like many hospitals in India, was overworked and under-equipped. James, too, had to spend some time in Calcutta and Bombay in June to complete his research and his absence, plus the childrens' distress, persuaded him to curtail the holiday. The Chinese rumblings along the Indian border provided the final evidence that now was the time to go.

At the end of July the Kennaways made their way back to London, the children gaunt and sickly, James on an upswing in mood because the three months away had given him enough new experience, he thought, for a new book. The result was "The Ends of the Earth" which he had completed in outline form by the end of October. Taking its text from a misquoted Acts I,8—"ye shall be witness unto me both in Jerusalem, and in all Judea, and in Samaria, and unto the uttermost part of the earth"—it tells the story of Dr Ian Lockhart, a Scots missionary doctor who performs an abortion on an Indian woman and is prosecuted. It had been suggested to him by what he had seen in the local mission hospital and the basic plot, that of a doctor committing an act that could either be seen as life for the pregnant woman or death for the unborn child, and the ethical problems involved, was to survive through many drafts to remain a vital component of *Some Gorgeous Accident.* By the following year the scene had been transferred to Calcutta and later still it was to be set in, respectively, New York, Glasgow and London, and in a changing gallery of characters, the one constant was Lockhart, the doctor who had become Fiddes by the second draft.

Once back in London, James put the finishing touches to *The Bells of Shoreditch* and sent it to John Guest on 19 August with the warning that "to be absolutely honest, I'm so disappointed and tired of it all I don't care whether you say yes or no. I certainly am not interested in publishing if it is, as I suspect, unreadable and you mustn't worry about losing me if I say 'no' to this. I'm not shopping around."[4] Guest was suitably cautious. Longmans would publish once the character of Andrew, Stella's feeble husband, was made more secure within the plot, but as a means of testing the market and discovering others' reactions, he sent the script to Pan to see if they wanted to offer for the paperback rights. Their report, which was shown to Longmans makes savage reading, tearing the novel apart for its "cryptic" dialogue and "drunken self-indulgent prose. "It seems to me," continued the anonymous reader, "that if Kennaway could acquire enough self-discipline to perform the graft work, the honest explanation to the reader, the solid construction that no novelist should despise, if he could control and use to its best advantages the obvious talents he has, then he could be a very formidable novelist indeed."[5] The report itself is over-blown and extreme but it shocked Guest and Mark Longman enough for it to be kept well hidden away in their Kennaway file. They knew that to have shaken James in his present brittle position would have both delayed his alterations to the novel and possibly also have knocked for six his writing ambitions. No writer likes reading hostile criticism of his or her own work: there are times when it can be safely ignored, there are others when it can hurt. Longmans were wise enough to understand that for James, the summer of 1962 was a time when adverse criticism could have stung.

Of more pressing concern to James in those film-less months was the fate of his play *Country Dance* (he had also toyed with the idea of calling it "Country Matters") which had found its way into the hands of Michael Langham, a fellow Scot from Kemnay in Aberdeenshire, who was then directing at the Shakespeare Memorial Theatre in Stratford, Ontario, in Canada. One of the principal reasons why the play had failed to find a producer to stage it was that it was not entirely clear which story was being told and on which generation was the main focus. In an effort to explain more clearly the Ferguson family background Kennaway had re-introduced from an early draft of *Household Ghosts*· the character of Mona, the alcoholic mother, and had made Stephen and David Dow brothers. Langham had rightly wanted them to be removed and he also suggested other ways in which the play could be cut and tightened. Kennaway, for his part, felt that he should go to Stratford in the autumn to work further with Langham and he arrived there on 5 September. Having conquered his feelings of angst about North America, he was delighted with the town, finding it to be "a cross between Crieff and Malibu, with, of course, a very special resemblance to the Avon, at Stratford, thrown in. Most shops are Crieff, most ladies like Mrs Macrae, most girls like Betty the maid at Chapelbank, but instead of pubs there are these dark and exorbitant cocktail bars."

The season was in full swing and Kennaway found time to enjoy it, being particularly impressed by Langham's direction of the *Taming of the Shrew*, "so good that it was if (I promise) I had never seen Shakespeare before", and there was also time allowed for "boozing with the actors in the wee hours". But then, a week after he had arrived, disaster struck. Mumps felled him and he was rushed into Avoncrest Hospital in Stratford for preliminary tests. To begin with, he had thought that he was merely suffering from a hangover of monumental proportions, and had been quite prepared to sleep off the pain and discomfort, but when his temperature had reached 104 degrees, Langham called in a doctor who, fearing that James was suffering from some unknown oriental virus, recommended that he be placed in an isolation ward. In hospital conditions were good but until mumps had been diagnosed, the medical caution meant that he had to endure a mild diet and a period of isolation from friends who tried to visit him. Then there was the physical discomfort and pain of the illness itself— the swollen glands below his left ear and the attendant fever and headaches—and like all men he lived in some fear that mumps would attack his testicles. However, he was saved on that score, and within five days the swelling had disappeared and he was declared well enough to leave hospital, having persuaded the administrators that funds were on their way from London to meet the accumulated bills.

He celebrated his release from confinement by going to Montreal on 29 September and planned to move to New York to continue discussions with Langham about the future of *Country*

Dance. While he was in Montreal he stayed with a French-Canadian couple whom he had met at Stratford and at their home he also met Anne —, a successful documentary film director. Her effect on him was electric. Not only was she attractive, and attracted to him, but she shared his intersts in film: Canada has a long tradition of documentary film-making and one of her colleagues was able to give James much useful advice on how realité techniques could be brought to bear on the film of the Kashmir story. James's affair with Anne was brief and passionate and fired by the whirligig of intense emotional drama. Perhaps he fell for her because she was able to stand up to him and face him on his own territory. Later he described to Susan "the fierceness of their lovemaking and the stormy rows which set him in such an excited spin"[7], both to wound her and also, as had become such a necessary ritual, to absolve his own feelings of guilt. To begin with the affair had started out as a brief sexual encounter—Anne was married, and James was going to stay with friends, the Bessies in New York—but by the time they had moved to the United States at the beginning of October, James was coming face to face with the reality that he was falling in love and that he might have to chose between Anne and his family. It was a high octane brew, fuelled by James's unnerving disappointments with his play—he became increasingly convinced that as his sexual activity burgeoned, so too did he become a better writer. He had confided earlier to John Guest[8] that he believed sex to be a creative energy and that an active sex life was the regenerative source of his literary and business success. Trapped in a writer's block, and beginning to fear failure, he took necessary refuge in his affair. The intensity be brought to the relationship was the cause of much emotional drama and this too be felt to be creative, giving him access to hitherto denied extremes of psychological distress. It seems that Anne realised this and the flashpoint of their rows would be her accusation that he was destroying her by insisting on channelling every emotion into his needs—"the hell I've created now around me", he wrote to her (in an unposted letter) during the period of marital breakdown, "can only be compared to the hell I created with you in New York".[9]

Deceit in relationships is rarely pleasant to recall; affairs long dead soon lose their significance. In James's case, his affair with Anne could safely have been condemned to time's wastepaper basket but for the lasting effect it had on him and his marriage. Far from killing his love for Susan, he claimed that the affair had enhanced it and having made the choice to stay with her, he no doubt felt a sense of relief, of coming home. Unfortunately, his confessions to Susan and his own insistence on continuing to have affairs—which he felt could be purged by a Calvinistic diet of hard work and denial (he once admitted to Graham Watson that during bouts of writing he set himself targets, so many pages without cigarettes, no alcohol until a chapter was finished, and so on)—had the reverse effect on his wife. Instead of becoming more understanding in the following year, she became increasingly withdrawn, "so that the hurt, if it should come, would not be so terrible".[10] Some marriages can survive affairs, and indeed, so did the Kennaway's; what frightened Susan about the affair with Anne was that, for the first time in her married life, she believed that it was possible for James to leave her for another woman.

She had good reason to feel concerned. On reaching New York at the beginning of October where he was supposed to be staying with his publisher, Kennaway dropped out of contact sufficiently long for Susan to cable Simon Michael Bessie: "Please send news if any of James Kennaway". It being crunch-time Kennaway replied that he was staying on in New York for the time being to try and complete the *Country Dance* script and to set up a film deal for the Kashmir story. Susan was used to James's absences from home: she was not prepared for what happened next, shortly after he returned at the end of the year. James told her quite unequivocably that he needed her love badly, that he expected her to love him, in spite of his behaviour, pleading with her that the artist within him had to be protected at all costs, a further extension of his belief that the artist is the child who must be cossetted. His chosen instrument was the pen, not the sword, a scrap of yellow paper containing a letter which he left on the kitchen table for her to read. Susan, he claimed, had interpreted his affair with Anne as being destructive, that "your reading of such indiscretions is that I am giving vent to forces of destruction within me, destroying you, lest I destroy myself. But all I have been trying to say is that the women are symptoms, not of course, the disease."[11] He continued his plea—the letter is an angry and convincing statement of his predicament—by saying, yes, he was wounding Susan, but that out of all that destructiveness would come forth creativity. If she kept faith—"Understand therefore that I commit no cruelty to you which is not properly directed at myself"—the rest would be unalloyed love. It was a plea for love and support both for himself and for his writing which so frightened Susan that she tore it up (although, later, she sellotaped it together again).

Although 1962 had come to a bad end (financially too, James claiming that without filmwork during the year, his income was only £400), it would be giving the wrong impression to suggest that the Kennaway marriage was being constantly rocked by a succession of dramas involving unfaithfulness and anguish. True, it had received a jolt from James's affair with Anne, and he himself enjoyed being out on the loose with his chums from the movie business but for the most part he was never more happy than when he was at home with his family. Friends of his like to remember Jim in his role as randy roisterer but that was a part of his life he preferred to keep in a separate compartment and one which Susan was not supposed to share.

That winter was to be spent skiing in Italy, in Cervinia, but the day was fast approaching when Emma and Jane would have to attend a proper school. Remembering with fondness his own Scottish schooldays, James thought that they too should be educated there, in Edinburgh, and at the beginning of January Emma was sent to St Denis's School. There was also a practical consideration to the choice: his mother was near at hand in case of any emergency and a boarding school education was the only sensible solution to the family's peripatetic lifestyle. But the sudden absence from home of his eldest daughter threw James into a panic. He may have remembered his own schooldays with a good deal of affection but he had not forgotten, either, the terror he had felt on being left at prep school. "As I was the most homesick boy Cargilfield ever experienced," he wrote to Emma's headmistress, Miss Ramsay on 17 January 1963, after leaving her at St Denis's, "I am obviously at present almost sleepless, terrified that my senior chicken is being bullied, tortured, poisoned, over-disciplined, locked in cupboards, half-starved and frozen to death. Could you drop me a line saying she is 1. 'unhappy', in which case I will at once fly up and remove her, with a great sense of relief and freedom from guilt, or 2. 'alright', in which case I won't believe you but will resign myself to a duodenal ulcer." (The British seem to be the only people who willingly send their children to institutions to be educated even though they have been unhappy at them themselves.) Jane followed Emma to St Denis's in September that same year and by then her father's letters to Miss Ramsay (by then Mrs Macdonald) were less taken up with fears for his daughters' homesickness than concern with their school reports. By April the following year he was imploring the school "that the thumbscrews may and should be applied" if carelessness crept into their work: "I have told them," he continued, "that no artist is ever careless—the two words are almost in exact contradiction—that girls who are all over the place in their appearance, manner, habits, letters and lessons are not so funny as they like to think etc., etc. Anyway, I have applied a little pressure saying we must now take lessons seriously, and work with attention and care. I also suggested that this care should come through their whole lives (Stanislavsky stuff!) and that if they were tidy with their books and pyjamas they might be more careful with their long division. In fact, Susan is a very tidy person and I think they have grown too used to things being done for them at home." Throughout his life, in fact, James would worry about their educations and also their behaviour and would seek out his friends' views about the advisability of putting the boys names down for Eton. In that respect, he had very conventional views about standards of excellence and moral behaviour.

At the end of February James returned to London from Cervinia for the première of *The Mindbenders*—"the reviews ranged from 'poor' to 'vitriolic'" he reported back to Susan—but, undismayed by the critics' reactions he threw himself back into the business of finding himself work. With Dirk Bogarde, star of *The Mindbenders,* he discussed the possibility of him playing the father figure, Alec White, in *Flowers,* the first treatment of which had taken shape during the early part of the winter. He also went north for Emma's half-term and to investigate possible locations for the film in Strathearn. For Talbot Hainault, an old Oxford friend, he was commissioned to write a *son et lumière* history for the Tower of London, *The Fair White Tower;* the idea was that it would be presented nightly after the Ceremony of the Keys and that its audience would view it from boats sailing from Westminster Pier to the Tower. It was produced for the London Tourist Board by Hainault's Pageantry Productions and concentrated on the period 1660 to 1667 when Richard Wallop was a prisoner there, although there were also scenes from Norman, Medieval and Tudor times. Much of the research material came from the diaries of Samuel Pepys and required a good deal of other reading and research all of which James rather enjoyed—he had taken to doing much of his writing in the Royal Institution in Albemarle Street, a gloomy tomb of a building which reminded him of Edinburgh. By far the most exciting project, though, was a treatment for a film commissioned by the Italian director Franco Zeffirelli. *The Ladies* or *Le Nemiche* was to have been set amongst the Anglo-Italian community in Florence during the fascist nineteen-thirties and the plot involved the disintegration of that society as seen through the eyes of a group of English ladies resident in the city. Zeffirelli, whom James had met the previous year in New York, also commissioned him to write a new translated version of Chekhov's play *The Three Sisters*. These deals gave James the confidence and the money to make secure his plans for the future and by April they were back in Alassio for the summer so that James would be free to attend script conferences with Zeffirelli in Florence—an experience he found unsettling as the Italian film industry was run on very different lines from anything he had encountered before. Meetings scheduled for the mid-afternoon could take place late at night and everything centred around the director. Films could be years in the making and some were developed to a fine stage of pre-production only to be dropped, a fate that befell *The Ladies,* even though it did re-surface under different titles and for different producers, including Milton Sperling.

While he was absent from home in the late Spring of 1963, Kennaway was missing at first hand one of the most extraordinary events of the decade, one that thoroughly shook the British Establishment and one that gave the British press (which James read avidly) a field day: the inquiry into the Profumo Affair. With each passing day the country shook with rumours of transvestism in judicial circles, Ministers of the Crown involved in unusual sexual practices, rampant homosexuality within the church and the wholesale distribution of British secrets to the Russians: all because Her Majesty's Secretary of State for War had been found out having an affair with a rather attractive but promiscuous call-girl. It had all begun in the summer of 1961 when John Profumo had met Christine Keeler at Cliveden, the home of Lord Astor, had fallen for her, and subsequently engaged in a short affair which ended shortly afterwards when he discovered her involvement with Stephen Ward, an osteopath friend of a Soviet diplomat. Keeler was then involved in a bizarre shooting incident involving two black rivals for her affections and was called as a witness at the ensuing Old Bailey trial. She then did a bunk to Spain and in the inquiry that followed, her affair with Profumo came to light, and the newspapers, alerted to the fact, trumpeted the story over their front pages together with an indiscreet letter Profumo had penned to end the affair. Some of the more sensational papers claimed that Profumo had assisted her rapid departure from London.

Faced by the dilemma of a member of his Cabinet being accused of adultery and with the hint that Profumo's mistress was both involved in underworld battles and in selling secrets provided by Profumo through Ward to the Soviets (this innuendo was untrue), Prime Minister Harold Macmillan hesitated. That same year he had mistakenly accepted the resignation of a minister, Tam Galbraith, during the Vassall Affair, another scandal that had rocked the Establishment. Vassall, a Soviet spy, had been employed by the Admiralty: at his trial it was discovered that he was a homosexual and it was claimed that the authorities should have been aware of this, and Galbraith allowed himself, wrongly, to be the scapegoat. Unwilling to face another scandal or to make another sacrificial victim, the Tory Establishment acted quickly and with as much solidarity as they could muster; a statement was prepared for the House which stated that although Profumo knew her, there had been "no impropriety in my relationship with Miss Keeler". This was a lie and in it lay the cause of Profumo's undoing. In the following maelstrom of Opposition questions and press demands for the truth, Profumo resigned and an inquiry into the whole affair—which now included the arrest, conviction and suicide of Stephen Ward—was conducted by the censorious Lord Denning.

The Profumo Affair, as it had come to be known, had a profound effect on Kennaway. Like many others, he saw it as firm evidence that the Establishment was willing and able to cover up its own sins of commission and that those in positions of authority could lead double lives provided that they did not make the mistake of being found out. It was also a further indication of the decline of Britain as a world power, as if its inner rottenness mirrored its enfeebled shell, of a nation unsure of its position in the world, of an old order having changed with nothing new to replace it. More importantly, he saw it as proof that society had become so amoral that a puritanical public morality was out of touch with people's private desires. The dichotomy between public and private standards he believed to be at the root of much that was wrong at all levels of society, although it became more magnified the higher the social strata, an understanding that he saw as being central to the theme of his next novel *The Bells of Shoreditch.*

> To find the source of power in England, it is necessary to observe very closely those things which are common to all the parliamentary parties, and characteristically, there is no evidence of this curious common caution, this infallible braking system which links them. One senses, rather than sees it in operation. It lies in a wink in the lobby or a nod in the Reform; in a "pairing" arrangement between M.P.'s of different parties; even in a Christmas card. There is some sort of tacit agreement lying behind the whole business of government which almost completely emasculates the rude and witty things which members shout at each other across the floor of the House.[12]

Central to the plot is a thoroughly scurrilous piece of banking practice involving just those winks and nods which Kennaway saw as exercising the real power, whether it be in parliament or banking, and he went to great lengths to research the background with merchant banking friends, including two from Oxford days, A.E. Rudd and the Hon. Angus Ogilvie. Basically, what happens is this (and he had beside him as he wrote an *aide memoire* describing such a hypothetical transaction): a Hamburg firm makes a bit for a Scottish engineering firm, Glasgow

Turbines, and employs a merchant bank, Sarsons Browne, to administer the deal, because the chairman, J.T. Sarson, is a member of the court of the Bank of England who can give permission for the sale without a parliamentary inquiry. The money is due to be paid on a Friday but Sarson delays signing the cheques, a definite break in the strict timetable of negotiations. During the weekend the Deutschmark is revalued and as a result of the new rate of exchange, Sarsons Browne makes a killing of £675,000. Sarson's two managers, his son-in-law Alisdair, and Andrew Vass, suspect, probably rightly, that their chairman has used his position with the Bank of England to find out about the revaluation, hence the delay, hence the profit. But when they make their claims they do so in ignorance of the solidarity of the Establishment. They are overheard discussing Sarson's complicity in a Glasgow hotel by a shipowner who passes on his knowledge to another merchant banker, who in turn threatens to sue Alisdair and Andrew. At that point Sarson is cleared by a fellow member of the court and the threats dreamed up by the young managers come to nothing. Alisdair is given a seat on the Board to keep him out of further mischief and Andrew is given the boot.

In that respect, the novel is ruthlessly accurate in its portrayal of the primacy of the wealthy and politically powerful in the city—J.T. Sarson is introduced as very much a Buchan man, in the mould of Edward Leithen—but as James had already remarked to Mark Longman, his problem lay in writing a poetic novel around such intricate, though necessary financial details. The result was a further exploration of the dynamics of the triangular relationship with, again, a strong-willed woman at its apex, Stella, the Glasgow-born wife of the weak-willed, though pleasant, Andrew Vass. Whereas Mary had ignored and bullied her husband, Stephen, because of his impotence, Stella has tried, throughout her marriage, to shake Andrew out of middle-class complacency by serving up an ill-digested view of socialist politics and memories of her proletarian Glasgow background, of a childhood imbued with the ideals of Jimmy Maxton and the other Red Clydesiders. By the time of her marriage, though, after her Oxford education and her residence in Hampstead Garden Suburb, those political beliefs are little more than shadows, a vague race memory of a past that she can no longer lay claim to in the land of the middle class. But Stella is nothing if not hard, an amazon who imagines that she controls not only her own destiny but also that of others. It is for Stella's ideals that Andrew takes on Sarson and is sacked: her response is to seduce Sarson in a brief and pointless affair with a man she thinks of as "the enemy", he of "the pussy-cat face . . . and . . . those big forearms with the blond, yacht-owning fur on them" (p. 13). Although she sees bedding Sarson as a rejection of her past and a re-affirmation of herself as an individual, nothing has changed. It is still Sarson who calls the shots. Sarson drops her, Andrew finds another job in the city and in so doing redefines himself with a Sarson-like hardness. The novel ends with Sarson telling Stella the simplest of truths—"as usual the nastiest blows came in a soft, almost vague tone"—Sarson knowing the rules of the game better than she.

> "When you came to me in the flat you were saying exactly the same thing, only putting it in a different tense, namely the future. You weren't going to sleep with me, because your scruples, of the most curious and muddled politico-moral order, prevented you from doing so, the implication being frankly jingoistic, 'I'm not going to sleep with you, dear, but by jingo if I do.' Consider your actions, coolly, and you will find that absolutely nothing has changed. You're up to the same old tricks. In the course of the last two weeks you have done the following things. You have sent, if indirectly, wild alarms to me by enrolling the help of a son-in-law quite famous for his indiscretion. You have employed your husband in anti-red flag land. You have told me, here, within a matter of seconds, dramatically and almost with those easy, easy tears of yours, that you have decided to live your life in conflict, which is to say frankly that you still haven't come to any conclusion whatsoever." (p. 206)

During that final visit, Sarson gives Andrew a clue about a financial killing he might make and Stella finds herself with a husband who has become as Sarson-like as his ex-employer and her now-lost lover. The ending to the tale has a harshly grandiloquent touch, similar to the conclusion of *Household Ghosts.*

> For a long long time, they remained like this, fixed and hostile, like brother and sister hoarse and naked in the back street; which is to say, reduced to that blazing attachment where passion starts.
>
> *When will you pay me?*
> *Say the Bells of Old Bailey.*

When I grow rich,
Say the Bells of Shoreditch. (p. 211)

Stella seems to be hard and ruthless, but she is also a great self-deceiver. Not all the shades of Jimmy Maxton, John Maclean and Willie Gallagher rolled into one can save her from her predicament: incarceration in suburbia, a stranger from her past. Having made her husband fight the system by employing crude rhetoric, she now enables him to join it. Having thought that she had seduced her capitalist "cat-man" lover, she now finds that it is he who is calling the shots. She is determined to use her sensuality as a weapon—"You big tart, Stella" is her oft-repeated litany, "Oh, you big one, Stella Vass."—at heart, and by the end of the novel, she betrays the essential femininity James demanded of his women characters.

The publication of *The Bells of Shoreditch* together with his re-engagement with screenwriting gave James a good deal of renewed financial security. The Zeffirelli deal alone was worth $50,000 and he looked forward to the future with some confidence as far as money was concerned. *Flowers* had moved on to a new stage of development with producer Michael Forlong, and James was determined that he should both write and direct it, as he felt that only he could provide the key to its intensely autobiographical scenes—"I want desperately to direct as well as write it myself and I haven't been doing nothing for two years with regards to preparing myself for that stiff ordeal".[13] As James envisaged it, the film would be shot on location in Scotland in spite of the lack of facilities; it would be a "small-unit" job with a low budget which he could control, and the film itself would be taut and lean.

Forlong took up the option on *Flowers* and a final treatment appeared in January 1965 but by then the producers had gone cold on the project, feeling that it was a period piece, out of tenor with the times. Other projects, though, re-surfaced, including an unlikely offer to re-make *The Ghost Goes West* as a Broadway musical, and at last it looked as if Michael Langham might be able to get *Country Dance* into the winter production schedule at Stratford, Ontario. At the end of July the Kennaways returned from Italy to London where James found waiting for him a letter from an American producer, Robert Emmett Ginna, which made

19. *John Mills as Basil Barrow and Alec Guinness as Jock Sinclair in the film of* Tunes of Glory

20. *James, Malibu, 1961*

21. *Writing, Villa Garassino, 1961*

22. *Mary Ure as Oonagh and Dirk Bogarde as Longman in the film of* The Mindbenders

23. *Official photograph, 1962*

24. *With Jane at Anzio, making* The Shoes of the Fisherman

him put aside some of his other projects: the opportunity arose of scripting a film about the life of the Hungarian-American war photographer, Robert Capa. Ginna's letter contained a brief outline treatment, a selection of Capa's photographs, including the famous portrait of a Loyalist soldier falling at the moment of death during the Spanish Civil War, and as bait a handful of compliments about James's work. James was hooked, not so much by the lure of another film deal—he already had enough on his plate—but by the chance of writing about a man with whom he had an inkling he could get on level terms.

> Capa comes at a time when I am totally engaged on a work which I hope to "realize" (I mean write and direct). But if Talent recognises Genius, then I was never so sure of my talent. The Capa you outline in your television handout—and I *intend* to be cruel—is of no interest to me at all. The Capa that searched, failed, and searched again to find the still photos you show fascinates me. The parallel with forgotten Hemingway and worshipped pseudo Heminghaironthechestaway is close. I would not be interested in concocting "good dramatic scenes" between a fictional Capa & fictional Lady Brett-type in Paris Ritz or anywhere else. But to make the film that Capa *should* have made; in other words to make his *stills* live (and show the man by reflection only) is a task which frightens me almost as much as it fascinates me. This could be the anti-war, yet the rebel story of our times.
>
> I am intolerable in collaboration. I am extremely opinionated; I am in other words, a bastard to cope with (except with regard to money, which I do not seek) & I question if we could ever fit, in spite of your beautiful remarks about my work, which I love & for which I say a true thank you. But am I interested? Look at the photos. I am not a fool. Of course I am interested.

It was a happy choice of subject and Bob Ginna and Kennaway were to enjoy a happy partnership with Capa and other projects.

Robert Capa had been born in Hungary in 1913 and, in 1932 had moved to Germany, where he studied photography and made his first forays into the new art of photo-journalism, a career that ended with Hitler's rise to power and his persecution of the Jews. Capa escaped to Paris and made his name as a war photographer during the Spanish Civil War. There he refused the safety of the trenches, preferring to take the same risks as the men he was photographing as they fought and died. His best work has that intensity which can only come in war photographs by observing the strange mixture of fear, exultation and boredom of men involved in the action of war. In 1941 he became an American citizen and spent World War Two as a freelance photographer in Europe and North Africa. He was killed in 1954 by a land-mine while covering the French colonial war in Indo-China (now Vietnam). But it was not the bare skeleton of a brave and unusual man's life that fascinated Kennaway: it was his work, the blazing passion he brought to his task and his involvement with men at the extremity of war, that finally convinced James. He was also much taken with the fact that Capa had died young, at the age of forty, and had lived life at a high pitch, was inordinately attractive to women and had had many affairs with beautiful women, including a much publicised relationship with the actress Ingrid Bergman. Capa had been fond of saying that it was the war photographer's indulgence to choose his spot, either out of fire or in it. That he would not be punished for opting for the former option, as would the soldier be, was his personal torture. In other words, to achieve the best, one had to risk everything, and that philosophy also extended to his life and to his relationships with women. It was a concept of living that was not very far removed from James's own theories, and he threw himself into the project with relish.

He spent a brief time in New York that November meeting Bob Ginna and Cornell Capa, the photographer's brother. It was agreed that if a treatment could be formulated that would satisfy the Capa family, the way would be open for Ginna's Sextant production company to swing into full script development. The go-ahead, after much wrangling about which personal details to leave in and which to omit, came on 27 January 1964 while James was skiing in Couchevel and he was summoned to New York six days later. Kennaway's treatment had depended on the idea of recurrence in Capa's life—the repeating pattern of wars, women, friendships and battles of all kinds—and he wanted to have a minimum of actors playing several parts. He also wanted to concentrate on the dynamism that fired Capa to take risks in his work and with his life. Ginna wanted a film that would be both logical and tragic. Together, the two men worked on a script at Ginna's summer house in Sag Harbour, an old whaling port on Long Island. Their method of working was deceptively simple. Kennaway would work on the script during the day while Ginna was in New York. When he returned he would work on it at night, using James's labours as the baseline, and slowly a collaborative script began to take shape without recourse to the rows that James had feared at the very outset.

As it was obvious that the Capa project would detain him in New York, James, after a good deal of searching, rented an apartment in upper Manhattan for Susan and the boys, "a really delightful apartment with a view of the river, a park alongside, big, old-fashioned rooms, fridge, telephone etc. It is vaguely reminiscent of Zeffirelli's flat, only the rooms are bigger and barer—and there's a lift. It isn't ideal for the children—they'll have to be good and there are quite a lot of things they must not break, but compared to other New York houses, it's good even for them. For us, I'd say it was first class. It has got a T.V. by the way."[14] At the same time, James was still seeing Anne, With her he still felt that he could promote the kind of passionate anger that he had come to think was the necessary fuel for his writing. With Susan, that intensity led to tears and anguish, to her belief that he was doing his best to destroy her.[15] But for all his continuing infatuation with Anne, he still adored Susan ("whom I love, the only one in the end"). Another quandary lay in the block that was affecting his work on the Kashmir novel, which was now called *Gorgeous Palaces,* and which he knew to be artificial and contrived. About his scriptwriting he entertained no qualms but he was beginning to fear that he had lost his touch as a novelist.

With so many strains in his life something was bound to give sooner or later, and the catalyst turned out to be another writer, David Cornwell, whom he had met in the autumn of 1963 through Susan's sister Gyll. There had been, according to Susan, an immediate attraction between the two men. Both were successful novelists—under his pseudonym of John Le Carré, Cornwell had published that year his extremely successful spy thriller, *The Spy who Came in from the Cold*—and both men were extremely wrapped up in their writing, Cornwell having decided to give up his career in the Foreign Office to concentrate on writing full-time.

After returning from New York—James stayed on a little longer to complete the Robert Capa script—Susan went back to her father's old house in Fairford, Gloucestershire, a nineteenth-century manor house which had been let to them at "peppercorn rent, as he liked us to visit him, but not stay".[16] There she met David Cornwell again and when James came home a few days later, Cornwell was invited to stay with them, and he soon became an important ingredient in both their lives.

> During that time we all got to know each other a little better, lots of jokes, funny voices, excursions; David looking in my cupboards, oohing and aahing at the tidiness; David telling stories to the boys, conjuring shillings out of their ears and generally making himself an extremely amiable guest. James and David were talking all the time, discussing George Orwell or Ortega Y Gasset or the film or the novel, or just themselves. I did not feel part of these conversations but there were the children to be looked after, the meals to be cooked and I enjoyed doing domestic things. After a time David went back to the Continent and we resumed our life in London.[17]

Theirs was a literary friendship, one that was undoubtedly close, but one that because of their callings, could, and did—on James's part at least—lead to rivalry. James looked on Cornwell as a friend, as a competitor; perhaps, as we shall see, as a man capable of loving his wife and in turn, of being loved by her.

For the most part, James had not bothered with literary society. He had not taken the trouble to get to know well his contemporaries who were also writers, to allow his publishers to puff his books or to appear in public as the literary lion. Instead, he preferred the company of acquaintances in the theatre or in movies and in the previous year he had become quite attached to Peter Finch and Christopher Plummer, and his distant cousin Susannah York, was a friend and *confidante* throughout his career. David Cornwell was, quite simply, the first man, who was neither producer nor publisher, with whom he felt able to discuss the intricacies of his own work—with the important proviso, that he was not a little jealous of his chum's success. "David Cornwell's book is the rage out here," he had written to Susan from New York, "but people have seen the *Time* photo and it has raised my sexual status at a time when my interest seems to be minimal". The photograph in *Time,* taken earlier in

California, was published on 31 January 1964 to accompany a highly complimentary review of *The Bells of Shoreditch.*

In August that year, after having spent part of the summer in France, James accompanied Cornwell to Paris for a script conference on the film version of *The Looking Glass War,* Le Carré's second major success, the successor to *The Spy Who Came in from the Cold.* It was due to be published in the early part of 1965. The book is dedicated to James Kennaway and it is clear from his notes and letters that James offered much help and advice in its creation (not all of it, of course, was taken). Having felt, no doubt, that he had a stake in the book, James was not shy about taking himself along to the meeting with the director who was interested in making the film, Karel Reisz, who had been associated with the British Free Cinema group of the nineteen-fifties. What happened next is difficult to decipher as James, apart from notes for the script, unaccountably, did not keep a record of the trip in his diary, and David Cornwell will not speak about it.[18] However, some hints about the expedition and its attendant shenanigans can be found in Le Carré's novel *The Naive and Sentimental Lover* (1971) which seems to be a partial and personal reflection of his friendship with James and of his affair with Susan (an account which Susan disclaims). Shamus, a writer and novelist, inveigles himself to Paris in the company of his friend Aldo, a pram manufacturer, and the days spent together, as they discover Shamus's Paris of "hydrants and cobble streets and rotten vegetables",[19] brings them to a new pitch of love and understanding. Other details seem also to coincide. Aldo tells Shamus about his unhappy past, Shamus cuts an eccentric and self-centered figure in the prim respectability of Aldo's business world which both men affect to despise, nights are spent in drunken revelry and womanising—these stories crept into James's account to Susan of what befell him and Cornwell.

What appears to have happened was that Reisz found James to be an intrusive presence, and made it clear that he did not take to him. "I am not enjoying Karel so much, but I think he will settle," James told Susan by letter after he had arrived in Paris, "he is just a little short of humour sometimes, taking himself fairly seriously". Then he wrote on the day before they left: "Nothing is simple. David and I are now inseparable chums but a the dramatics that went on with Karel were of Ealing proportions and the story is a bastard to adapt . . . The frustration period has been the worst with a good deal of late night drinking." Six months later James admitted in his notebook that one of the things that had angered him in Paris was Reisz's attitudes to him, coupled with the distinct impression that the director did not rate him as a writer.

> David's (I'd known him marginally before) appearance in my life had several effects, envy, love, the idea that I was after all an artist of integrity who could help, and a man to set others free, that I was growing older etc. Paris meeting in August included a political triangle situation with the director who wanted to get rid of me, which David firmly refused; even resented. Of me, he said, "Well, some of us seem to find it very hard to grow up . . ." That stung, because in many ways I found this to be true: yet in others, I knew and know that it is not in the least true. I grew up at 12, so school reports record, soon after my father's death; becoming head boy, belt of honour cadet, youngest prefect etc., etc. The remark saddened me. I hate that director. I hated David for not having defended me more strongly.[20]

James's resentment at what had happened in Paris was made worse by the suspicion that Reisz was indeed correct in his assessment—in spite of all his literary and social successes, James had been cocooned from the harsher realities of the world, and he knew it—and so he proceeded to behave in a destructive way as if to prove to everyone that he was immature. But it was not all black. The experience had brought both men closer together, as writers and as friends. In James's notebook, at the conclusion of the notes for the script of *The Looking Glass War*, Cornwell had written: "Jim. You have done more for me in a week than I have done for anyone else in my lifetime."[21] Kennaway had already returned the compliment by writing to Susan from Paris: "I'm truly amazed by David. Believe me, he didn't get there by luck. The head is strong and the heart a much hunted one."[22]

That James would have taken the upper hand in scripting the film is evident from the diaries. That his professionalism had been called into account saddened him and added to his conviction that he was a failure as an artist, despite David Cornwell's corrective assertion that he was "an artist of integrity". On the way back to England with Cornwell James became ill with glandular fever. At home he suffered extreme physical discomfort brought on by fever associated with the illness and he also experienced terrible, disquieting dreams, nightmares involving struggles between white and black horses, the light, innocent side of his nature in contention with the dark, shadowy side. it also brought on a new lethargy that he found hard to conquer. *Gorgeous Palaces,* which was now called *Maclaren's History,* had been moved in setting to Glasgow and introduced Annie—based on a girl James had met there—a prostitute upon whom Fiddes, the doctor, performs an illegal abortion, but Kennaway was so fixed on the crisis of conscience brought about by the doctor's clash between the abuse of medical ethics and the claims of love and humanity, that he found the other characters difficult to develop. Many of the drafts are unreadable[23] and they betray Kennaway's inability to pull together the different strands in the work—which contains too many disparate ideas—and to weld it into a coherent whole.

In November that year, while visiting Britain—he was then living in Vienna—Cornwell stayed with the Kennaways and found that he was falling in love with Susan. James had always hinted that she should have affairs, perhaps in an attempt to assuage his own guilt. What he did not expect was that, when she did have one, it would be with his best friend and that she would fall in love with him, thus establishing in real life the triangular love relationship that had so intrigued him in his novels. It is not altogether surprising that Susan should have fallen for David Cornwell. He was considerate, charming and caring at a time when James was being sullen, self-centred and flaunting before her his own unreasonable behaviour. They fell in love with each other at a dance after coyly stepping around their mutual attraction, and, significantly, drawing James into the relationship as the polarity between them. Susan wanted "a small revenge" on James: Cornwell knew his friend well enough to know the kind of life he had enjoyed. As James had always said, in a love affair, there was always a second man present, the "best man", the woman's second choice against the possibility that passion might destroy the relationship, or she be destroyed by the first man. And as Susan herself admitted[24] at the time, she would have found it very difficult to have chosen between the two men.

But her affair with Cornwell, however enhancing it might have been and however understandable her motives, had to be kept discreet, and discretion bred deception. With the three knowing one another so well, the affair was a powder keg which the slightest spark could blow sky-high.

~ 9 ~

Some Gorgeous Accident

THE story of what happened when the affair did become known has already been told in *The Kennaway Papers,* and it is an unsparing account of love and infidelity, of passion and total self-regard as the three protagonists struggled to come to terms with the violence that erupted around them. In January 1965 the Kennaways made their, by now, annual skiing trip, not to Couchevel but to Zell-am-See, south of Salzburg in the Kitzebüheler Alps, where their villa was a gaunt lodge, the Haus am Berg, perched halfway up a mountainside. James was in good spirits. A film deal had emerged for *The Bells of Shoreditch* which contained the possibility that Rex Harrison would play the leading role of Jakie Sarson and *Country Dance,* having failed to take off at Stratford, Ontario, was now in the hands of Prospect Productions, one of Britain's leading touring theatre companies. During the holiday James maintained his strict regimen of skiing early in the morning and working for the rest of the day so that pleasure would not interfere with his work.

Later in the month the Cornwells came from Vienna to ski, but the visit was not a success, nor could it be for Susan or David Cornwell. The strain of the affair placed great demands on both of them and, both being unwilling to break up their respective marriages, they decided to take each day at a time, being "foolish enough to think that we could make do with a meeting here and there, from time to time, hello and goodbye".[1] The only way to keep in touch would be by letter and after the Cornwells had left, James found one of the letters that Susan had been writing.

His reactions were extreme, but, in the circumstances, perhaps understandable. Although he had felt it to be perfectly in order to tell Susan about his own affairs; to find himself on the receiving end was quite alien and so, having expressed his anger and dismay in the plainest terms, he ran away from the problem, taking with him their car, a red Citroen, and all their money. For the next week, at the beginning of February, he drove furiously up and down the Italian Riviera attempting to find friends to help in what he was sure was his hour of extremity. To Susan he kept up a barrage of contradictory telegrams and telephone calls, reaffirming his love with one and then denying it in the next. Like a stuck pig he ran from one place to the next in an angry and bewildered attempt to ease his pain. Two weeks later Susan went back to Britain to see the girls during their half-term in Edinburgh, leaving the boys with the governess, and while she was away, James chose his moment to return to the Haus am Berg, determined to repair some of the damage.

It was then that the final act in the drama was played out. Susan arrived back in Zell am See with Denys Hodson who had earlier arranged to spend a skiing holiday with them, but was now placed in the unenviable position of acting as a referee. There followed terrible rows in the villa as James prompted post-mortems on the affair and stimulated scenes that led to tears and anguish. Then, feeling that the only solution to the story—for he now felt that in some dreadful way, he was its only author—he arranged for David Cornwell to come from Vienna to discuss the matter. He agreed and what began as a fairly tense evening with James pushing events along at an "impossibly high fever" became a curious mixture of low farce and tragedy as the party made their way from the gloomy villa to the nearby town. In a restaurant James decided that the only way he could preserve his love and friendship for them both was to present Susan to David Cornwell, a "transaction" he attempted to complete in the foyer of the late-night station against the background of the sinister, dark and snow-covered streets. Eventually Denys Hodson pulled James away from the scene and there followed a night of near mental breakdown as James collapsed in the villa, all passions spent. From Susan's account in *The Kennaway Papers*, she felt sure that James had engineered a series of events to win back David Cornwell as a means of saving his own marriage, to get to his wife through his friend, and so to prevent her from leaving. The following day she and Cornwell "climbed the hill again and we went into the big bedroom, where James was curled on the bed in his vest and pants, unshaven, in the foetal position, crying. It had been snowing in the night and the white flakes piled up high against the window panes caused both a strange lightness and a shadowless gloom in the room. David went straight to the bed and sat across the end of it. "Old Jim, old chumbo, old chum, come on,' he said, and James peeped through his fingers, and their conversation began. I walked out of the room and I knew then that my little affair had ended."[2]

James may have won the battle which in his mind he had been fighting for Susan, but he had not won the war. Cornwell, showing much tact and discretion, left the villa and went back to Vienna, leaving Hodson, James and Susan in the Haus am Berg. There the quarrels and recriminations continued until, unable to take James's coldness and perversity any longer, Susan returned to England with the children after little David had been involved in a skiing accident. James threw himself into local society with some enthusiasm and set about amassing a barricade of acquaintances against the loneliness and depression that was threatening to overwhelm him. But the artificial *politesse* of the ski slopes soon palled, and James took himself off to Munich where he rented a room in the Hofbrauhaus and spent much of his time at a bar-cum-brothel, the Petit Paris where he met a new set of acquaintances, including Rolf, a student of psychiatry for whom James wrote a series of rambling notes describing his predicament[3]. There was also a series of casual affairs with the girls who frequented the bar, including Sylvie, a blonde German girl, and Jacqueline, a beautiful black girl who looked like "Eartha Kitt in a white furry collar and white leather coat". In their entourage James whiled away the rest of the month in introspection, booze and sex, falling with ease into the sleazy environment of the bar and its occupants. In April he left Munich with Jacqueline in tow and made his way back to England through France. In the uneasy truce that followed he went to live in Fairford while

Susan, who refused to crack up under the strain, lived in Highgate.

The break-up had provided James with a period of rumination during which he had attempted to find an answer to the question that, how at that stage in his life, when to all intents and purposes he was considered a success, he should have found himself in such a plight, and, more to the point, how he had involved those he loved in the same predicament. His analysis of the position was first and foremost self-centred. After returning from Hollywood in the autumn of 1961 he felt that he had been a failure as a writer and that others too recognised his shortcomings. This led him to believe that he was also less than a success as a man, and his petty sexual affairs and his one big love affair with Anne reinforced that notion. Feeling that he might be destroying Susan through his unreasonable behaviour he wrote the "yellow letter" which, far from appeasing her, made her feel that she had to withdraw her love in order to survive, to protect her first need, security. ("Living with James is rather like being a moth caught in a lighthouse lamp: the glare and intensity of his attention could be terrifying. It was fun but it wasn't the sort of peace and contentment that I was looking for then."[4]) David Cornwell's appearance in their lives, firstly as a successful writer, a competitor, then as his wife's lover, a rival, only served to underline his sense of imperfection, he being able to offer Susan that "peace and contentment"; hence the belief in Zell am See that he, James, should withdraw, leaving them together. It was only when that scenario became a possibility in the station, late at night, that James fought to regain control in the only way he knew: by manipulating a new scene in which he could play on both their emotions, one in which he would be the only director. In his own words: "I have not tried to be a man. Not except in sabre-toothed defence."[5]

The reasons for his behaviour went back, he reasoned, to his childhood when the trauma of his father's death had been swallowed up by a sense of premature responsibility. While that side of James's personality ruled, passions were kept under control, thus precluding the follies of youth, so necessary for a person's mental and spiritual growth. It was when Jim was in the ascendancy—and James had been aware of the division since his schooldays at Glenalmond—that the darker side of his behaviour was betrayed. James was the mature man, Jim the boy who had never grown up, the boy who had to be protected, or, as he also put it, James was the sophisticate, Jim the "nasty wee Scot". Later, he came to characterise the split as James the domesticated man constrained by society and Jim the artist who should be allowed any amount of licence. There were other portents that he felt backed up his belief that he was two men. Before his father's death he had been fair-haired and open; when his hair fell out after a bout of ringworm, it grew in again, dark, curly, and as he put it, demonaic. His astrological sign was Gemini, the twins; the dreams that haunted him involved the struggle between white and black horses, the two polarities of his emotions. He was fascinated by the androgynous nature of man and viewed with awe the female side; all normal enough interests, but in his case, a further evidence of the duality of his personality and nature. At the height of the hysteria in Zell am See the division became clear—"James et Jim, man and artist, wild boy and introvert"[6]. And the nature of that separation was made clear to him through the insight that the "artist is the baby", that it was his duty to protect the creative within him, hence his self-centred behaviour, hence, too, his blatant lack of regard for those around him.

> Left to my own (in Zell am See, February 1965) I got in with new people, one of whom noticed that in trying to prepare a new life for myself I divided very sharply the artist and the man, refusing to defend the behaviour of the man, being fairly ruthless and arrogant in the protection of the artist. I actually wrote down words in this notebook for them to describe my reasons for refusing "control": "let me scream like a child if I write like a man: let me die if I write like a god."[7]

The dramatisation of his life in those terms, the man being responsible to society, the artist only to himself, was a satisfying exegisis and one whose articulation helped the healing process within him. But its revelation was less important in an understanding of James's work than the accompanying discovery that he was losing all sense of distinction between his fiction which, from the evidence of his notebook, had come to embrace all fact, and his life which he now felt he was living in order to gain the raw materials for his novels.

> It's quite certain to me now that an Author is not a character worth talking about, worth analysing because the contradiction is one too many: he is the actor to end all actors because he is driven by the people within, that vast family of cousins . . . He's a kind of rickety candelabra (there was just such a one in the Haus am Berg) in which all the lights don't work all the time. They come off and go on again due to outside circumstances. The man in the street, the girl in the bed, whatever sets a light. She or he resembles closely enough the character already hidden in the head for there to be illumination bright enough to demand attention: to be written about or *acted out,* so close do fiction and fact become . . .[8]

Then, a few days later in the same notebook he magnified that thought to include a statement about the indivisibility of his art and his life.

> How wonderfully close fiction and life have suddenly become. And all moving to reality. It seems a blessing suddenly, the whole thing (though I suspected it from the start) and I seem to be moved not to recollection in the lock-up Proustian sense, of which I've been so afraid, but to a different kind of belated loneliness. The lights are going on and off in that candelabra much more frequently, and they blaze, blaze, blaze, each and every one. My real fear, what makes me really cry is that I may fail to grasp this hour which some authors may never even know. I fear I'll shamble back and lay my head where my life has been, to Susan's belly and pad. But I know I shall love her much more if I don't: even if I don't see her again.[9]

The result was a more-or-less rewrite of *Maclaren's History*. Kennaway had introduced in that draft the notion that Maclaren, Annie's pimp, would fall in love with Fiddes, the doctor who commits the abortion. To win back her husband Maclaren's wife "did the only possible thing—made a dive at Fiddes which Fiddes could not resist, fundamentally because he wanted to deny what went on between himself and Maclaren".[10] But that consequence had never seemed totally feasible to Kennaway and the triangular relationship of Fiddes, Maclaren and his wife had a false ring to it: now he had much firmer evidence. Instead of setting it in Glasgow, the one sure piece of writing with its suggestive setting of grey buildings against the sleet and snow of winter in the north, Kennaway moved the novel to London, to the "swinging London" of the mid-sixties. The period references are tipped in by a deft hand—Mary Quant, LSD, Bob Dylan, Vietnam—but this is also a London of sleazy private clubs, cheap backstreet trattorias and broken telephone kiosks, the soft underbelly of the ad-man's dream.

Into that authentic no-man's-land comes James Link, American-Irish, war photographer, fortyish and scared of growing old (a loose portrait of Robert Capa) and friend of Fiddes, ex-missionary doctor, a puritanical yet humanitarian man who hides his good works behind a withdrawn and laconic manner. Link is a self-deceiver and destroyer—"Link had evil's illegitimate quality, its pure beginning, its ironic regret, its obscenity, vitality; but not its self-knowledge, not its 'no' side. Link still loved Link: which is to say that he still had a private, savage appetite for life." (p. 3) He has been in love with an Austrian aristocrat called Furstental—she has been killed in a skiing accident—but has now transferred his affections to Susie Steinberg, a trendy young fashion editor with an international magazine. During the course of the novel, and in a series of flashbacks, he submits her to the Link treatment of extremes of love and pain, but by the time that he discovers that he really does love her, he has lost her to his straightforward friend, Fiddes. Link's jealousy is frightening and it terrifies him: "But then, in a glimpse, he saw it again, that Surgery rug. Saw the pain of them making love. He heard a sigh he'd never heard and knew it as Susie's sigh of love." (p. 117) He engineers a plot—but refuses to take a direct part in it—that leads to Fiddes being hauled before a B.M.A. committee for committing an abortion on Mandy-Margaret, a prostitute. This is Link's final cry for independence and he is let off the hook when Fiddes allows himself to be struck off in order to prevent Link and Susie being involved in the case. What happens is rather different. Susie, unable to involve herself in Link's gorgeous accident, leaves both men and Fiddes's sacrifice binds him even more closely to Link, the truth being revealed in the novel's penultimate page.

Within the bare bones of that story Kennaway had thrown much personal experience. The down-at-heel College Girls Club where Mandy-Margaret works, is based on the Petit Paris. Link's first love, Furstental, died in a skiing accident at Zell am See in circumstances remarkably similar to David Kennaway's own injury—both ran into passing army lorries at the edge of the ski slopes. Link suffered from many of James's dreams. The station scene when Fiddes and Susie try to get away from Link may be Victoria but its origins are Zell am See and the ensuing renewal of friendship between Link and Fiddes is an echo of what happened between James and David Cornwell in the Haus am Berg. James made it clear that he had written the book as Link/James, Fiddes/David, Susie/Susan in a letter to John Guest: "That bloody novel really took it out of me. No wonder, if you have to live so much of it out first."[11]

Kennaway felt that it was quite legitimate to use real life as the raw material for fiction—most novelists do. After all, he reasoned, there are very few original plots and after *Tunes of Glory* he had been much taken with the closing words of Ortega Y Gasset's *Notes on the Novel*: "Not in the invention of plots but in the invention of characters lies the best hope in the novel."[12] In his brief essay Ortega Y Gasset put forward the theory that the novel could only survive by developing character and motive, that stories as such were dead, and that the novelist had to be a man of experience to be able to write with the kind of depth that raised the novel of the future to an impressionistic form, above the simple, or as he put it, primitive, telling of tales.

> To enjoy a novel we must feel surrounded by it on all sides; it cannot exist as a more or less conspicuous thing among the rest of things. Precisely because it is a pre-eminently realistic genre it is incompatible with outer reality. In order to establish its own inner world it must dislodge and abolish the surrounding one. . . . a novelist should never attack a subject unless he knows it thoroughly. He must produce *ex abundantia*. Where he finds himself moving in shallow waters, he will never make good.[13]

Ortega Y Gasset was not advocating a simple "I am a camera" *realité*. Rather he stated that it was the duty of the novelist to transmute experience into art, to create a world into which he invites the reader to enter and about which the reader will care greatly. Although the world would have to be kept separate from the novelist's "real" world (his view of reality is never explained) it would owe its life to it, hence his belief that a novelist is a man writing his own life.

In *Some Gorgeous Accident* Kennaway went a stage further by making inseparable his own life and the lives of his fictional protagonists. For the first time in his life, Kennaway had experienced the bitterness of love lost, the late-night anguish of personal failure and the hurly-burly of painfully expressed emotional drama. He had also run the gamut of mental breakdown, or at the very least, of emotional collapse and had kept a careful record of the conflicting emotions that haunted him, and which had brought him to the conclusion that he now felt he could understand love, that life could begin again. Those notes formed the basis for the re-fashioning of *Some Gorgeous Accident*, and during the madness of Zell am See it was revealed to him that the James/David/Susan triangle was a drama, almost a piece of art, being acted out for his own benefit, and one that he himself controlled.

> "We're puppets," she said. "We're the puppets of that bastard Link." He tried to comfort her. Maybe taking a leaf from Mandy's book, she swore at Link again. When she paused and looked round the station there were very few people there and she couldn't quite believe in it.
>
> Clarke and Link then arrived on the scene and the couple stood up, hand in hand. Link roughly grabbed her spare hand, pulled her and said, "You're coming come. Come to your senses, woman." All his remarks might have come from a retired major, at this point.
>
> Fiddes didn't let go the hand she held so tightly in his.
>
> Link said, "If you'd stop leading poor Kildare by the nose and —"
>
> (p. 179)

(The "leading by the nose" comment is a direct reference to the taunt James had thrown at Susan in the station at Zell am See, that she should be ashamed of herself, leading a young man like David by the nose.)

As a work which interprets James's attitudes and acts as a flarepath on the route towards an understanding of what happened to him and Susan in early 1965, *Some Gorgeous Accident* is an interesting enough novel. In its own right, it is not without recommendation. The style is cinematic with quick cuts, dissolves and flashbacks creating a sense of space and time that is both past and present; and to link the scenes he used the silent cinema technique of placing captions to help the reader through the action. *"But we were outside one of those swell hotels up the street." "Plus cą change." "Then, a couple of days later, maybe three, maybe four, Clarky rang up."* Their employment was attacked by some critics as being a pretentious gimmick but in a novel in which most of the "action" unfolds through the reader's growing understanding of the characters, those brief, and often sardonic, directions merge easily into the general staccato tone of Kennaway's language.

The atmosphere of mid-sixties London has already been remarked upon; the other scene of tense realism takes place during Fiddes's hearing and James had invested considerable research in getting it right by poring through reports of B.M.A. tribunals; but what makes *Some Gorgeous Accident* work as a novel is the creation of the three central characters and his examination of their motives and conflicting ideals. Link has all the mannerisms of his period; he is shallow and articulate, a-legend-in-his-own-lifetime success, conscious of the responsibility of preserving that legend. He is also ruthless and destructive, a hazard to those who swim into his orbit. Susie is equally unappealingly drawn, "a smooth-walking, cool-talking, coon-meeting, all-happening chick" (p. 17), a trendy product of the sixties, a loser drawn intro the harsh glare of Link's myth-making. Fiddes is also a loser who ony excites the reader's sympathy for his mistaken chivalry during the hearing—by then we are given to realise that Fiddes's "trial" is an event that should never have happened. All are unsympathetic and confused, incapable of facing the obligatory scenes that should dominate their unsatisfactory lives, but by then James's interest was less the creation of dramatic fiction than the drawing of characters with all their complexities.

> Because I am to some extent a confused character, but moreover believe that the serious scene of today is one of confusion, I keep writing about characters who other people find "unsympathetic", or more to the point, "incredible". To simplify them—"clarify them" as every other author seems to do is to impoverish them and also to betray myself.[14]

Only Mandy-Margaret, the prostitute, retains the primitive edge of James's earlier female characters, Mary and Stella, by acting as a gutsy foil to the weak and indecisive Susie. She was inspired by a prostitute James had met in Glasgow and was Annie in earlier drafts: she also owed her existence to Christine Keeler whom James had contrived to meet, and by coincidence, Paul Mann, the documentary film-maker in the novel, also turned out to be the real-life friend of Christine Keeler. (James only discovered this after the novel had been published, and when he was reading Lord Denning's report on the Profumo Affair). James, though, could not separate himself entirely from his creation of Link. Like Link himself, he too perhaps believed too strongly in the Linky-legend. And perhaps that is why he came to dislike the novel, to hate "its hero Link, hate everbody in it, its atmosphere, what it says, what it stands for. It makes me sick."[15] *Some Gorgeous Accident* suffers from being too compressed a book, and given its genesis from so many different, and at times conflicting, drafts, that is not unexpected. The triangular relationship is somewhat contrived and intrusive, based as it is, so firmly in the author's own experience: nevertheless, its creation and publication did open the way to the later novels and to a new belief in the kind of fiction he wanted to create.

(Similar scenes to those enacted in *Some Gorgeous Accident* find their way into Le Carré's *The Naive and Sentimental Lover*. Shamus presides over a mock wedding between Helen, his wife, and Aldo Cassidy, but then stage-manages her return by persuading them that he is capable of committing suicide. It is all there: the villa—here placed in the Swiss village of Saint Angele—the desolate background of the snow-covered Alps, the rows and tantrums, the jealousies, Aldo admitting that he provided Shamus with material for his novel, even the presence of an outside party to the affair, the Eldermans, friends of Aldo Cassidy. At the novel's end, Cassidy loses both Shamus and Helen and retires from public life. When Shamus's novel "Three for the Road"—*Some Gorgeous Accident*(?)—is published, Aldo does not read it, and in time comes to forget its author "entirely".)

On settling back into the Manor House at Fairford, James set himself the task of writing the script of *The Bells of Shoreditch* which had been commissioned by M.G.M. Rex Harrison had now dropped out of the reckoning but James's Hollywood producer, Bernard Smith, hoped to get either Marlon Brando or Richard Burton to play Sarson and he was given notice to go to Culver City to work on the script editing later that year. James was determined that his marriage should be made to work before he set off for another bout of transatlantic nail-biting in movie-land, and his letters to Susan that summer—he spent much of it in Fontainebleau in France in the cottage of a friend of the Edmonds—are an honest reflection of that desire, wanting her to "come through this horrid nightmare to green fields again, because the fields are so lonely without you". Susan was in London undergoing psychiatric treatment, originally intended for James, but which he manipulated she should have instead. "In the shock that followed," she remembers, "I also found a friend. I really needed someone who could tell me I wasn't the cold, callous person that James told me I was."[16]

James was still finding the withdrawal from his god-like position as manipulator difficult to achieve, he still wanted to have the final control not only over his, but over other people's destinies. The final pages of his notebook betray that sense of ambition and they also clarify his own feelings about the split within him. He was finally coming to terms with that.

> Now I stick to two facts, One, Susan, Denys, David and others have insisted on the James/Jim dichotomy or schizophrenia in myself. In other words a familiar James is becoming an unfamiliar, unpredictable and unlovable Jim.[17]

In September he went to New York *en route* to California and while there he considered writing to Anne to arrange a meeting "to lay all the ghosts", begging her to give him the necessary "courage to say goodbye".[18] It was written in the Algonquin Hotel, but wisely, perhaps, he chose not to post it. The ghosts of his own past were now becoming too painful: he wanted a quieter and less frenetic time ahead, free of the kind of emotional battles that had disfigured his year.

> Odysseus is missing home very much. I know I have to search N. York for this book, maybe for the following play, but then I hope and pray that we will be together for a little while, because there aren't, I know, so many more little whiles ahead for all of us together. I do not prognosticate particular doom: I speak of man's estate. But of all families we have the least to complain about. It has been super and with luck there are as many years of freedom ahead as we have behind us, until Emma is 21. They've been long but such wonderful years and recent storms now only mark the summer that preceded such a thunderous fall. In ten years you will be little different to look at: very little, I guess and so long as Wasser photographs me, I won't be too bad. Odysseus feels that by packing so much (and that implies deceptions, of course it does) into such a

> short time he may have gained a little on time. But were time to turn on me now, and kill me, nothing would have been lost, except the possible books and plays. I have beaten time that way. I have seen the world and, my darling, you know, you don't have to be told what a massive proportion of that world (though not all of it) has been seen through your eyes. Thank you.
>
> Have no fear. I love you too. The difficult years are behind. There remains a year of two of insistent journey and search and I know I must not avoid that—tired as I am becoming, wishing for an island for you and your children with me—and then, you wait; the triumphal march.[19]

(Odysseus had become his *nom d'amour* during the subsequent, tremulous courtship of Susan.)

His second trip to California was less frenetic than the nightmare of four years earlier. Gone was the angst about the size of the place and the speed of its lifestyle. Gone too was his own playboy sense of enjoyment ("The height of our sins has been middle-aged sexual anecdotes told in a bar with topless waitresses after dinner at Frascatis."): this time he had come determined to work. *The Bells of Shoreditch* progressed far enough for it to be agreed that in 1966 he would spend most of the year in California working on the script. He returned to England on 4 October and went back to Gloucestershire determined to spend the winter writing. At that time he was still working on the drafts of *Some Gorgeous Accident*—then called tentatively "A Sense of Disorder" or "Ego Link"—and his play, *Country Dance* was still very much on his mind.

While staying at the Manor House, living apart, still, from Susan, James made a number of new friends locally. He had that chameleon ability to adapt himself to almost any society and enjoyed not only being with people, but also collecting them. For the most part, his new friends were intrigued by James's dark looks and by the sheer energy he brought to relationships; and once in his orbit few wanted to leave. Impulsively generous, both with his patience and with his money, he believed in the community of mankind, that because we are all in many ways dependent on one another, it was the duty of each and every one to care about the well-being of the people in our lives. That sense of love and consideration extended outwards to a whole range of different friends, all of whom he kept in quite separate compartments, but it began with his family, especially his children. Typical of this feeling was his concern for his Scottish relatives, some of whom he suspected he neglected too much.

> Even if I am guilty of failing to write letters (he wrote to one of the Craig Dhu aunts in Crieff) I would like you to know that whenever I remember a long and happy childhood, much of it is re-enacted for me in Craig Dhu . . . . . .I have lived, am living a life which is fuller and more exciting than my grandfather could have dreamt of, and while I love it, like this and the prospect which is offered to the children, I have no complaint. But none. Perhaps the clemency of those early days (in spite of some of the tragedies that went with them, with my father and Eva going so early when they were so close) affects me beneficially in the end. At any rate, I can speak of nothing other than the understanding and generosity of my aunts which is more than most can say, and your gift to Emma is yet another confirmation of this unrestrained love. It is therefore not all *unexpected,* but it is none the less appreciated for that.[20]

Not all of his friends were show-biz. John Browne, to whom he dedicated *The Cost of Living Like This,* was a charming and staunch friend, and he and his wife Jennifer were frequent visitors with their children. With him, James could relax, free from the competitive strains of his professional life, and he remained a close friend and companion until the end. (He was killed in a motoring accident long after James's own death.)

James's critics, and there were those who refused to be charmed by him, believed that the energy and commitment he brought to friendships was part of his overwhelming need to find the raw material of his fiction and there is some truth in their observations. He did enjoy entering people's lives, finding out about them and about what motivated them; and at times he would even try to order their lives, offering a helping hand here, advice there, not all of it useful. But he enjoyed seeing what happened next, once his counsel had been taken.[21] It was not done maliciously—but it is difficult to avoid the impression that sometimes his manipulations went too far (especially where romance was concerned), that the real-life needs and aspirations of people whom he knew took over those of the "people within, that vast family of cousins".

After Christmas, Susan went skiing in Wengen, Switzerland and James moved into Holly Terace until the end of February when he took off for California again. Through his previous stay he had been contracted by Universal to write an original North-West Frontier story set in the days of the British Raj, an opportunity he embraced with some enthusiasm, claiming that he would write it as an adventure story for his son, Guy. *The Bells of Shoreditch* was also moving forward with M.G.M. who wanted him to lose some of the "Britishness" in the original script and also to strengthen the character of Andrew whom they felt was still a cardboard cut-out of attitudes, without a fully rounded personality.

Once he had arrived in Los Angeles he moved into the Sportsmen's Lodge Hotel on Ventura Boulevard in North Hollywood, near Studio City, and Universal's studios. With its Olympic-size swimming pool and luxury apartments, the hotel gave James the seclusion he needed, even though he wondered if it were not all a busman's holiday, offering too much idleness and gracious living, "an absolute paradise with eight hours clear sunshine every single day". Faced by such ennervating affluence, James set himself a number of hurdles which had to be cleared each day before he allowed himself any enjoyment: a swim before breakfast, followed by a long stint writing, no sunning or drinks until so many words had been written, and so on.

At Easter he was back in London for a three-week break in April and when he returned on 5 May he moved out of his Sportsmen's Lodge Hotel into an apartment on Malibu Road at the north end of Malibu Beach. Little more than an apartment in a wooden clapper-board beach house, it looked out directly onto the beach and the ocean and at high tide the waves lapped over the stilts below. It was a perfect place for work, offering solitude and a sense of calm, and for James it had the added attraction of being beside the sea, allowing him to be near the ever-changing tides.

> I don't think I can be happier than walking barefoot down the shore, in and out of the edge of the sea, a literary beachcomber, poet-manqué. I was thinking of the end of the world and all that, because impressed lately with Jung's dictum that the second part of life is ruined unless we are prepared to welcome death. But I'm afraid if the sea should grow still. If the sea's going to stop, then I can't bear death. Which is to say, cornering myself, that I, like every other person who has known happiness, believe in life everlasting. The mystery of infinity should itself reassure us. The waves come infinitely, infinitely. Life, and with it therefore hope, is everlasting.

> We are not cheated. There is no end. End is a term which we have invented, it did not exist in the beginning.[22]

The sea was not only the well-spring of all life: in some half-imagined and mystical way, it was also a source of inspiration, and in his present mood, a place of spiritual rebirth. He had all ways loved seascapes and been attracted to the coast—in Malibu he felt that being near the sea and hearing it creak against the timbers of the house with the ebb and flow of the tides, was a vital element in his renewal.

By the end of the month, heady figures were being bandied about his head. Rex Harrison had become warm again on playing the part of Sarson and with the possibility of him leading and Mackendrick directing, M.G.M. forecast that *The Bells of Shoreditch* would be a big budget movie. As he told Susan on 1 June, "if it went well, 17½% would be worth anything up to £200,000 over the ten years". There was also the possibility of adapting Brian Moore's novel *The Emperor of Icecream* for Ronald Neame, and Harry Salzman, too, had come up with an offer to do some script-doctoring in North Africa that summer. James, having fired his agents, was taking his wheeling and dealing seriously, anxious to build up sufficient funds so that he could leave the business and return to London to concentrate on the novel and drama for a couple of years. As he had told Mark Longman earlier, he was determined that Kennaway the movie man should not sell short Kennaway the novelist. As so often happens, though, not all the deals came off. M.G.M. blew hot and cold and told him to wait for a year, he turned down the Brian Moore deal, tired of the North-West Frontier story, and only Harry Salzman came up with a definite offer, not to doctor scripts, as it turned out, but to work on a new film he wanted to make to celebrate the Battle of Britain.

Initially, Kennaway was sceptical, wondering if he was being asked to create a film that would be similar in theme to *Tunes of Glory*, and, more to the point, if a film celebrating heroes of World War Two could be made in serious vein in the flippant world of the mid-sixties. It was also not his intention to write an epic with cameo roles that would help the production company, Paramount, to make huge profits, while truth was made to jump out of the window. However, he reasoned, if he was allowed to make a film about the people who fought in, and lived throughout the battle, about their relationships, their hopes and fears, then he was in. Salzman was suitably re-assuring and James returned to London in August to begin work on the script.

Typically, his research was painstaking and thorough. As well as building up a cuttings archive, he spent many days in viewing theatres looking at wartime footage and at other films that had been made, seeping in the atmosphere of the tension under which everyone was forced to live during those momentous and perilous days. He was paid $75,000 for writing the script and the deal brought him into contact with one of the best known producers of the day—Canadian-born Harry Salzman had cemented his reputation by making the phenomenally successful James Bond films which were as much a product of the sixties as was "swinging London". It was a good time for James to move into that league. Before he left Hollywood he had also put in hand a number of moves designed to protect his interests there. With James Hill, a former M.G.M. producer and a partner with Ben Hecht and Burt Lancaster in the Hill-Hecht-Lancaster company, Kennaway had formed a business partnership, and H.W. Swanson, the distinguished agent, agreed to represent him on the West Coast.

At the end of the year the Battle of Britain project ran into trouble. Paramount had become a wholly-owned subsidiary of Gulf and Western and changes in the management structure had brought about a swing in attitudes towards major projects, of which *The Battle of Britain* was perhaps the most prestigious. One of the points of contention that had blown up between Paramount and Salzman was Kennaway's draft script which had been described by Paramount boss Charles Bluhdon as being "awfully English"—it was, in fact, and so remained, remarkably fair to the German point of view, but that was not the real thrust of Bluhdon's argument: he wanted more American interest. The Battle of Britain had been a British victory; the producers were American; Salzman refused to make a film smacking of Errol Flynn heroics, as *Objective Burma* had been. (This film, showing Flynn and the Americans winning the war in Burma single-handed, had caused considerable comment, not all of it favourable, when it had been shown to British audiences.) The row caused a good deal of heart-searching in Britain; first of all from a sense of dented pride that it had taken an American production company to give the backing for a film about a notable British historical event, and secondly, that the British film industry was either unwilling or unable to raise the money and the expertise to make a $10 million blockbuster. Eventually, by the Spring of 1967, Salzman had won the support of United Artists and Rank, and much of the film was shot at Pinewood where the Rank technical department manufactured a whole air force of static World War Two planes. Most of the film was shot in the summer of 1968, ironically, one of the worst summers on record, preventing filming, in Britain at least, of the blue September skies that had characterised much of the actual battle. Other sequences were shot in the south of France and in Spain and that country's air force provided some of the pilots for the German military planes of the period.

Susan skied in Switzerland again that winter and while she was at Wengen, James telegraphed her excitedly to say that the long saga of *Country Dance* was finally coming to an end. It would be produced by Michael Codron at the Hampstead Theatre Club that June with James Roose-Evans directing. It opened with a gala première on 27 June and in the programme note James made much of the play's long history, that it had been "bought and funked by five managements" before finding a home at Hampstead. He protested, perhaps, too much. In its early drafts, the play was unproduceable. It was too long, told too many stories from the points of view of too many characters, and it tried too hard to maintain the ethos of the novel, *Household Ghosts,* in stage terms. Kennaway only got it right when he reduced the cast to four characters: Pink (played by Edward Fox), Hilary, his sister, a recreation of Mary (played by Jane Merrow), Douglas Dow, an amalgamation of Stephen and David (Stuart Mungall) and Rosie, a dairymaid (Janet Michael). In his notes for the final draft, James made due obesiance to his debt to Chekhov in writing a play about the declining aristocracy—"the puzzle is why the cherry orchards haven't been chopped down (in rural Perthshire)"—and there is a hint, too, of Ibsen, but Kennaway's dialogue was too self-consciously brittle to allow the characters to have more than a surface interest in their fates. Pink, though, like Osvald in Ibsen's *Ghosts,* is a burnt-out case, haunted by the sins of his family's past and by a dark hint of incest with his sister Hilary. He tries to assert a romantic view of that past with all its shared rituals, in preference to the grey contemporary world (typified by the meritocrat Douglas with his vulgar Jaguar motor car), by returning to the private mythology of his childhood. But that route leads to madness as Hilary is forced to choose between his fantasy and the hard-edged reality offered by her husband. Hilary then becomes the central character, the pivot upon which their lives revolve, the woman created as myth-maker and life-giver.

> No mattter how we dress it up, the one and only positive value in life is survival, and on the whole it is woman, not man who instinctively recognises this. Survival in this sense includes marriage and procreation which are the theme of practically every country dance.[23]

(The dance referred to in the title and in Kennaway's note is "Hamilton House", a lively Scottish reel in which the woman sets to one partner and then dances with the other.) Hilary turns away from the sterility of the past but Pink is swallowed up by it after a botched suicide, his epitaph being taken from Rabelais's supposed last words: *Tirez le rideau, la farce est jouée.*

For all its verbal pyrotechnics—Pink addresses an early morning hangover as "Dear Dawn, you silvery old tragedy"—the play was not a complete success, most critics shielding their mild dislike with the observation that they hoped for better things next time. Their disquiet appeared to spring from two related reasons: firstly the relationships between the characters created by Kennaway seemed to have no foundation, and secondly, it was considered to be somewhat unfashionable to write a play about the foibles of the landed gentry at a time when most playwrights were exploring other territories. A third criticism, which need not detain us, as it says more about the critics themselves than it does about James's talents, was that the play was "too literary", a "fault" which many playwrights would be only too willing to take on board! There was some basis to the criticisms, though. Pink's incestuous love for Hilary in the Hampstead production was contrived and the script had little to give Rosie, the dairymaid, who is central to the plot (she is left to care for Pink and acts as a sounding board for Hilary and Douglas); there was also the ever-present danger, never entirely corrected, that the play, set in a Perthshire "big house" could descend into drawing-room comedy, for much of the play is very funny indeed.

The play was booked to play at the Edinburgh Festival that year—it took the place of a première of Tennessee Williams's *The Two Character Play*—and James set about repairing some of those faults. He amended the script to make Pink more dedicated to booze and kept within himself as a character, while Hilary became more aristocratic in her bearing. "Ah it's serious," James wrote to Roose-Evans about what he hoped would be the audience's reactions, "a tense situation between the patient Scots boy and his bitchy wife." The play was in fact a great success in Edinburgh where it ran during the week of 4 September at the Royal Lyceum Theatre with Joanna van Gyseghem taking over the role of Hilary from Jane Merrow, and it attracted generous notices.

> The novelty of seeing a play that is concerned with contemporary Scotland is exhilarating. When it also happens to be vividly written and performed, there is cause for celebration. . . . James Kennaway is an exile who cannot conceal his affection for home, but is sardonic rather than sentimental in his attitude. Reversing the usual trend of our native dramatists, he puts an historical conflict into modern terms. In observing the split in the Scottish character between romance and realism, he creates latter-day Jacobites and Covenanters —the degenerate but picturesque aristocracy versus the dour and diligent middle class.[24]

The Scotsman's review of the play (written by its drama critic, Allen Wright) was typical of the enthusiasm displayed by the Festival press and Kennaway, who was in Edinburgh for the performance, was delighted by the favourable reaction. While in Edinburgh he gave a celebrity lecture at the International Film Festival on Saturday 2 September, taking as his theme 'The Obligatory Scene" and illustrating it with extracts from the films, *Tunes of Glory, On the Waterfront, Un Homme et Une Femme* and *My Fair Lady*. It was a great success and it was typical of the man that he remembered to come back before he left Edinburgh to thank the staff of the Film Festival, then trying to free the event from its documentary-film orientation: Kennaway's lecture and the significance of *Country Dance* to contemporary Scotland was not lost on the Festival's director, Murray Grigor.

> I am sorry I was out of the Festival office when you called. I was

> probably upstairs; attending to "Films of Scotland", the other part of the Film Festival job, doctoring the national image. The lack of tickets did not stop us all seeing "Country Dance". for me it more than purged a host of Scotch-bred ills. If rumour is right it ought to make an even better film—a score of obligatory scenes.

Rumour, for once, was correct. James had sold the film rights to Bob Ginna before coming to Edinburgh and so successful was the Festival run that Frederick Coe, a New York theatre producer and friend of Ginna's, had taken an option on the U.S. rights.

While in Edinburgh for the opening of *Country Dance*, Susan had been laid low by a dose of meningitis, and to help her recover they spent the rest of the month in Venice where James worked on "Boswell and Begg", the novel that was to become *The Cost of Living Like This*. Its other titles were "The Lengths to Which we Go", "A Damned Serious Business" and "Glasgow Role", and it was to have been set in a university medical school, its themes student revolt and the love of a don for a younger student. In October they went back to California with their son David and took a house again at Malibu. The marriage that had seemed doomed was back on course again and they had found a new love and respect for each other after the traumas of the past two years—"We wanted to be together, not to keep James out of trouble but because we found each other such good company. Such an upswing."[25]

Holly Terrace was sold on their return and they decided to move permanently to Gloucestershire, keeping a flat on in London which James began converting into a film studio to further his directing ambitions. Prudence Downing, who had worked in the Foreign Office, came to work as secretary and personal assistant as life became more complicated—at the time he was working on a novel and four filmscripts as well as conducting a number of lengthy and time-consuming deals. Having sacked his agents he had come to rely on his lawyer, William Forwood, to help him on contractual matters. 1967 was a year of renewal and re-awakening but it was not without its upsets. Beryl Edmonds, Susan's step-mother, died of cancer before Christmas—her father had died in the previous year—and James himself had been seriously ill. In June, while returning from one of his writing bouts in Fontainebleau, he and Susan had stopped at Barfleur on the Normandy coast. Shortly before lunchtime on the Sunday, when they were due to catch the ferry at Le Havre, James suffered a severe attack of angina. Throughout his life he had betrayed mild hypochondria—every cold and sore throat from school to Hollywood found their way into his correspondence—but he also thought doctors a waste of time. (He was scathing about the profession in *The Cost of Living Like This.*) When he got back to England the following day he did go to the family doctor but made little of the attack, preferring instead to take up a strict régime of punishing distance running, in the circumstances the worst possible course he could have taken. He refused, too, to cut back on his breakneck style of living.

Some Gorgeous Accident had been published in New York in July and in London in September and it had immediately become a hot film property. Apple, the Beatles' production company, made a bid for it and James Hill tried to interest M.G.M. in it as part of a two-film deal in the long-lasting saga of *The Bells of Shoreditch.* Columbia and the newly-formed C.B.S. film group also expressed their interest and inquiries came in from a number of independent producers in London and Los Angeles. For once, Kennaway did not want to be involved in the writing of the script and amongst the writers approached was Melvyn Bragg, a young novelist who had made his name with his first novel, *For Want of a Nail.* The excitement of involving himself in film deals had waned, though, and James had come to the weary conclusion that scriptwriting was the icing on the literary cake, providing him with a good deal of wealth but little in the way of substance.

He went back to California twice in the following year, in January to work on the script of *Country Dance* with Ginna, and in July to work on *The Shoes of the Fisherman* for Michael Anderson which was made with Anthony Quinn in the leading role of Pope Kiril I, the first communist pope. It was based on a novel of the same name by Morris West. James spent Easter in Rome to capture the background flavour and he was in Europe again in October and November, visiting Denmark and East Germany, when he completed the drafts of his novella, *Silence.* Travel and living abroad had by now become an essential part of the creative process. Towards the end of 1968 the Robert Capa film project—which was to have been called "The Wars of Robert Capa"—was sold to M.G.M. and in December James was commissioned by Castle Films to write the screenplay for a new version of *Wuthering Heights* which would star Christopher Plummer as Heathcliff. James went up to Haworth, the Bronte's home in Yorkshire, and came back shortly before Christmas excited by his interpretation that the narrator, Mr Lockwood, was a medium who could summon up the dead Catherine, that her knocking on the window pane was a plea to her family and her real love, Heathcliff, to be let into "your hearts and to your imagination for ever by listening to my story".[26] It was a good way to end the year. At home, plans were afoot, too, to convert the stables of the Manor House into a cordon bleu restaurant: Susan had arranged a dinner party on Saturday 21 December to discuss the project with a visiting French lady and the Hon. Victoria Lawrence who was to be her partner.

That day James went up to London to meet Peter O'Toole who had been cast in the part of Pink in the film of *Country Dance* which would begin production the following year. He set off home again early in the evening in his grey Volvo taking his usual route out of London, the recently built M4 motorway. At about seven o'clock near the Langley roundabout he had a massive coronary and his car spun out of control. It veered twice into the fast lane and back onto the hard shoulder before drifting across the central reservation into the paths of three cars travelling in the opposite direction. None of their occupants was hurt. James Kennaway was dead, as he had frequently prophesied, at the early age of forty. At the Manor House his absence went unremarked until later in the evening when Susan and the dinner party guests began to worry, and at ten-thirty John Lawrence, Victoria Lawrence's husband, called the police. They were on their way, they said, to report the accident.

~ 10 ~

Aftermath

IT is idle to speculate what might have become of James Kennaway had he not suffered from a heart attack that December's night on the M4, or what he would have made of his life and work had be managed to bring his car under control, or if he had been persuaded to consult a doctor on his return from France the previous summer. In a very Scottish way, which he would doubtless have appreciated, it is also perverse to speculate thus, Scottish history having been littered with more "if onlys" than any other nation's. Most of his friends, on hearing the news on the Monday morning, felt that a very great presence had been removed from their lives. Alexander Mackendrick, perhaps the only man to have influenced him, felt a flash of anger when he heard the news in London, a feeling of bitterness that James should have died with so much undone, his talents never completely fulfilled. Other associates experienced similar emotions, allied to a deep grief that so energetic a man should have died so suddenly, that he should have left them with so little warning.

At the Manor House, the sad little party dispersed, leaving Susan alone with her brother-in-law Philip and sister Gyll. Outside, the rose bush which grew against the house banged its branches in the wind, tap-tapping against the drawing room window, until, at four o'clock, unable to endure the sound any longer, Philip went outside and cut back the offending limbs. In both their minds, though, the tapping persisted, an eerie echo of Catherine's plea to be let in in *Wuthering Heights*. Later, James would often return to Susan in dreams telling her that he was alive and well, that he had not been in his car that fateful evening, that he was now free of the frustration of film deals and that he was writing what he had always wanted to write. Other friends experienced similar dreams and "hauntings"[1], all common enough happenings in a period of bereavement. James was buried after Christmas in the churchyard of St Mary's Church in Fairford, a compact fifteenth-century structure with a Norman tower, renowned for the elegance and piety of its stained glass windows. From the west side of the tower, a Christ of Piety, carved in archaic style stares down on those who rest below.

At low points throughout his life, James had pondered much on the mutability of life and on the prospect of an early death which was one of the reasons, he admitted to those near him, why he had chosen to live his life so intensely. His unposted letter to his mother, written in September 1956, had made that perfectly clear—"Just now I want to blaze, in every direction, right or wrong, just so as I shan't sink with too much left undone, too much never tried, too many sensations missed"—and any hint of mortality further increased his belief that life was too short and constrained to contain all his many energies. In one sense, that feeling was born of his father's early death and the suddenness with which it visited itself on James's young life. And yet, tuberculosis is a virus, not a hereditary disease: there was no medical reason why he should have feared a similar fate, and, in any case, both Kennaways and Ewings enjoyed longevity, which is a hereditary factor. Partly, he liked to dramatise the notion of the artist dying young. Partly, too, he remembered the untimely death of his friend Alasdair Hilleary, the Lycidas he could never quite forget. For all those reasons, the fear of early death was a pall over his blackest moments.

When his posthumous novel, *The Cost of Living Like This,* appeared in September 1969, the rumour grew that James, like his central character Julian, was dying of cancer when he had the accident. Not so. It was a major coronary that killed him—whether or not he was dead by the time the cars collided is immaterial. He was a classic candidate for a heart attack, somewhat overweight, a smoker with a high voltage lifestyle. He could have eased up, but then, argue friends like Douglas Rae, he would not have been James, he would not have been able to keep writing in the style that suited him best.[2] He was dead; those who lived on and who had loved him, had to live with the hopelessness of the "if onlys".

The Cost of Living Like This which had begun its life in 1967—"Boswell and Begg", "The Lengths to which we go", "A Damned Serious Business" and "Glasgow Role" were amongst its working titles[3]—marks a departure in Kennaway's techniques with its shifts of narrative and its cinematic intercutting of scenes combining flashback, interpretation, illusion and harsh reality. Julian, an Oxford don and an economist of importance—by now the Kennaway reader was used to seeing his men portrayed as occupying positions of authority, men of the world who have made their mark upon it—is married to Christabel who is bright and pretty and amusing. Julian is dying slowly of cancer and in his pain and his misery he tries to find renewal in Sally, a seventeen-year-old black-eyed, pert Cockney swimmer who remains ignorant of Julian's struggle with "the Crab"—throughout the novel he addresses his illness as if it was some kind of homunculus with whom he can strike up a bargain. Only Christabel knows of the struggle and of the game that he plays to keep himself in the land of the living.

> And Lord, the economist thought, the games we play, even when we're sick like this. perhaps *because* we're sick like this.
>
> The wicked games, the weapons we use to destroy others with ourselves: there is no measuring the lengths to which we go in order to avoid the loneliness of death. . . . Lord, the games. . . .
>
> . . . No one really guesses the games which are so special to the dying. No one would believe them, if they were told. No one has mastered them, except the dead. (p.6)

But Christabel knows the games and has mastered their rules, that the illness must never be mentioned, that there must be all the time left in the world to make plans for the future. It is that knowledge that sends her to bed with "The Mimic", a man "who made a lot of money working the commodity market from a telephone number which was London Wall" (p. 65), a grubby affair which takes place shortly after Julian's exploratory operations and one which gives him the strength to find a new lease of life with Sally. There is a further twist to this familiar triangular relationship—our expectations in the motives of all Kennaway's characters are always being turned upside down—when Sally conjures up a tortured rivalry with Christabel, and flaunts a Californian lover, all blond hair, single and mindless, in front of Julian.

Much is made clear by the development of the characters who have not been conceived either by pure description, rhetoric or the planting of evidence, but by their discovery of each other in dialogue, or in Julian's case, by his intense conversations with the Crab. (Some of James's knowledge of the effects of cancer had come first-hand from watching Beryl die the previous year.) This method leads to a shifting viewpoint in which the characters betray themselves by the odd gestures so that Sally, whom we have come to look on as a typical teenager whose flat is all empty Coke bottles and discarded Beatles records, becomes hard-edged and knowing; and Christabel, the sophisticated one, attempts to take her life before the novel's end. What happens next in the novel is scant enough: a necessary marking out of the old triangle. Through a series of fortuitous accidents, Julian, Christabel and Sally fetch up in Glasgow which is evoked as a disarmingly murky *mis-en-scène* where Sally is due to take part in a swimming competition and where there is a ghastly scene involving all three protagonists. (Scottish critics tut-tutted their disapproval over Kennaway's description of Glasgow: Partick Thistle's football ground, a necessary part of the plot, is given as Furbank, not Firhill.)

At this point, Mozart Anderson enters their lives, a Glasgow football referee—made credible against all the odds—so called because he plays "sweet and profound inglorious tunes" (p. 133) on his clarinet, a reference which may have been the author's mocking note at the title of his first novel. Mozart picks up Christabel in an echoing cafe "of particularly Scottish texture: formica, tartan, linoleum and carbohydrate" (p. 44), and proceeds to put her through her paces in another sort of game in which she is the candidate, he the inquisitor. His interpretation of the Julian/Christabel/Sally triangle acts as a chorus to the tragedy that is being played out: like his tunes, his insights are sweet and profound and act as healing balm to Christabel. when she attempts suicide by drinking Julian's "jungle-juice" (the morphine-based concoction that keeps pain at bay), he turns his attention to Sally who has been caught up with Julian in a students' revolt at the Allan Ramsay School of Art, a vividly-drawn scene which summons up the spirit of revolt in in a series of flashbacks. Slightly wounded in the riot, Julian is taken into hospital where the Crab, throwing the last card, ends the game by killing Julian in front of the two women who have battled for his love.

> They were with him, together, when the end came. Two or three times, he stopped breathing for so long that they thought it was over and almost rose from their places each side of the bed. Then suddenly he shuddered and breathed and that awful muscular contraction happened again. They both had an arm over his body to try and quieten the painful jerks. It was as if he had hiccoughs of the spine. He groaned and whimpered. Sally hardly dared look at him, but held onto his right hand, and occasionally put her cheek down against his fingers. Then she sat up and saw that Christabel was in exactly the same position on the other side. She also was exhausted. (p. 193)

Thus the savage competition between the two women is brought to an end and ultimately the laurels go to Christabel. Sally, who later, and unsatisfactorily, withdraws into guilt, commits suicide in her bedsitting room in Half Moon Lane, London S.E. 24. The competition between two lovers for the loved one was never so violently expressed as it was in this novel, and that theme of rivalry runs throughout Kennaway's fiction. Sinclair and Barrow struggle for the regiment; Stephen, David and Pink for Mary's soul; Andrew Vass and Jakie Sarson battle it out for the right to own Stella; Link and Fiddes are locked in friendship and in rivalry for Susie; even Taylor Two and his chums enjoy the power-struggle within the school. Kennaway was fascinated by the dynamism of power, by the ways in which his characters would react in the ever-changing shifts of emphasis that entailed. What makes *The Cost of Living Like This* such an impressive novel is that for the first time Kennaway was able to detach himself from that rivalry, to allow the characters to tell their own story without his own voice intruding.

Predictably, perhaps, the reviewers' response was one both of respect for the book and a sense of regret that its author was no longer alive. "With this author's death," Janice Elliot ended her review in the *Sunday Telegraph* of 7 September 1969, "a novelist of macabre, disturbing and anguished vision has been lost." "A sad triumph," was Isobel Murray's comment in the *Financial Times* of 11 September, at the conclusion of a most favourable review. "It is sadly ironic that the last novel from the finely perceptive James Kennaway should be largely concerned with death"—Jeremy Brien in the *Bristol Evening Post* of 11 September, and other reviews made much of the connection between Julian's death from cancer and James's own death in an accident, hence the rumours that James himself had also died in the clutches of the Crab. The film rights to the novel were sold to Bob Ginna and he began looking for suitable locations in Scotland during the summer of 1970, the year in which *Country Dance* was shown at the Edinburgh Film Festival, but as so often happens after a writer's death in the movie business, producers quickly lost interst in his work and the film was never made.

Country Dance, on which he had lavished so much care and attention in its different forms since 1961, was not well received and M.G.M. gave it a limited distribution, thereby condemning it to more-or-less instant oblivion. In writing the script from the play, Kennaway had lost the big scenes, the obligatory ones that had so distinguished the novel, so that the relationships between the protagonists are seen as being mannered and shallow. The scenes that are hinted at, those between Pink and Hilary, played respectively by Peter O'Toole and Susannah York, all appear to have happened in the past and so the film hinges on a series of disparate scenes which lead up to their final separation and Hilary's improbable reconciliation with her husband, played by Michael Craig. Pink's love for his sister is played as being merely brotherly (significantly, it was released in the United States under that title, *Brotherly Love*), all hint of incest gone, so that the film becomes so tasteful and light-hearted that it begins to bore. Another problem was Peter O'Toole. Fine character actor though he is, he was not Pink, and his ingratiating histrionic charm in playing him as a drunken, aristocratic buffoon, was very different from James's understanding of "the unpredictability, the laughs, the upside down picnic of Pink's orbit and Pink's world". (Hilary to Douglas) Pink may be full of fun and he has some splendidly funny lines but his loss of Hilary has to be seen as being the one tragic event in his life, as sad as all the family ghosts who haunt him.

There were also stories of disagreement between director J. Lee Thompson and O'Toole who, by contract, had final say in the script. If James had lived, claimed Thompson and his leading actors, it would have been a very different film. If only. The film itself was shot on location in Strathearn and at Ardmore Studios at Bray in Ireland, Scotland not having the necessary studio facilities to complete the production.

James's other film project, *Battle of Britain,* was completed by Wilfred Greatorex and released in September 1969. Guy Hamilton's direction was praised both for its brilliant aeronautical sequences and for its faithfulness to the period it was representing, but otherwise the film received more respect that critical adulation.

With the money from *Country Dance* Susan was able to open her restaurant within a year of James's death. Called "Pink's" in honour of her husband's most vivid literary creation, it was run in partnership with Victoria Lawrence and quickly gained a good reputation for its high standard of cuisine and service. It was sold in 1976 when Susan went into commercial film production in London, but she built a new house nearby at Mallam Waters, making a large and attractive landscaped garden out of one of the many gravel pits that dot the area. In 1980 she married Stanley Vereker.

It is unusual for a writer's reputation, especially a writer like Kennaway whose output was so small, to be resurrected quickly after his death. Critics generally like to have a decent breathing space before they risk pronouncements on the newly dead; but in James's case it was slightly different as he had left work in progress that could be retrieved and published with proper care and attention to his own intentions. Amongst his papers were two partially completed novels, *My Colonel and I,* and *Round and Round the Wedding Ring* which both exist in manuscript drafts[4]: these and the rest of his papers (apart from his private letters) were deposited in the National Library of Scotland in 1972, the year that his novella, *Silence,* was also published. It was edited and prepared for publication by Lynn Hughes, a friend whom James had met in the London offices of M.G.M., and so tersely is it written that it could equally well have been the outline for a possible film. For some years, James's American friends and colleagues had been suggesting to him that he write a novel set in America. *Silence* was the answer—although, paradoxically, it was his only novel never to achieve transatlantic publication. Perhaps it struck too near the heart of America's racial problems.

Kennaway had written the first draft by the middle of September 1968 when he was in Berlin, and a second draft was finished by midnight on 1/2 October, James ending the holograph script with the words, "and not a bad day's work, though I say it myself".[5] The setting for the opening of the novel was the Harvard Club at West 44th Street in New York—he had stayed there in 1964—and the action takes place in the ghettoes of Harlem, although, later, he added a note: "Doesn't need to be in New York—no man's land".[6] Those first versions were to have been a tale told by an advertising man, Bob, on his return to New York from Paris: by 2 December he had become a doctor, Larry Ewing, the club had become anonymous, and the setting changed so that it resembled Chicago more than New York, although by then he was less concerned with the setting than with the story about a white man who finds love with a black woman during a period of violence and tension between the two races. She is called "Silence", but the silence is also that point of stillness when they reach love and understanding together.

At the opening of the novel, the weather is bleak and uncompromising, the snow, as ever, sinister—"sixteen below zero and the wind was blowing hard across the lake" (p.13)—but in the Club men of action and authority drink warming Bloody Marys, called, ironically in the light of later events, Club's Blood. When the doctor enters the club he finds his son-in-law, Michael Angel, plotting a raid of revenge on a black youth who has sexually assaulted his wife, Ewing's daughter, after she had completed some kind of charity work in the ghetto. The doctor is a good man, or at the very least tries to be a good man, but when he sees his son-in-law and his vacuous son engaged in revenge, willy-nilly, he is drawn into the action.

> The doctor thought how strange it was that a certain type of rich man often believed that fathers had been castrated. He wondered if

> it was his profession, his income or merely his age that led them so brightly to this insulting assumption. He finished his vodka and very gently asked the question, "Do I take it that we are leaving at five?"
>
> In putting it that way, he was being less than true to himself. He was answering Angel and his friends in their own terms. He knew that. Almost as he said it he asked himself, Why on earth should I have done that? How inconsistent we are.
>
> "Good for the Doc," one of them said generously, thereby applauding him for having made the worst decision in his life. (p.20)

The result is both farce and tragedy. The raid is made into a mockery by a minor car crash, a black boy is badly injured, shots are fired, a race riot erupts and the doctor is left stranded with a wound in his side, a rich picking for the enraged blacks. Then follows a period of memorable grace which turns the novel from being a tale concerned with contemporary violence and the murdering cruelty of man, into a religious allegory. Ewing takes refuge in a tumble-down slum apartment where he is taken in hand by an athletic, amazonian yet graceful, black called, as he discovers, Silence. She is dressed, bizarrely, in a flimsy dancer's outfit, smokes pot, listens to scratched Sinatra records, and says nothing. All her instincts suggest that she should hand over Ewing to the mob, but this Mary Magdalen cares for him, as a mother for a child, as a lover for the loved one. They play games together, eat and drink together in a celebration of their common humanity. When their lair is discovered, Silence leads him to a dentist's surgery where the full effects of the riot are made plain to him in a magazine article: following the death of the black boy, rioting leads to blood-letting and his son, Lawrence Junior, has been strung up and lynched in revenge. Silence, he also learns, is wanted by the police for her part in that crime. (Presumably she committed it while caring for him: as Kennaway makes it clear that the lynching ocurred two days after the riot.) It is then that the doctor realises how flimsy has become his hold on past reality, how separate he has grown from those around him, Silence now is his only reality; he cannot mourn his son's death. Silence enables him to escape but it is only when he has reached partial safety that he realises his life has been bought at a terrible price. He makes his way back to the surgery and finds it destroyed with Silence in the middle of a cruel parody of a pietà scene.

> She was naked. They may have gang-banged her first, but probably not. Nobody will ever know. she was standing or almost standing, stark naked. Her back was like an uncooked steak that had been thrashed by a tennis racket strung with wire.
>
> And the doctor thought, maybe it *is* Sunday, but there is no longer any belief. So help me, they didn't do as much to Christ.
>
> Yes, it could be called standing. She was bowed, but she was on her feet, not on her knees, exactly between the waiting room and the surgery, in the doorway. She was making absolutely no sound. Not a moan. No sound at all. . . . . .Then the doctor saw that she wasn't tied to the door as at first he'd thought. Her hands weren't tied there, just a few inches above her big head. They were nailed. Nailed to the lintel with one big square nail. (pp. 79-80)

Now it is the turn of Ewing to care for Silence. They walk blindly through the streets—"Look what's become of Adam and Eve; that's what the doctor thought" (p. 84)—through the city's park until they reached the stockyards and are discovered there the following day, the religious symbolism being made complete when they are found asleep amongst the animals and the hay, outcasts from the world of man. Silence is put in a police hospital, and when the doctor hears a spokesman say that she may not speak, but she'll talk, he decides that because she had become his partner in a kind of suffering that is as old as mankind, he has to ease that pain in the only way that is left open to him: he kills her by slitting her jugular vein to preserve her silence, and thereby her own identity.

> Then there was blood over everybody and a hell of a lot of people seemed to be there. He stood. He kept his eyes on her until he knew suddenly and gloriously that she was dead. He wiped his tears from his face with his sleeve, then he spoke. He said levelly, "Notice the blood. It is also red."
>
> He now seemed to be beyond sadness. Then he turned and looked at the others, who were still standing round in an appalling silence. He said, "Now, please will somebody take me away?"
>
> There followed a bloody accusing confusion and crying noise. (p. 93)

The final phrase came from the last pages of his last notebook and had been written a day or so before he died. In the third draft, Ewing would only have left the scalpel for Silence to use if *she* wanted, and although that ending is weaker—Ewing's existential act of murder is redolent of the same grace afforded him by Silence—that earlier version does contain a more complete statement of Kennaway's intention, even though he had by then realised the impossibility of Silence being allowed to surrender to man's far-from-tender mercies.

> I met passion. I made no passionate love. I was the object of this extraordinary passion. I am therefore honoured beyond most men. I do not say, "'I learnt from the experience such and such about the colour bar, or the Police, or the black threat." I am not in the area of saying any of that.
>
> Silence, I pray. I pray for Silence. No, to be true to the end. I pray for the sculptor. Yes, I do. I have neither the power nor the right, nor even the appetite to put her into the hands of a blind God. I want to put her—I want to put my dark passionate Silence, forever and ever, into the compassionate hand of man.[7]

Silence's tight intercutting of scenes against a backcloth of the harsh North American winter betrays Kennaway's apprenticeship in the cinema, but this is not a script disguised as a novel, as some critics had described his previous two novels. It is rich with poetic insight and religious allegory, of the notion of a terrible second coming, all expressed in the terse, telegraphic prose style of the later Hemingway. In spite of a few minor flaws—it is never fully explained why Silence, too, is on the run, nor how she became involved in Lawrence Junior's lynching—*Silence* is a tautly told, poetic novel which fully justified its publication from Kennaway's drafts. *Silence* was republished by Penguin in 1977 and 1979 and to a new generation of readers came to represent all that was best about Kennaway's style, "a view of the world as an arena bleak and emptied of love".[8]

Curiously, when Kennaway came to be honoured officially, it was for his work as a scriptwriter that he was chosen to be remembered. In April 1970, the Scottish Arts Council "as small recognition on our part of his very important contribution in the two fields of literature and film"[9], established a screenplay competition in his honour and named it for him. For a prize of £500, contributions were invited for a thirty-minute script which could then be developed further. Amongst the judges were Bruce Beresford, then of the B.F.I. production board, who later became a distinguished director in Australia, Murray Grigor, director of the Edinburgh International Film Festival, and Neil

Paterson, another Scottish novelist who, like Kennaway, had enjoyed a successful career in films (his screenplay for John Braine's novel, *Room at the Top,* had received an Oscar in 1959). The response was enthusiastic—most Scottish writers had been hitherto denied access to feature film-making, Scottish film-makers being still steeped in the Griersonian documentary tradition—but the judges later had to report that standards were not of the highest and the award was divided amongst three writers: John Lloyd, Robert Nye and Jack Withers. The competition was not repeated.

A more lasting form of recognition came in 1980 and 1981 when Mainstream Publishing, a new Edinburgh-based firm, re-issued the five major novels, each with a critical introduction by a Kennaway contemporary and admirer. The two Taylor Two stories were published together, and *The Dollar Bottom,* which had been filmed in the previous year, received a 1981 Oscar for the Best Short Feature Film of the year. Roger Christian directed, Robert Urquhart played the headmaster and Rikki Fulton gave a fond interpretation of Karl, the shrewd housemaster. Sadly, the link with Glenalmond was lost when the school's governors could not see their way to allowing the college to be the rightful setting: it was shot instead in Edinburgh at Cargilfield and Fettes and the extras came from Daniel Stewart's and Melville College and from the Scottish Youth Theatre.

Acknowledgement of a more sensational kind also came in 1981 with the publication in January of *The Kennaway Papers,* a selection of writings, edited by Susan from James's notebooks and linked to extracts from *Some Gorgeous Accident,* which tells the story of their marriage break-up and renewal of love and understanding. Its publication was the signal for a short season of bally-hoo in which the identity of "David" was guessed at by some and coyly hinted at by others. In fact, so popular a novelist had Le Carré become that media interest was concentrated more or less entirely upon him with the result that James tended to appear as a shoddy second-best. Censure, said Jonathan Swift, is the tax a man pays to the public for being eminent. James's shade was about to pay in full. Critical interest in the book ranged from the disgust shown by Paul Bailey in *The Observer* who denounced it as being "strictly for the snoopers" to the reason of Philip

Oakes in the *Sunday Times* who saw it for what it was, "a courageous and healing book", truth-telling of the highest order.

The book is painful and in parts embarrassing to read. In the Petit Paris bar in Munich during that Spring of 1965, James does indeed sound demented and the scene at the railway station at Zell-am-See was appalling with drunken shouts and screams and gross behaviour as James attempted to present Susan to Le Carré. And yet, for all those dramas, so vividly and horridly recalled in James's diaries and Susan's eloquent linking narrative, for all the sorry tale of cruelty and mistaken motives, *The Kennaway Papers* is a necessary document for cathartic reasons and as a key to James's own writing. Until it was published, *Some Gorgeous Accident* was a wryly told, Sparkish celebration of a shallow man's fascination with a love triangle and his over-reaching need to lead other people's lives. With the publication of the "papers" it was possible to see, in James's words, "how wonderfully close fiction and life has suddenly become. And all leading to reality . . . my real fear, what makes me really cry, is that I may fail to grasp this hour which some authors may never even know". (p. 100)

As we have seen, Kennaway used the Susan/David relationship as a means of bringing to fruition a novel he knew to be bad. Accordingly, life came to the rescue of fiction and the story told in *The Kennaway Papers* is of a writer who made no differentiation between the two. Consider the moment in *Some Gorgeous Accident* when Link returns to London to meet his friend, Fiddes,

> "Nothing's changed, has it, Link?" That's what Fiddes' face said. And Link's smile was warm.
>
> "Of course not. Nor ever will. You're my partner. No women, no war, no God can break that up."
>
> And Fiddes was glad about that: Link was his only friend. (p. 9)

with the awful reality of Susan's description of David Cornwell's arrival in the chalet at Zell-am-See,

> Arriving back from his abortive trip to the station, angry as he was, James was nevertheless pleased to see David and rushed to the case of wine, popping corks as if it were Christmas. It all seemed so friendly and jolly. (p. 54)

And the results of the affair seeped into his other novel, *The Cost of Living Like This,* with Julian testing to destruction his relationships with his wife Cristabel and his mistress Sally. It leads us to a new understanding, too, of Julian's anguish when he discovers that Sally herself has had an affair with Josh Reynolds, the young, bright Californian boy.

> Jealousy is wild and filthy, we know; is demanding, obsessive, leading always to thoughts of violence; but Lord, it is a living emotion. We are never more totally alive than when the loved one is lying in someone else's arms. (p. 26)

This is very different from the "flatness of jealousy" betrayed by Stephen in *Household Ghosts* (p. 57) and displays a strength of feeling created by a man whose writing had become essential to his emotional make-up, a man who felt that he might be writing his own life. Diaries and journals are an essential tool in literary history. James's diaries would have revealed to future generations some of the clues and keys to the obligatory scenes in his novels; what *The Kennaway Papers* disclosed through Susan's careful editing and notes of explanation was the extent to which her husband's life and his writing had almost become one and the same thing.

Its publication also assisted the publicity for the re-issue of the novels (although that was not its primary intention) and for a while there was a brief spate of interest in Kennaway and his work. But for all that, he remains a difficult writer to place. It is unlikely that he will receive more than a passing mention in any history of the novel. In a sense, he wrote too much and published too little before his early death prevented him from finding his true voice (which is only hinted at in *Silence*). One part of him told him that, like Stephen, he had been "cheated of failure by limited success" (p. 10), another that he had achieved a great deal in the novel that he never saw in print, *The Cost of Living Like This*. *Tunes of Glory,* by which he is chiefly remembered, both for the film and the book, gave him his reputation and yet he felt that it had been a cheat because it had been so easy to write. As novel and film it would be ample epitaph for any writer, but James was too restless to be satisfied with that as his memorial, hence the shift towards the three skeletally-constructed and sparsely muscled novels of his later years: *Some Gorgeous Accident, The Cost of Living Like This,* and *Silence*. In respect of these, he was an innovator, a believer in employing techniques that would tell simple stories on the surface but which would also express the totally contradictory nature of his characters who tend to behave just as human beings do, in all their frailty.

In Scotland, Kennaway's place in the critical canon, for the forseeable future at least, has been assured by the prominence given to his work in recent critical works,[10] a judgement which would no doubt have amused him, as to the end he remained suspicious of Scottish cultural life. The verdict of the writers, though, is not misplaced. *Tunes of Glory* has an authentic atmosphere, from small-town Scotland with its Thrums-like windows peeping out onto snow-covered streets to the creation of Jock Sinclair as mac-machismo man. On one level, *Household Ghosts* is a Scottish Gothic novel, and, as Francis Russell Hart has pointed out,[11] the relationship of Pink to Mary is an echo of Clara's to her brother in Sir Walter Scott's *St Ronan's Well*. In *The Bells of Shoreditch*, he introduced Stella Vass, a myth-maker and life-enhancer in the mould of other Scottish heroines, notably Chris in Lewis Grassic Gibbon's trilogy, *A Scots Quair*, and Mozart Anderson, however improbably named he might be, voices Kennaway's interest in the Humean belief that the cause of order in the universe bears no analogy to human intelligence. ("The point I am making," he tells Christabel, "is that the only way to cure a man who is consumed by this kind of passion is to inspect the conditions that existed before he took the jump, then change them.") (p. 114) These are satisfying critical conceits: for Scottish writers more than, say, their Irish counterparts, are made to test their Scottishness, or have a test of Scottishness made upon their work even though it is an examination which James Kennaway would have found irrelevant. (It is illuminating to note that while he was creating his novels, other Scottish writers, Gordon Williams, Alan Sharp, Archie Hind, William McIlvanney, amongst others, were engaged in the school of proletarian romanticism[12], novels springing from their working-class childhoods in the west of Scotland, novels that are as different from Kennaway's as D.H. Lawrence's are from Anthony Powell's, the Scottish tradition being as divisable as the English.)

By accident of birth, upbringing, and, later, of talent, Kennaway came to live as an expatriate, yet, personally, and although he may not have admitted it, in his work he was deeply affected by his sense of being Scottish. Much of his work he thought worthless, having subjected it to that savage self-criticism he believed created great art, but he wanted to be remembered as a writer. He was a man of paradoxes, whose energies and delightful nature are held in great regard by his closest friends: in his heart of hearts he frequently doubted if he was worthy to be called either an artist of integrity or a man of honour. Failure haunted him; success claimed him. He was James the charmer, and Jim the deceiver. During his lifetime he frequently despaired of critical success as a novelist and yet, as so often happens in the nature of things, that acclaim is his after his death. Original, poetic, talented, powerful: these are the familiar terms used by critics and friends to describe his writing. They are also not a bad verdict on his life.

Notes

The bulk of James Kennaway's manuscripts, literary notebooks, letters and diaries form 28 boxes of Accession 5540, and 4 boxes of Accession 5696 in the National Library of Scotland. Other papers are contained in the Longman Archive held by the Library of the University of Reading and amount to 11 files listed under the titles of the novels published by that firm between 1961 and 1969. Other papers quoted within the text are in the private possession of the family. Where the quotation is also included in *The Kennaway Papers,* I have provided both references. References to the published novels are made to the Mainstream reprints, and, in the case of *Silence,* to the Penguin edition. All are in print, with the exception of *The Mindbenders.*

Chapter One: Kennaway Country

1. J.K. to his mother, 6 February 1944
2. ibid
3. J.K. to Edith Shaw, 1 March 1947
4. Alan Ross, *London Magazine,* December, 1961
5. Treatment for *Flowers,* p.1, in NLS Acc 5540, Box 23
6. *Tunes of Glory,* p.9
7. ibid, p.91
8. J.K. to his mother 31 January 1943
9. J.K. to Edith Shaw, 19 September 1949
10. Notebooks for *Household Ghosts* and *Country Dance* in NLS Acc 5540, Box 28
11. *Household Ghosts,* p.174

Chapter Two: A Scots Childhood

1. Treatment for *Flowers,* NLS, op. cit.
2. George Malcolm Thomson, *Caledonia, or the Future of the Scots* (London, 1926), p.41
3. Charles Kennaway, *Gentleman Adventurer* (London, 1951), pp.17-18
4. *Peoples Journal,* 4 October 1958
5. NLS, Acc. 5540, Box 28; quoted in *The Kennaway Papers,* p.76

6. ibid: quoted in *The Kennaway papers,* p.82
7. *The Kennaway Papers,* p.105
8. Evelyn Waugh, *Put Out More Flags* (Penguin Edition, Harmondsworth, 1966), p.45
9. Conversation with Hazel Bolton (nee Kennaway), 10 February 1981
10. J.M. Johnson, *Tor-na-dee Magazine,* no. 1, October 1921, p.2
11. Notes for treatment of *Flowers,* NLS, op. cit.
12. Conversation with Mrs Sheila Kittermaster and Mowbray Pearson, 3 May 1983
13. Notes in the possession of Mrs Sheila Kittermaster
14. *The Kennaway Papers,* p.99

Chapter Three: Glenalmond

1. G. St Quintin, *The History of Glenalmond: The Story of a Hundred Years* (Edinburgh, 1956), p.6
2. ibid, p.16
3. Reminiscences of Charles Millar, December 1981
4. J.K. to his mother 11 October 1942
5. St Quintin, op. cit. p.2
6. St Quintin, op. cit. p.274
7. Letter from J.S. Liddell, 9 December 1980
8. Letter from Jeremy Bruce-Watt, 7 January 1983
9. *The Kennaway Papers,* p.76
10. J.K. to his mother, 26 November 1944
11. *The Glenalmond Chronicle* no. CCCLVI, January 1946, p.7
12. *The Dollar Bottom & Taylor's Finest Hour,* p.62
13. *The Scotsman,* 3 February 1969

Chapter Four: The Complexion of a Soldier

1. J.K. to his mother, 27 September 1948
2. J.K. to his mother, 10 October 1946
3. W.C. Hayward to Marjory Kennaway, 29 September 1946
4. J.K. to his mother, 5 October 1946
5. J.K. to his mother, 25 October 1946
6. J.K. to his mother, undated, but probably end of October 1946
7. Maj. W.K.B. Crawford, *Training the National Service Officer at Eaton Hall,* Journal of the Royal United Service Institution, vol XCVI, no 581, February, 1951, p.138
8. Letter from Major Allan Cameron, 16 January 1983
9. Hesketh Pearson, *Bernard Shaw: His Life and Personality* (London, 1961), p.472

10. Christopher Sinclair-Stevenson, *The Life of a Regiment: The History of the Gordon Highlanders,* vol 6, (London), 1974, p.9
11. J.K. to his mother, undated, but probably March 1948
12. J.K. to his mother, Easter Monday, 1948
13. J.K. to his mother, 9 April 1948
14. Sinclair-Stevenson, op. cit.

Chapter Five: An Oxford Vintage

1. J.K. to his mother, 13 May 1948
2. J.K. to his mother, 26 April 1948
3. *The Kennaway Papers,* p.106
4. George Scott, *Time and Place* (London, 1956), p.145
5. Evelyn Waugh, *Brideshead Revisited* (Penguin edition, Harmondsworth, 1962), p.23
6. J.K. to his mother, 13 May 1949
7. Naomi Mitchison, *Memories of an Edwardian Childhood* (London 1973); *All Change Here* (London, 1975)
8. *The Kennaway Papers,* pp.66-69
9. J.K. to Susan 14 January 1950
10. Jan Morris, *Oxford* (rev. ed., Oxford, 1978), p.123
11. Kennaway's unpublished stories are contained in NLS Acc 5540, Box 26 and consist of: 'The Actor Manager', 'Acquaintances', 'An English Hero', 'The Artist's Cottage', 'The Summer Game', 'Coming of Age', 'Dik', 'An Economical Holiday', 'The Girl who wanted to eat', 'The Grand Tour', 'Gravitation', 'An Italian has Lunch', 'Ladies Foursome', 'London Cry', 'The Long Unblinking Stare', 'My Little Grey Home in the North-East', 'Scottish Highland Dancing', 'A Sunny Honeymoon', 'Unconverted', 'The Wake'. The box also contains seven plays, listed as 'Flops and Juvenilia': 'Cosmopolia' (as Charles Stretron), 'In the News', 'Personal Friends', 'The Poker', 'Political Pieces', 'Snakes and Ladders', 'Writing for Sound'. Those in Acc 5696, Box 3 consist of 'Monday through Thursday', 'Country Cousins', 'Letter to a Rusticated Friend'.
12. Letter from Denys Hodson of 27 March 1983
13. *The Mindbenders,* p.54
14. Hodson, op. cit.
15. J.K. to his mother, 1 April 1951

Chapter Six: Publisher's Clerk

1. J.K. to Susan undated, September 1952

2. *The Bells of Shoreditch,* p.27
3. Guy R. Williams, *London in the Country* (London, 1975), p.32
4. *The Bells of Shoreditch,* p.158
5. Godfrey Smith, Introduction to *Tunes of Glory* (Edinburgh, 1980)
6. *The Kennaway Papers,* p.69
7. J.K. to his mother, 16 September 1952
8. Notes for *Old Alliance* in NLS Acc 5540, Box 16 (i)
9. *The Kennaway Papers,* p.72
10. J.K. to Susan 5 May 1955
11. A.E. (sic) Kennaway, 'It pays to advertise', *Courier,* June 1953, p.99
12. see note 11, chapter five
13. *The Kennaway Papers,* p.70
14. Conrad Wilson, 'Kennaway writes in a room at the top', *The Scotsman,* 10 June, 1962, p.4
15. The full story is told in Trevor Royle, *Death Before Dishonour: The True Story of Fighting Mac,* (Edinburgh, 1982)
16. Dorothy Laird, 'Dynamic Man of Letters', *Scottish Field,* March, 1963, p.33
17. Reported in *The Bookseller,* 12 May 1956
18. Duncan McAra, 'James Kennaway', *London Magazine,* February 1978, p.40

Chapter Seven: Movie Man

1. NLS Acc 5696, Box 4; quoted partially in *The Kennaway Papers,* pp.70-72
2. Michael Balcon, *Kinematograph Weekly,* January 1945
3. Michael Trueman to Sir Michael Balcon, in NLS, Acc 5540, Box 22
4. George Melly, *Revolt into Style* (London, 1970), p.26
5. George Melly, *Owning Up* (Penguin edition, Harmondsworth, 1970) p.233
6. conversation with Alexander Mackendrick, 27 May 1983
7. NLS, Acc 5696, Box 3
8. University of Reading Library, Longman Archive, 'Household Ghosts', part II, 256/13
9. ibid
10. see Francis Russell Hart, *The Scottish Novel* (London 1978), pp.290-291
11. William Archer, *Playmaking* (London 1912)
12. NLS, Acc 5540, Box 28
13. JK to Susan, early June 1961, partially quoted in *The Kennaway Papers,* p.75
14. conversation with Mackendrick, op cit.

15. *The Kennaway Papers*, p.9
16. conversation with J. Lee Thompson, 29 May 1983
17. NLS op cit.
18. Longman Archive, op cit.
19. NLS op cit.
20. BBC Scotland interview, TR with Susan Kennaway, 29 January 1981

Chapter Eight: All You Need is Love

1. University of Reading Library, Longman Archive, 'The Bells of Shoreditch', part II, 266/15
2. *The Guardian*, 12 May 1979
3. Longman Archive, op cit.
4. ibid.
5. ibid.
6. J.K. to Susan, 9 September 1962
7. *The Kennaway Papers*, p.27
8 conversation with John Guest, 22 September 1981.
9. *The Kennaway Papers*, p.49
10. ibid, p.28
11. ibid, p.29
12. NLS, Acc 5540, Box 8
13. J.K. to Michael Forlong, 23 May 1963, NLS, Acc 9696, Box 4
14. J.K. to Susan, undated, probably February 1964
15. *The Kennaway Papers*, pp.25-30
16. ibid, p.21
17. ibid, p.22
18. letter from David Cornwell, 29 April 1983: 'I think that my memories of James are best told in my own way and in my own time, and you will forgive me if I say that I am not prepared to entrust them to third parties. At the moment, anything I say is liable to be blown up and taken out of context, however sensitively it may be reported.'
19. John Le Carré, *The Naive and Sentimental Lover* (London 1971), p.182
20. *The Kennaway Papers*, p. 103
21. ibid, p.18
22. ibid, p.17
23. NLS, Acc 5540, Boxes 9-16
24. *The Kennaway Papers*, p.32

Chapter Nine: Some Gorgeous Accident

1. *The Kennaway Papers*, p.36

2. ibid, p.58
3. ibid, pp.102-108
4. ibid, p.36
5. ibid, p.108
6. ibid, p.106
7. ibid, p.104
8. ibid, p.97
9. ibid, p.100
10. NLS, acc. 5540, Box 28
11. University of Reading, Longman Archive, 'Some Gorgeous Accident', 312/18
12. José Ortega Y Gasset, *The Dehumanisation of Art and Notes on the Novel*, trans. Helene Wehl (Princeton 1948), p.103
13. ibid, pp.96-97
14. NLS, op cit.
15. Longman Archive, op cit.
16. *The Kennaway Papers*, p.127
17. ibid, p.129
18. NLS, Acc 5696, Box 4
19. J.K. to Susan, 1 September 1965, quoted in *The Kennaway Papers*, p.141 where it is dated 1967
20. NLS, op cit.
21. conversation with Tony Cox, 9 July 1983. Cox had met Kennaway in Paddy's Bar in Edinburgh in 1964 shortly before his own marriage. J.K. had offered much help and advice, Cox being fifteen years his junior, and had acted as best man at the wedding.
22. NLS, Acc 5540, Box 28, quoted in *The Kennaway Papers*, pp.10-11
23. NLS, op cit.
24. *The Scotsman*, 6 September 1967
25. *The Kennaway Papers*, p.139
26. ibid, p.12

Chapter Ten: Aftermath

1. see Frank Delaney's introduction to *The Bells of Shoreditch*.
2. conversation with Douglas Rae, 16 February 1983
3. NLS, Acc 5540, Boxes 17-19
4. NLS, Acc 5696, Box 2
5. NLS, Acc 5540, Box 21
6. ibid
7 ibid
8. Alan Bold, *Modern Scottish Literature* (Harlow, 1983), p.256
9. Ronald Mavor, Director of the Scottish Arts Council, to Susan, 13 April 1970

10. see especially Bold and Hart.
11. Hart, op cit, p.291
12. Bold, op cit, pp.233-241 for discussion of this genre.

Selected Bibliography

There is no complete bibliography of the literary works of James Kennaway. The following lists his published books, the other principal manuscripts are located in the National Library of Scotland and exact references to them are listed in the Notes.

1. BOOKS BY JAMES KENNAWAY

Tunes of Glory, London: Putnam, 1956; New York: Harper and Row, 1956; London: Corgi, 1959, 1967; Edinburgh: Mainstream, 1980, with an introduction by Godfrey Smith.

Household Ghosts, London: Longmans, Green, 1961; New York: Atheneum, 1961; London: Four Square, 1964; Edinburgh: Mainstream, 1981, with an introduction by Magnus Magnusson.

The Mindbenders, London: Longmans, Green and Pan Books, 1963; New York: Atheneum, 1963; New York: Signet, 1964.

The Bells of Shoreditch, London: Longmans, Green, 1963; New York: Atheneum, 1964; London: Four Square, 1965; Edinburgh: Mainstream, 1981, with an introduction by Frank Delaney.

Some Gorgeous Accident, London: Longmans, Green, 1967; New York: Atheneum, 1967; London: Panther, 1972; Edinburgh: Mainstream, 1981, with an introduction by Melvyn Bragg.

The Cost of Living Like This, London: Longmans, Green, 1969; New York: Atheneum, 1969; Harmondsworth: Penguin, 1972; Edinburgh: Mainstream, 1980, with an introduction by Frederic Raphael.

Silence, edited by Lynn Hughes, London: Jonathan Cape, 1972; Harmondsworth: Penguin, 1977, 1979.

The Dollar Bottom & Taylor's Finest Hour, edited and introduced by Trevor Royle, Edinburgh: Mainstream, 1981.

The Kennaway Papers, by James and Susan Kennaway, London: Jonathan Cape, 1981; New York: Holt Rinehart and Winston, 1981.

II. CRITICAL REFERENCES

Alan Bold, 'Kennaway and Character', *Modern Scottish Literature,* Harlow, Longman, 1983, pp.249-256

Francis Russell Hart, 'Kennaway, Spark and After', *The Scottish Novel,* London, John Murray, 1978, pp. 287-294

Duncan McAra, 'James Kennaway', *London Magazine*, February 1978, vol. 17, no. 8, pp.37-55

Hugh Mackay, 'The Novels of James Kennaway', *Library Review*, Summer 1972, vol. 23, no.6, pp. 230-232

Allan Massie, 'The Artful Art of James Kennaway', *New Edinburgh Review*, November, 1980, no.52, pp.13-16

Michael Pye, 'James Kennaway', *The Scotsman*, 23 May 1970, p.i

Trevor Royle, 'The Power and The Glory of Kennaway', *The Scotsman*, 11 July 1981, p.i

Trevor Royle, 'James Kennaway', *Companion to Scottish Literature*, London, Macmillan, 1983, pp. 162-163

Godfrey Smith, 'James Kennaway's Legacy', *Sunday Times Magazine*, 4 October 1970, pp.53-56

III. OTHER PUBLISHED SOURCES

Charles Barr, *Ealing Studios*, Newton Abbot, 1977

Dirk Bogarde, *Snakes and Ladders*, London, 1979

James Cameron, *Memory Lane*, London, 1980

B.S. Johnson (ed,), *All Bull: The National Serviceman*, London, 1973

Bernard Levin, *The Pendulum Year: Britain and The Sixties*, London, 1970

Maurice Lindsay, *A History of Scottish Literature*, London, 1977

George Melly, *Owning Up*, Harmondsworth, 1970; *Revolt into Style*, London, 1970

Naomi Mitchison, *Memoirs of an Edwardian Childhood*, London, 1973; *All Change Here*, London, 1975

Leonard Mosley, *Battle of Britain: The Making of a Film*, London, 1969

Jan Morris, *Oxford*, rev. ed., Oxford 1978

José Ortega Y Gasset, *The Dehumanisation of Art and Notes on The Novel*, trans. Helene Wehl, Princeton, 1948

Trevor Royle, *Death Before Dishonour: The True Story of Fighting Mac*, Edinburgh, 1982

G. St. Quintin, *The History of Glenalmond: The Story of a Hundred Years*, Edinburgh, 1956

George Scott, *Time and Place*, London, 1956

Robert Speaight, *Francois Mauriac: A Study of the Writer and The Man*, London, 1976

George Malcolm Thomson, *Caledonia, or The Future of the Scots*, London, 1926

Nigel Tranter, *The Queen's Scotland: The Heartland*, London, 1971.

Index